MW01294011

Peace Without P
International State-Building in Bosnia

Ten years on from the signing of the Dayton Peace Agreement in November 1995, the legacy of the Bosnian war still shapes every aspect of the political, social and economic environment of the tiny state. This is highlighted by the fact that Bosnia is still under international control, with the Office of the International High Representative regularly using its powers to dismiss elected presidents, prime-ministers and MPs and to impose legislation over the resistance of elected legislatures at national, regional and local level. What has changed in the ten years since Dayton? Is international regulation helping to establish a sustainable peace in Bosnia? What lessons can be learned for nation-building in Bosnia?

This volume was previously published as a special issue of the journal *International Peacekeeping*.

David Chandler is Senior Lecturer in International Relations, Centre for the Study of Democracy, University of Westminster.

THE ROUTLEDGE SERIES ON PEACEKEEPING
General Editor: Michael Pugh
ISSN 1367-9880

This series examines all aspects of peacekeeping, from the political, operational and legal dimensions to the developmental and humanitarian issues that must be dealt with by all those involved with peacekeeping in the world today.

Peace Without Politics?
Ten Years of International
State-Building in Bosnia

Edited by

David Chandler

Routledge
Taylor & Francis Group

LONDON AND NEW YORK

First published 2006 by Routledge
2 Park Square, Milton Park, Abingdon, Oxon, OX14 4RN

Simultaneously published in the USA and Canada
by Routledge
270 Madison Ave, New York NY 10016

Routledge is an imprint of the Taylor & Francis Group

Transferred to Digital Printing 2008

© 2006 Taylor & Francis Group Ltd

Typeset in Times by Techset Composition Limited

British Library Cataloguing in Publication Data
A catalogue record for this book is available from the British Library

Library of Congress Cataloging in Publication Data
A catalog record for this book has been requested

ISBN10: 0-415-34822-6 (hbk)
ISBN10: 0-415-46382-3 (pbk)

ISBN13: 978-0-415-34822-5 (hbk)
ISBN13: 978-0-415-46382-9 (pbk)

Contents

Notes on Contributors

Roberto Belloni is Lecturer, School of Politics and International Studies, Queens University, Belfast. He was a Research Fellow at the Kennedy School of Government and the World Peace Foundation at Harvard University 2002–2004.

Florian Bieber is Senior Research Fellow at the European Centre for Minority Issues, a Visiting Professor, Nationalism Studies Programme, Central European University, Budapest, co-editor of the journal *Southeast European Politics*, editor of the electronic network *Balkan Academic News*, and author of *Post-War Bosnia: Ethnic Structure, Inequality and Governance of the Public Sector* (Palgrave, 2005).

Sumantra Bose is Reader in Comparative Politics, Department of Government, London School of Economics, and author of *Bosnia after Dayton: Nationalist Partition and International Intervention* (Oxford University Press, 2002) and *Kashmir: The Roots of Conflict, Paths to Peace* (Harvard University Press, 2003).

Richard Caplan is University Lecturer in International Relations and Official Fellow at Linacre College, Oxford University, and author of *International Governance of War-Torn Territories: Rule and Reconstruction* (Oxford University Press, 2005) and *Europe and the Recognition of New States in Yugoslavia* (Cambridge University Press, 2005).

Gemma Collantes Celador is a doctoral candidate, Department of International Politics, University of Wales, Aberystwyth. Her thesis analyses the reform of police forces in post-Dayton Bosnia.

David Chandler is Senior Lecturer in International Relations, Centre for the Study of Democracy, University of Westminster, and author of *Bosnia: Democracy after Dayton* (Pluto Press, 1999), *From Kosovo to Kabul* (Pluto Press, 2002) and *Constructing Global Civil Society* (Palgrave, 2004).

Adam Fagan is Senior Lecturer in the Department of Politics, Queen Mary College, University of London.

Daniela Heimerl is a Researcher at La Documentation Française, Paris, a Research Associate at the LASP Research Centre, University of Paris X-Nanterre, and a member of the editorial staff of the *Courrier des pays de l'Est*.

Michael Pugh is Professor of International Relations, University of Plymouth and Director of the Plymouth International Studies Centre. He edits the journal *International Peacekeeping* and the Taylor & Francis book series on Peacekeeping. He is lead ESRC researcher on the Transformation of War Economies project and co-author of *War Economies in a Regional Context: The Challenge of Transformation* (Lynne Rienner, 2004).

Vanessa Pupavac is a Lecturer in the School of Politics, University of Nottingham. Her recent research has analysed the rise of international psycho-social approaches. She was awarded the 2003 Otto Klineberg Intercultural and International Relations Award.

Dominik Zaum is Rose Research Fellow in International Relations, Lady Margaret Hall, University of Oxford, and has worked for the Office of the High Representative in Bosnia and for the Lessons Learned and Analysis Unit of the UN Mission in Kosovo.

Abbreviations

BBC	British Broadcasting Corporation
BiH	Bosnia and Herzegovina
CAFAO	(European Commission funded) Customs and Fiscal Assistance Office
CARDS	(European Commission) Community Programme of Assistance for Reconstruction, Development and Stabilization
CAS	Country Assistance Strategy
CEDAW	Convention on the Elimination of Discrimination against Women
CFSP	Common Foreign and Security Policy
CoM	(EU) Council of Ministers
CRS	(EU) Catholic Relief Services
DEI	Directorate for European Integrations
DFID	(UK) Department for International Development
EC	European Commission
ESI	European Stability Initiative
EU	European Union
EUFOR	EU Stabilization Force
EUPM	EU Police Mission
FBiH	Muslim-Croat Federation
FDI	Foreign Direct Investment
FRY	Federal Republic of Yugoslavia
FTA	Federation Tax Administration
GDP	Gross Domestic Product
GFA/GFAP	General Framework Agreement for Peace
HDZ	Hrvatska Demokratska Zajednica (Croatian Democratic Union)
IAG	International Advisory Group
ICG	International Crisis Group
ICTY	International Criminal Tribunal for the former Yugoslavia
ICVA	International Council for Voluntary Agencies
IDPs/DPs	Internally Displaced Persons
IEBL	Inter-Entity Boundary Line
IFIs	International Financial Institutions
IFOR	NATO Implementation Force
ILO	International Labour Organization
IMF	International Monetary Fund
IPTF	UN International Police Task Force
KM	Konvertibilna Marka (convertible marks)
MIP	Mission Implementation Plan

NATO	North Atlantic Treaty Organization
NGO	non-governmental organization
ODA	Overseas Development Agency
OHCHR	Office of the High Commission for Human Rights
OHR	Office of the High Representative
OSCE	Organization for Security and Cooperation in Europe
PFSAC	Public Finance Structural Adjustment Credit
PIC	Peace Implementation Council
PLIP	Property Law Implementation Plan
PMC	Permanent Mandates Commission
PRSP	Poverty Reduction Strategy Paper
RRTF	Reconstruction and Return Task Force
RS	Republika Srpska
SAA	Stabilization and Association Agreement
SAP	Stabilization and Association Process
SBiH	Stranka Za Bosnu I Hercegovinu (Party for Bosnia and Herzegovina)
SDA	Stranka Demokrastke Akcije (Party of Democratic Action)
SDS	Srpska Demokratska Stranka (Serbian Democratic Party)
SFOR	NATO Stabilization Force
SRS	Srpska Radikalna Stranka (Serbian Radical Party)
TALDi	Tuzla Agency for Local Development Initiatives
UK	United Kingdom
UN	United Nations
UNDP	UN Development Programme
UNPF	UN Population Fund
UNHCR	UN High Commission for Refugees
UNICEF	UN Children's Fund
UNMIBH	UN Mission in Bosnia and Herzegovina
UNMIK	UN Mission in Kosovo
US	United States
USAID	US Agency for International Development
WTO	World Trade Organization

Introduction: Peace Without Politics?

DAVID CHANDLER

It is ten years since the Dayton peace settlement, which formally ended the war in Bosnia and Herzegovina (BiH) in November 1995. Since then there has been much discussion about the steep learning curve necessary for the new international tasks of state-building and post-conflict peacebuilding. BiH was the first such extensive international project since the post-Second World War US-led occupations of the defeated Axis powers Germany and Japan. Today, with the end of cold war geo-political divisions, BiH has become widely seen as a template for new experiments in international administration and external assistance in state reconstruction and post-conflict reconciliation. The contributions in this specially commissioned collection seek to probe the lessons of the BiH experience and highlight the nature of the problems confronted by international policy-making institutions; exploring the limitations and possibilities for external influence and drawing attention to some of the unintended consequences of projects of this kind.

The in-depth analysis offered by the contributors to this volume comes at an important time when the issue of post-conflict state-building and international attempts to prevent and manage the consequences of state failure have become major questions on the international policy agenda. In the wake of 9/11 and the problems of international intervention and administrative regulation in Afghanistan and Iraq, international engagement in state capacity-building initiatives has become central to international concerns.

This interventionist desire to shape the political process and reconstruct state institutions, where states are perceived to be 'failing', is in marked contrast to the political norms and possibilities of the cold war period where the geo-political divide between the Soviet Union and the United States meant there was little international consensus on how states should be governed or on which policies they should follow in the domestic realm. In the second half of the twentieth century, the reaction against colonial practices meant that the United Nations upheld the formal political equality of all sovereign states, regardless of their level of political, economic or social development or of the capacity or willingness of their regimes to uphold the rights of their citizens.[1] Changed international power relations and changed political sensibilities have meant that today there is much less of a divide between how states are treated internationally and what they do domestically.

A new normative framework has emerged which has placed international regulation of, and intervention in, the domestic affairs of states firmly on the agenda. However, even in leading policy-making circles there is a concern that the development and assessment of international practices has lagged behind the demand that international actions be undertaken.[2] After ten years of international experience and experimentation in state-building in BiH, the successes and failures of the international post-war administration of BiH should be at the centre of debate regarding the development of new international policy practices. It is to be hoped that this collection can assist in helping analysis of state-building initiatives catch up with the world of state-building practice.

Politics as a Barrier to Peace

The one theme that comes out clearly in the contributions below is that of the tendency for the international administrative authority in BiH to separate state-building from politics. There is a tendency to see state-building as a technical or administrative process, one which does not require building a popular consensus for policy-making. The post-Second World War external administrations of Germany and Japan engaged the local populations in a major project of social, economic and political reconstruction and, through doing so, won a high level of popular legitimacy and support. In contrast, the international administration of BiH has excluded all but token local input in the making and implementation of policy, criticizing the programmes and personnel of the main political parties and asserting that the BiH electorate is not yet to be trusted with a meaningful vote. Rather than deriving policy from Bosnians' concerns and needs, the legislative process has been driven by technical and administrative 'experts' in Brussels and Washington. Policies have then been imposed through the international Office of the High Representative, forcing locally accountable political leaders to accede to demands under the threat of being dismissed on the grounds of 'obstruction'.

The powers of the international administration have grown in an ad hoc way since Dayton, reflecting a greater international consensus behind new, and more interventionist, state-building practices. BiH, unlike Germany and Japan, was not defeated by its administrating powers in a war; there was no formal ceding of sovereignty and political control over decision-making. Close international oversight was intended to last for one year only, until the first state elections in September 1996. However, ten years on from Dayton, not one piece of substantial legislation had been devised, ratified and implemented by Bosnian politicians and civil servants.[3] This is in marked contrast to Japan and West Germany where, in the first case, the external occupation lasted nearly seven years and in the latter, there were four years of occupation, and full control over industrial and security policy was returned ten years after the end of the war.[4]

A decade on from Dayton – in a context where external state-building is taking place with the maintenance of the trappings of formal sovereignty – the lack of political autonomy for Bosnian representatives, and of political accountability for Bosnian citizens, is possibly the most remarkable feature of the Bosnian settlement. However, the lack of democracy in BiH has posed little barrier to negotiations over the European Union accession process. In fact, the European Union has given its formal blessing to the maintenance of a highly restricted political sphere, with the establishment of the EU's Special

Representative as the international High Representative in 2002. There would appear to be a clear international consensus that, for state-building to be a success, rule by externally-appointed bureaucrats is preferential to rule by Bosnian representatives accountable to BiH's citizens.

The contributors to this volume vary in their assessments of the results of this experiment in external oversight; however, whether they ultimately judge this approach as useful or as counterproductive, all the authors highlight the secondary importance of the participatory political process in today's discussions of state-building and post-conflict reconstruction. It is this aspect which this Introduction seeks to briefly examine before outlining the contributions themselves.

States without Politics?

In the past, the political process was generally understood as key to the creation of stable and viable states. Samuel Huntington's pioneering late-1960s study, *Political Order in Changing Societies*, was the key text for students of political development studies during the last 30 years of the twentieth century.[5] His concern was not the creation of states, which had the stamp of international approval because the ruling clique supported the policies of those in power in Washington, nor was he trying to design the perfect constitution for export around the world, with a bill of rights and a separation of powers and human rights protections. For Huntington, the key to state stability was a political question of building a domestic consensus, a sense of political community, and establishing a government with popular legitimacy. Huntington argued that bureaucratic rule or government by isolated cliques may be able to produce stability in simple pre-industrialized societies but that modernization and the development of democratic, participatory societies depended on the strengthening and institutionalization of the political sphere.

Political institutions could only cohere society if they emerged out of existing social forces, if they represented real interests and real clashes of interest which then led to the establishment of mechanisms and organizational rules and procedures which were capable of resolving those disagreements.[6] It was the links between political institutions, political parties and individuals which were considered key to strengthening the state both institutionally and in terms of its popular legitimacy. Huntington's findings challenge those who argue that international bureaucrats can draw up all the necessary legislation for state-building and post-conflict reconciliation. He argued that the powerful were always tempted to bypass the political sphere:

> Inevitably a ruling monarch tends to view political parties as divisive forces which either challenge his authority or greatly complicate his efforts to unify and modernize his country... The modernizing monarch necessarily sees himself as the 'Patriot King' who is 'to espouse no party, but to govern like the common father of his people'.[7]

The desire of those in power to avoid popular accountability and to legitimize their authority on the basis of their direct and unmediated representation of the 'public interest' will sound familiar to anyone who has read the statements of the succession of internationally-appointed High Representatives in BiH. High Representative Carlos Westendorp saw the Bosnian Presidency, Council of Ministers and Parliamentary Assembly as 'painfully cumbersome and ineffective' when compared to the alternative possibility of the swift signature of his administrator's pen.[8] Westendorp thrived on being the unaccountable judge of his own policy-making prowess, arguing: 'You do not [have] power handed to you on a platter. You just seize it, if you use this power well, no-one will contest it.'[9] Lord Paddy Ashdown, the current incumbent, has used very similar phraseology, for example, in his inaugural speech of May 2002, stating:

> I have concluded that there are two ways I can make my decisions. One is with a tape measure, measuring the precise equidistant position between three sides. The other is by doing what I think is right for the country as a whole. I prefer the second of these. So when I act, I shall seek to do so in defence of the interests of all the people of BiH, putting their priorities first.[10]

For Lord Ashdown, as for his predecessors, rather than facilitating consensus-building between the three main political parties – representing Bosnian Muslims (also referred to as Bosniacs), Bosnian Serbs and Bosnian Croats – his own personal perspective of 'what I think is right' was held to directly coincide with the interests of the population as a whole.

This high-handed approach, which has marked the ten years of international regulation in the tiny post-war state, is at the centre of the analysis in the collection here. While some commentators focus on the achievements of this approach and others on the shortcomings, all the analysts suggest that there are important lessons to be learned in the study of the efficiency and sustainability of policy-making by international imposition. That this is the case should not be altogether surprising considering earlier accepted wisdom on the importance of the political process to strengthening state capacity. To return to Huntington:

> The administrator opposed to parties accepts the need to rationalize social and economic structures. He is unwilling, however, to accept the implications of modernization for broadening the scope of popular participation in politics. His is a bureaucratic model; the goal is efficiency and the elimination of conflict. Parties simply introduce irrational and corrupt considerations into the efficient pursuit of goals upon which everyone should be agreed. The administrative opponent of parties may wear any dress, but he is less likely to be in mufti than in uniform.[11]

For Huntington, leaving aside the acuteness of his observation on the link between the military-mindset and the administrative one – captured well by Ashdown the ex-Royal Marine Commando who had never enjoyed elected government office – the point is that hostility to the political sphere is essentially counterproductive. While kings and bureaucrats understand their legitimacy as existing independently of society, links between individuals and the state – provided by the political sphere, and the mediation of political party competition – are crucial both to creating identities which transcend parochial and particularist groupings and to legitimizing state-level institutions.[12]

Huntington's assertion of the centrality of the political sphere and the need for strong connections between states and their citizens is entirely missing from today's international policy documents outlining 'best practices' for international administrations. In fact, where his 1960s work is referred to, his points about the importance of strong state institutions are taken out of any political context. This later approach is exemplified in Roland Paris's well-received book, At War's End, published in 2004.[13] Paris critiques the idea that a market economy and liberal democracy are the two preconditions for a stable peace. He argues that it is necessary to have 'Institutionalization before Liberalization', to focus on strong institutions, the rule of law and human rights protections before giving post-conflict societies the right to have a say in their own affairs.

For Paris, elections are important, but secondary. The process of political reconciliation and the development of a shared sense of political community should precede competitive elections: 'Peacebuilders' should proceed with elections only when there is evidence that "moderate" parties...have sufficient popular support...to prevail over "immoderate" parties at the polls.'[14] This interventionist project attempts not merely to reconstruct a state but also to transform the attitudes of the inhabitants of a post-conflict state. This latter task is to be undertaken through: civil society building; the encouragement of cross-cutting links and interests; international attention to educational curricula from primary school through to university level; the strict control and regulation of the media; trauma counselling and other therapeutic practices; and through punishing political parties or elected representatives held to be 'obstructing' progress. Clearly this state-building agenda is an ambitious one, but one that reflects the existing practices of international institutions, states and non-governmental organizations in BiH.

State-building practices are increasingly informed by the assumption that democracy is good for Western states but tutelage is better for non-Western states variously judged to be 'under stress', at 'risk of failure' or in post-conflict 'recovery'. This assumption rests on a transformed view of centrality of the political process to state legitimacy. The argument that it is possible to create the institutional framework of a strong and stable state before liberalization – that is, opening up the political process to democratic competition – suggests that citizens (and states) can be socially-engineered by correct practices of external regulation. The assumption is that the problems of politics can be resolved outside the realm of the political, in the realms of law, social policy and administration.[15] It would seem, as Alejandro Bendaña notes, that 'good governance or state-building...has deep ideological presumptions which purport to offer technical solutions to what in essence are political problems'.[16]

It is this view of the feasibility of 'peace without politics' which has been central to current discussions of the external state-building agenda: an agenda which asserts that it is possible to have good governance without democratic participatory politics. In BiH, the international administration argues that the rule of law and even 'respect for democracy' can be developed before elected representatives are allowed to assume political responsibility. In the wake of the US-led Iraq occupation, High Representative Ashdown toured Western capitals arguing that the 'rule of law' had to precede elections and political liberaliza-tion.[17] This view of 'sequencing' formally relegates the political process to an optional extra, to be considered only after the mechanisms of governance are already firmly established.[18]

War without Politics?

The new international dispensation for military intervention – the undermining of state sovereignty in the case of gross human rights abuses and international support for intervention to address the threats posed by 'failed states' – has reflected broader calls for a reconsideration of the relationship between Western military intervention and international law. For example, there has been a growing tendency for international theorists and international security actors to perceive internal conflicts in the non-Western world as crimes to be judged and righted rather than as political conflicts to be mediated.[19] Kalevi Holsti captured this new perception of conflict as 'wars of the third kind', stating that: 'In these wars, ordinary cost-benefit analyses that underlie wars as a "continuation of politics by other means" no longer apply.'[20] Mary Kaldor developed Holsti's themes with the concept of 'New Wars'.[21]

Politics was removed from the understanding of conflict in two ways. First, conflict in the non-Western state was held to be the domestic product of irrational, rapacious or criminal elites representing their own private interests – and there-fore lacking any political legitimacy. Second, the intervention (military or other-wise) of Western powers was also divorced from any political interest and equated with a universal or ethical interest. Interventions of this sort were now likened to domestic policing, that is, merely the enforcement of pre-existing norms and laws.

War – understood as a conflict of political interests – was replaced by either war crimes and human rights abuses (conflict in the non-Western world) or poli-cing and law enforcement (armed conflict undertaken by Western powers).[22] Neither non-Western state 'failure', nor the international response to this, was conceived in traditional terms of political interests. This discursive dichotomy, between the failed state and the post-national or post-political intervention, in one move delegitimated the political process of the state intervened in, while at the same time setting up the intervening powers as being beyond or above political interests. Rather than being neutral observers of a legitimate conflict of interests, the international intervener became the judge, jury and administrator in a situation where there were no legitimate political interests to be taken into account.

The relationship between external intervening powers (increasingly seen as legitimate) and domestic political actors (now increasingly portrayed as pursuing illegitimate interests) has been transformed through a succession of innovative international policy-shifts since the end of the cold war. At the heart of this trans-formation has been the United Nations itself, which has extended its remit and reinterpreted the formal restrictions of the UN Charter while increasingly giving free reign to self-selected 'coalitions of the willing' to set their own conditions on when and how interventions should take place and be formally brought to an end.[23]

Ten years on from Dayton, a process that developed in BiH in a relatively arbitrary and ad hoc way has been increasingly institutionalized. At the end of 2004, the Report of the UN Secretary-General's High-level Panel on Threats, Challenges and Change, *A More Secure World: Our Shared Responsibility*, advised the establishment of a Peacebuilding Commission to oversee the international administration of failing and post-conflict states.[24] According to the UN advisers and the Secretary-General Kofi Annan, a select committee of the 'great and the good' from around the world, acting under UN auspices, would have the requisite skills to help co-ordinate a panoply of international intervention mechanisms – from early warning, through preventative action, and onto post-conflict transitional administrations – where states were held to be 'under stress or recovering from conflict'.[25]

The 'Ethical Turn' in International Theorizing

The rejection of the domestic political sphere as a constitutive sphere – in which social and political bonds are shaped and strengthened – and the re-representation of this sphere as purely one of corruption and conflict has received relatively little critical evaluation from academic commentators involved in international relations and international security studies. In fact, since the end of the cold war, new approaches to theorizing security have stressed that states are part of the problem rather than part of the solution to conflict and political and social division.[26] Many of these critical approaches draw on post-structuralist theorizing and follow Foucault's widely cited inversion of Clausewitz, seeing 'politics as a continuation of war by other means'.[27] The existence of states, in this reading, is the result of war and domestic social conflict, with the domination of victorious elites being enforced and reproduced by political processes of representation rather than military force. For these theorists, states inevitably engage in war and internal conflict as they are based on domination and relations of exclusion and exclusivity.[28]

For critical, post-structuralist and normative theorists of international relations and international security, the political sphere is the problem to be addressed, not the sphere where solutions are to be found. Rather than starting from politics – from social forces and the clash of interests in society, as many realist theorists did[29] – many theorists start from ethics and norms and then seek to derive (non-exclusionary) political frameworks from this basis.[30] The approach of privileging ethics above the political process, central to the 'ethical turn' in international theorizing, fits closely with international state-building practices which privilege bureaucracy, law and administration above the political and may in part explain why there is little critical focus on these developments in many academic circles.[31]

The focus of 'human security' doctrines is no longer on the defence of states but on the rights of individuals wherever they might be in the world. This is construed to be a moral or ethical duty, placed upon the powerful, to take responsibility for the protection of the rights of those elsewhere.[32] The 2004 Barcelona

Report of the Study Group on Europe's Security Capabilities, *A Human Security Doctrine for Europe*, argues, for example, that: 'A human security approach for the European Union means that it should contribute to the protection of every individual human being and not focus only on the defence of the Union's borders, as was the security approach of nation-states.'[33] Here it is assumed that the EU has risen above the politics of state interests and that, as a post-national or post-political entity, it is capable of judging upon and acting in the interests of 'every individual' regardless of which state they happen to be a citizen of. The UN High-level Panel Report, referred to above, also explicitly awards might with the badge of righteousness, suggesting that when it comes to the new tasks of external state-building, 'all those in a position to help others...[have] the responsibility to do so'.[34]

It could be argued that the ten years of state-building experience in BiH serve as a symbol of the return of liberal faith in the science of law and administration, analogous to the inter-war period of the last century. This is evidenced in the return of the idea of conditional sovereignty, reminiscent of the Versailles restrictions on the sovereignty of the new states established in central and eastern Europe, and in the renewed faith in the powers of international conferences and committees to establish the borders of states (the European Community Badinter Commission did this for the former Yugoslavia) and to appoint external governors (as the Peace Implementation Council did for BiH and the United Nations for Kosovo). There is without doubt a growing consensus that international experts and bureaucrats can better govern a country than politicians accountable to the people who have to live with the consequences of their policy-making.

However, in our post-colonial era, there is little support for the return of traditional empire, for a new network of colonial protectorates bringing 'order' to the regions of the world threatened by failing states. Rather, new international administrative regimes are, in the terminology of Michael Ignatieff, most often run on the basis of 'Empire Lite'.[35] International administrators are loath to be held to account for the policies they pursue or the outcome of their interventions into the political process. At the same time, local actors are denied the political autonomy to reach their own compromise solutions and assume accountability themselves. BiH highlights the contradictions of having the existence of a formally sovereign state with regularly contested elections at state, entity and local levels and, alongside this, the existence of a parallel administration headed by unaccountable international appointees with the power to draw up and impose legislation and sack elected officials.

Uniquely, the political process is squeezed from above and below. There is no accountability for policy-making either domestically or internationally. In this sense the borders between the domestic and international have been effectively erased. However, the external regulation of Bosnian people as 'humans', rather than as 'citizens' with rights of political equality, has done little to overcome the 'politics of exclusion'. Bosnian political representatives who have been elected are accountable to international overseers rather than to Bosnian voters, reducing political institutions to irrelevant talking shops. In this context, elections are not a judgement on government policies; in fact, the inverse relationship is in play. Elections are openly seen as educational exercises whereby Bosnian voters submit to the judgement of the international administrators as to their political capacities.

A few international analysts have stood out against the view that the political process can be short-cut or replaced by bureaucratic and administrative edict. Amitai Etzioni and Francis Fukuyama have, for example, questioned 'over-ambitious societal engineering'.[36] Gerald Knaus and others at the Brussels-based think tank, the European Stability Initiative, have attempted to initiate a debate on the 'Travails of the European Raj' in BiH, highlighting the limitations of the high-handed approach taken to post-conflict reconstruction.[37] William Bain has also challenged the 'New Paternalism' of the failed states discourse and highlighted the return of a more hierarchical world order with the institutionalization of new forms of political inequality between states and between individuals.[38] Simon Chesterman's study of post-conflict international administrations points out that today's international rule over BiH provides even less local accountability than the last century's mandate system or that under the presently defunct UN Trusteeship Council.[39] Chesterman's in-depth comparative study also concludes that current international state-building practices are prone to a number of fundamental flaws which stem from the inequalities built into the relationship of political pedagogy and external regulation: the means are often inconsistent with the declared ends; the resources are often inadequate to achieve the ends sought; and finally, much policy-making is more declaratory than practical, being largely irrelevant to the tasks at hand.[40]

This collection hopes to extend this discussion of the questions and contradictions raised by international state-building in the specific 'post-imperial' context of our times. It is for this reason that the collection focuses on the case-study of BiH, where the greatest amount of international institutional effort has been expended in developing new techniques and state-building practices. The contributions analyse both initiatives from above, by international administrators and other external actors, and initiatives at a local level which seek to encourage or reflect Bosnian political initiatives or to empower and give voice to those otherwise excluded from the political process. Having established the context for the collection, the following section outlines the structure of the volume and the layout of the individual contributions.

Structure and Content

The volume is divided into four sections. Part 1, 'Reassessing Dayton' contains two introductory essays which assess the development of the Dayton process from 1995 to 2005. In Part 2, 'Imposing Reform from Above', three contributions assess international reforms in the key areas of economic reform, police reform and refugee return and the resettlement of internally displaced people. Part 3, 'Encouraging Reform from Below', contains four contributions which analyse initiatives seeking to achieve change at a local level through the reform of local government, or attempts to empower or give voice to those otherwise excluded from the political process at a local level, such as refugee return groups, women's groups and civil society voices. Part 4, 'Bosnia Today' concludes with two essays which seek to understand, and move beyond, the current stasis of the state-building process – in both the economic and political spheres.

In 'The Bosnian State a Decade after Dayton', Sumantra Bose examines the post-Dayton process through raising two central questions. First, whether the federal consociational power-sharing framework, established at Dayton, has proved to be viable. He answers in the affirmative, arguing that attempts to impose a unitary structure without any social consensus between the three main ethnic groups would be undemocratic and unworkable in practice, while greater secession for entities or regions would be equally unworkable. Second, he addresses the crucial role of the international community in constructing and enforcing the Dayton settlement. Bose highlights the extent to which international pressure, or direct enforcement, has contributed to the major state-building measures undertaken over the last decade, from refugee return to the issue of Bosnian currency.

In the following contribution, 'From Dayton to Europe', David Chandler highlights that while, on the one hand, Dayton institutionalized a complex mechanism of consociational federalism, it also created a free hand for international administrators to set the limits to their own authority and establish a further set of complex and ad hoc mechanisms of policy development and implementation. I trace the reforms to administrative mechanisms such as the High Representative, illustrating how the international administration has increasingly come under direct European Union administrative control from 1999 onwards. While the governance side of the Dayton framework – under international control – has been extended and transformed, there has been little change to the government side – the input into policy-making by Bosnian citizens or their representatives.

The following three contributions highlight the advantages and problems of post-conflict administration and state-building which, in the context of external authority, is inevitably driven at least as much by externally- as by domestically-generated concerns. One of the key themes to emerge is the instrumental use of policy to support and encourage aims outside of the immediate sphere of policy concern. In the cases below – of economic reform, police reform and refugee return – the contributions draw out the potential contradictions caused by subsuming these policy areas to wider strategic concerns of the international peacebuilding and state-building process.

Dominik Zaum, in his contribution on 'Economic Reform and the Transformation of the Payment Bureaux', argues that economic reforms, which have had a major impact on the political authority of the Bosnian entities (and on the living standards of the population), have been pushed through as technical and managerial necessities. While, on the one hand, international coordination in this area has seen major successes in implementing reforming legislation, Zaum raises a cautionary note that taking the politics out of economic reform has done little to give Bosnian people a stake in the reform process or to strengthen the legitimacy or authority of Bosnian political institutions themselves.

In her contribution, 'Police Reform: Peacebuilding through Democratic Policing', Gemma Collantes Celador suggests that police reform, while valuable in its own terms, has produced unnecessary pressures on the institution through raising unrealistic expectations that multi-ethnic policing can act as a catalyst for broader social change. Her research suggests that the instrumental use of police reform for social engineering purposes, in isolation from broader social changes, has been unsuccessful and, indeed, counterproductive. She further argues that the 'democratization' of the police force, demanded by external administrators, has undermined the morale and efficiency of the police.

Daniela Heimerl, in 'The Return of Refugees and Internally Displaced Persons: From Coercion to Sustainability?' suggests that the international administration's attempt to use the return of refugees and internally displaced persons as a mechanism for undermining the electoral hold of nationalist political parties has necessitated a very restrictive and prescriptive approach to the question. This approach is seen as problematic in that it does not take into account the economic and social needs of the vulnerable or the lack of alternative options available to many choosing to return. She also suggests that international returns policy fails to take into account the changed social, political and economic circumstances in Bosnia: these necessitate a forward looking agenda rather than the unrealistic desire to turn the clock back to the status quo ante of 1991.

The following four contributions analyse international policy attempts to encourage reform from below and consider the impact of Bosnian activity at the local level. The authors suggest that international policy has often had the unintended effect of institutionalizing political and social fragmentation rather than overcoming it.

Vanessa Pupavac, in her analysis, 'Empowering Women? An Assessment of International Gender Policies in Bosnia', argues that international policies in this area have shifted away from seeing women as victims, in need of counselling, towards an emphasis on empowering women to play a greater role in Bosnian politics and in civil society. However, her research highlights that these policies have, in effect, institutionalized women's subordinate role in society rather than challenging it. This has particularly been the case with attempts to increase women's political participation through quota regimes – which have merely reinforced dominant political influences, whether domestic or external – and with the reliance on micro-credit and small business initiatives which have tended to cohere social and economic relations in which women have little economic independence.

In 'Civil Society in Bosnia Ten Years after Dayton', Adam Fagan reassesses international policy aimed at encouraging a vibrant NGO sector capable of political advocacy in the civil society sphere. He suggests that international policy has changed in two directions: first, there is, today, greater emphasis on internationally-supported NGOs working more closely in tandem with Bosnian local authorities, often through involvement in training and educational regimes; second, there has been a shift away from a project-focus, where international needs are foremost, to an emphasis on NGO sustainability through skills-training. He concludes that despite a shift in the language of NGO and civil society development policies, the Bosnian NGO sector remains heavily reliant on international sponsorship, making it difficult for these institutions to play a normal civil society advocacy role through engaging and advocating on behalf of Bosnian people's needs.

Florian Bieber's contribution, 'Local Institutional Engineering: A Tale of Two Cities, Mostar and Brčko', considers the impact of local political and electoral arrangements in post-conflict peace-building. He compares two different approaches at the local level: Mostar, where international administrators allowed regular elections and, alongside, developed complex mechanisms of ethnic quotas; and Brčko, where the international arbitration commission created an 'autonomous district' run directly by an international appointee who selected Bosnian officials, enabling a greater emphasis on imposing consensus-building at a local level. Bieber suggests that direct international regulation was a major factor in encouraging important policy reforms in Brčko, but that neither direct regulation nor complex ethnic quotas have facilitated the creation of political frameworks capable of breaking down post-war ethno-political divisions.

Roberto Belloni's contribution, 'Peace-building at the Local Level: Refugee Return to Prijedor', provides an example of the importance of international policy-makers considering Bosnian people, especially refugee groups, as political subjects in their own right, rather than just as objects of political intervention. He suggests that international policy regarding refugee return after Dayton was often counterproductive, institutionalizing rather than overcoming ethnic segmentation. His research highlights the role of groups of refugees and displaced persons in forcing the agenda of minority return, against the wishes of international agencies, and the important political role of minority returnees in challenging the post-war political establishment in Prijedor.

The concluding two contributions provide an overview of the situation in BiH today. Michael Pugh, in 'Transformation in the Political Economy of Bosnia since Dayton', analyses the impact of internationally-imposed economic policies and questions the elitist view of Western policy-makers who often portray the problems arising from their promotion of market economic policies as the result of a clash between neo-liberal modernity and a pre-modern 'Balkan way'. He makes the point that this perspective is problematic in its dyadic assumptions and in its underestimation of the important linkages between the spheres of neo-liberalism and nationalist-clientism. Ironically, international policies in the economic sphere appear to have reinforced the social and political fragmentation of Bosnian life, further undermining the policy-making capacity and political legitimacy of the BiH state.

In 'Who Guards the Guardians? International Accountability in Bosnia', Richard Caplan considers the limited political accountability which the international administration has to its Bosnian subjects. Importantly, he highlights a number of contradictions in the operation of an externally-appointed international administration above the level of elected Bosnian institutions. These contradictions are not open to any easy resolution, and he contends that attempts to make these external institutions of governance more accountable to the people of Bosnia would only further undermine elected political institutions. He suggests that, while international administrations cannot be liberal democracies and there-fore cannot be judged on this basis, there is a need to increase both the level of local accountability of external institutions and Bosnian 'ownership' over policy-making.

The contributions to this volume establish that, in the case of BiH, it is undoubtedly true that it is possible to have peace without politics. Dayton itself established that peace could be achieved through the external pressure of military intervention and economic and political sanctions. This external pressure created a state, but one with no real basis in Bosnian society and little popular legitimacy. Since Dayton, external administrators have built roads and schools, issued bank-notes, restructured economic institutions, provided incentives for refugee return, banned political parties or removed their elected leaders, and pushed through a broad package of external policy proposals. The successful assertion of external influence is, of course, hardly surprising considering the small size of the Bosnian state, its dependency on external assistance and direct international control over the mechanisms of governance.

However, as is clear from the contributions here, it is also becoming apparent that state-building requires more than the largess – and coercive power – of exter-nal benefactors. Ten years after Dayton, the Bosnian state still lacks a secure basis in Bosnian society and commands little social or political legitimacy. To this extent, the critics of the Dayton settlement – who allege that Dayton ended a war but did not create a state – have a justifiable point. Post-Dayton Bosnia has changed relatively little in this respect. The Bosnian state still bears the imprint of its creation by powers external to the region, and it seems unlikely that Bosnian society can move forward until this legacy has been overcome. While the international administration has been able to institute a large number of administrative and policy reforms to meet the externally-decided needs of 'good governance', it has been unable to establish Bosnian institutions of *government* – those institutions which are crucial to legitimizing the Bosnian state and are capable of overcoming the divisions of the war. In this respect, the international experiment in state-building without politics has revealed major short-comings.

ACKNOWLEDGEMENTS

I would like to thank all the contributors to this volume, especially Michael Pugh, for their part in encouraging and supporting this project. I would also like to thank the British Academy's South East Europe Partnership Programme, for funding in the period 2003–05, which facilitated the seminar proceedings at which some of these essays originated.

NOTES

1. See for example, United Nations General Assembly resolution 1514 (XV) of 14 December 1960, 'Declaration on the Granting of Independence to Colonial Countries and Peoples', at www.unhchr.ch/html/menu3/b/c_coloni.htm.
2. See for example, RAND Corporation, *America's Role in Nation-building: From Germany to Iraq*, Santa Monica, CA: RAND, 2003; The Conflict, Security and Development Group, *A Review of Peace Operations: A Case for Change*, London: Kings College, 2003; M. Lund, 'What Kind of

Peace is Being Built?': Taking Stock of Post-Conflict Peacebuilding and Charting Future Directions', discussion paper for the International Development Research Centre, Ottawa, Canada, January 2003, at http://web.idrc.ca/uploads/user-S/10527469720lund_final_mar_20.pdf.

3. For further reading on the post-Dayton international regime see the website of the international Office of the High Representative, at www.ohr.int/; see also D. Chandler, *Bosnia: Faking Democracy after Dayton*, 2nd edn., London: Pluto Press, 2000; E.M. Cousens and C.K. Cater, *Toward Peace in Bosnia: Implementing the Dayton Accords*, Boulder, CO: Lynne Rienner, 2001; D. Sololović and F. Bieber (eds), *Reconstructing Multiethnic Societies: The Case of Bosnia-Herzegovina*, Aldershot: Ashgate, 2001; S. Bose, *Bosnia after Dayton: Nationalist Partition and International Intervention*, London: Hurst, 2002.

4. For background on post-war state-building in Germany and Japan, see for example, J.W. Dower, *Embracing Defeat: Japan in the Wake of World War II*, New York: W.W. Norton, 1999; D.G. Williamson, *Germany from Defeat to Partition, 1945-1963*, London: Longman, 2001.

5. S. Huntington, *Political Order in Changing Societies*, New Haven: Yale University Press, 1968.

6. Ibid., p.11.

7. Ibid., p.403.

8. *Office of the High Representative Bulletin*, No.62, 11 Oct. 1997.

9. J. Rodriguez, 'Our Man in Sarajevo', *El Pais*, 29 March 1998 (trans. Office of the High Representative).

10. Lord Ashdown, 'Inaugural Speech by the new High Representative for Bosnia and Herzegovina', BiH State Parliament, 27 May 2002, at www.ohr.int/ohr-dept/presso/presssp/default.asp?content_id = 8417; see also discussion in Chandler, 'Bosnia's New Colonial Governor', *Guardian*, 9 July 2002, at http://politics.guardian.co.uk/comment/story/0,9115,751918,00.html.

11. Huntington (n.5 above), p.404.

12. Ibid., p.405.

13. R. Paris, *At War's End: Building Peace after Civil Conflict*, Cambridge: Cambridge University Press, 2004.

14. Ibid., pp.189–90.

15. The potential hubris of the desire to externally reshape 'failed states' in isolation from social forces, is captured in the RAND Corporation recommendations for Iraq, (n.2 above), which suggest that rather than co-opt existing Iraqi institutions, the sounder approach is that of a 'root and branch overhaul of state and political structures', involving 'the creation of wholly new organizations at the local and national levels and the recruitment, training, and management of new staff', p.205.

16. A. Bendaña, 'From Peace-building to State-building: One Step Forward and Two Backwards', presentation at 'Nation-building, State-building and International Intervention: Between "Liberation" and Symptom Relief', CERI, Paris, 15 Oct. 2004. See also, J. Demmers et al. (eds), *Good Governance in the Era of Global Neoliberalism: Conflict and Depolitisation in Latin America, Eastern Europe, Asia and Africa*, London: Routledge, 2004.

17. See, for example, Ashdown, 'What Baghdad can learn from BiH', *Guardian*, 22 April 2003; and 'Broken Communities, Shattered Lives: Winning the Savage War of Peace', speech to the International Rescue Committee, London, 19 June 2003, at www.ohr.int/print/?content_id = 30130.

18. See further, Chandler, '"Imposing the Rule of Law": The Lessons of BiH for Peacebuilding in Iraq', *International Peacekeeping*, Vol.11, No.2, 2004, pp.312–33.

19. See A. Colombo, 'Asymetrical Warfare or Asymetrical Society? The Changing Form of War and the Collapse of International Society', in A. Gobbicchi (ed.), *Globalization, Armed Conflicts and Security*, Rome: Cemiss-Rubbettino, 2004, pp.111–27.

20. K. Holsti, *The State, War, and the State of War*, Cambridge: Cambridge University Press, 1996.

21. M. Kaldor, *New and Old Wars: Organized Violence in a Global Era*, London: Polity Press, 1998.

22. See further, Chandler, *From Kosovo to Kabul: Human Rights and International Intervention*, London: Pluto Press, 2002.

23. Holsti (n.20 above), pp.190–91. For an excellent survey see S. Chesterman, *Just War or Just Peace?: Humanitarian Intervention and International Law*, Oxford: Oxford University Press, 2002.

24. Report of the Secretary-General's High-Level Panel on Threats, Challenges and Change, *A More Secure World: Our Shared Responsibility*, New York: United Nations, 2004, at www.un.org/secureworld/.

25. Ibid., p.83.

26. See for example, K. Booth, 'Security and Emancipation', *Review of International Studies*, Vol.17, No.4, 1991, pp.313–26; K. Krausse and M.C. Williams (eds), *Critical Security Studies*,

London: UCL Press, 1997; K. Booth (ed.), *Critical Security Studies and World Politics*, Boulder CO: Lynne Rienner, 2005.

27. M. Foucault, *Society must be Defended: Lectures at the Collège de France 1975-76*, trans. D. Macey, London: Allen Lane/Penguin, 2003.

28. See, for example, D. Campbell, *National Deconstruction: Violence, Identity and Justice in Bosnia*, Minneapolis: University of Minnesota Press, 1998; R. Keane, *Reconstituting Sovereignty: Post-Dayton Bosnia Uncovered*, Aldershot: Ashgate, 2002.

29. Where 'realist' theorists often highlighted the autonomy of the political and the limits of bureaucratic attempts to impose law and administration over clashes of power and interest, today's intellectual fashion is to focus on the indeterminacy and socially constructed nature of power and interest, emphasizing the importance of norms and law. For 'realist' critiques of the privileging of law and administration above the political, see, for example, the classic texts, E.H. Carr, *The Twenty Years' Crisis, 1919-1939*, Basingstoke: Palgrave, 2001 [orig. 1939]; and H.J. Morgenthau, *Politics Among Nations: The Struggle for Power and Peace*, New York: McGraw-Hill Education, 1992 [orig. 1948]. For a more in-depth discussion, see Chandler, *Constructing Global Civil Society: Morality and Power in International Relations*, Basingstoke: Palgrave, 2004.

30. See, for example, R. Falk, *On Humane Governance*, Cambridge: Polity Press, 1995; D. Archibugi and D. Held (eds), *Cosmopolitan Democracy: An Agenda for a New World Order*, Cambridge: Polity Press, 1995; A. Linklater, *The Transformation of Political Community*, Cambridge: Polity Press, 1998.

31. Kenneth Minogue highlights the despotic dangers of 'political moralism', which sees autonomy and independence – i.e., the political sphere – as a barrier to ethically-derived notions of justice, and argues that this approach to politics is especially strong in discussions of international relations. See, for example, his *Politcs: A Very Short Introduction*, Oxford: Oxford University Press, 1995, pp.104–5.

32. International Commission on Intervention and State Sovereignty, *The Responsibility to Protect*, Ottawa: International Development Research Centre, 2001.

33. Study Group on Europe's Security Capabilities, *A Human Security Doctrine for Europe*, Barcelona: 15 Sept. 2004, p.9, at www.lse.ac.uk/Depts/global/Human%20Security%20Report%20Full.pdf.

34. Report of the Secretary-General's High-level Panel on Threats, Challenges and Change (n.24 above), p.18; see also Chandler, 'The Responsibility to Protect: Imposing the 'Liberal Peace'?', *International Peacekeeping*, Vol.11, No.1, 2004, Special Issue: Peace Operations and Global Order, pp.59–81.

35. M. Ignatieff, *Empire Lite: Nation-building in Bosnia, Kosovo and Afghanistan*, London: Vintage, 2003.

36. A. Etzioni, 'A Self-Restrained Approach to Nation-Building by Foreign Powers', *International Affairs*, Vol.80, No.1, 2004, p.15; see also F. Fukuyama, *State Building: Governance and World Order in the Twenty-First Century*, London: Profile Books, 2004, p.123.

37. See, for example, G. Knaus and F. Martin, 'Lessons from Bosnia and Herzegovina: Travails of the European Raj', *Journal of Democracy*, Vol.14, No.3, 2003, pp.60–74; see also the European Stability Initiative website at www.esiweb.org/.

38. W. Bain, *Between Anarchy and Society: Trusteeship and the Obligations of Power*, Oxford: Oxford University Press, 2003.

39. Chesterman, *You, the People: the United Nations, Transitional Administration, and State-Building*, Oxford: Oxford University Press, 2004, p.45.

40. Ibid., pp.238–49.

The Bosnian State a Decade after Dayton

SUMANTRA BOSE

Free institutions are next to impossible in a country made up of different nationalities...It is in general a necessary condition for free institutions that the boundaries of government should coincide in the main with those of nationalities.
John Stuart Mill, *Considerations on Representative Government* [1]

[State-building in Bosnia] was a watershed experience... Aware of the powers of the High Representative to impose laws and remove obstructive officials, both...Bosnian intellectuals and international observers... demanded that I extensively use such powers... 'You have to impose the right solutions', I heard over and over again. But to my mind 'imposing' democracy and civil society seemed a contradiction in terms. However, during the first one-and-a-half years of my mandate I indeed had to act as the most interventionist High Representative ever.
Wolfgang Petritsch, High Representative in BiH, 1999–2002 [2]

Will the Bosnian state wither away, a doomed victim of its foundational and fundamental contradictions? Or will it prove sceptics wrong and turn out to be sustainable after all? A decade ago a straw-poll on the question would have elicited predictably polarized answers, depending on the respondents' views on several interconnected issues – the historical character of Bosnia and Herzegovina (BiH) as a society and the nature of relations between its three major peoples, the relative importance of external instigation as opposed to internal conflict in the causation of the 1992–95 Bosnian war, and the legitimacy and efficacy of international intervention in the most representative and most broken of the former Yugoslavia's federal units. The debate continues of course. A decade on it is somewhat clearer, nonetheless, that the Bosnian state is not about to wither away, if only because its inherent weakness is compensated in part by the resolve of the 'international community' that a Bosnian state should survive, and the protracted effort invested by the 'community' of powerful states, regional European institutions and multilateral organizations to ensure that survival.

This being the case, I ask two questions in this essay. First, is the consociational and confederal paradigm established by the Dayton agreement, and subsequently institutionalized, the appropriate framework for the Bosnian state?[3] The choice of this framework has been the focus of severe criticism and bitter argument, from Bosnians and interested foreigners alike, ever since it came into being. I claim here that this framework does provide, in the rather daunting circumstances that prevail, the most feasible and most democratic form of government for Bosnia's precarious existence as a multi-national state. With the twin-benefits of some more time and limited rationalizing reform, its construct of layered sovereignties, porous borders and multiple citizenships *may* prove in the near-term future to be both model and bridge for the larger post-Yugoslav region in south-eastern Europe, and it *may* also gradually facilitate the conditions that will allow for a less segmented polity to emerge and function within BiH.

My second question is inextricably linked to the first. Bosnia is a state of international design that exists *by* international design. Is this international engagement with state-building and democratization an example, indeed exemplar, of liberal internationalism at its best – or liberal imperialism at its worst? In assessing this debate, I argue that while the rose-tinted view of a benign liberal internationalism dispensing democracy and human rights is deeply naïve, extraordinarily uncritical and, in some versions at least, blindly arrogant, its antithesis – the view that this is an essentially malign liberal imperialism at work – is also flawed, exaggerated and tendentious in that it does not take sufficient account of the context of post-war BiH and of some real benefits that have accrued to Bosnians from international presence and activity. This presence and activity has had many aspects deserving of serious criticism but on balance has done more good than harm. Bosnian society would clearly have been worse off without the international community in its midst.

Failed State or Multi-national Democracy?

John Stuart Mill's pessimism about prospects of democracy in non-homogenous societies is dated. Contemporary scholars typically assert that 'the possibility of…multiple identities' – involving complementary loyalties to state and ethno-national community – 'makes…a multi-national democracy possible',[4] and that multi-national states will merely face somewhat 'different challenges in democratic transitions'.[5]

But BiH's 'stateness problem' puts it in a different category from states which have substantially succeeded in democratically accommodating ethno-national difference and conflict, such as Switzerland, Belgium, Canada, Spain or India. According to political scientists Juan Linz and Alfred Stepan, who coined the term, 'a stateness problem may be said to exist when a significant proportion of the population do not accept the territorial boundaries of the state...as a legitimate political unit to which they owe obedience'.[6] BiH is a fragment of a failed state, the former Yugoslavia, and itself fragmented violently as a result of the incompatible agendas of national self-determination unleashed by the collapse of the Yugoslav framework.[7] Hence, international intervention in BiH after Dayton aimed at nothing less than 'setting up a state on the basis of little more than the ruins and rivalries of a bitter war',[8] in the words of Carl Bildt, the first international High Representative to supervise the process. That is a challenge of such magnitude that John Stuart Mill might appear prophetic in retrospect.

It has been pointed out that clashing preferences regarding the legitimate boundaries of sovereignty tend to generate 'the most intractable and bitter political conflicts'.[9] The political theorist Robert Dahl argues that 'we cannot solve the question of the proper domain of sovereignty' where such disagreement exists over 'the rightfulness of the unit', although 'a crisp, unimpeachable solution... would be a marvellous achievement of democratic theory and practice'.[10] *However*, Dahl also says that although:

> It does not seem possible to arrive at a defensible conclusion about the proper unit of democracy by strictly theoretical reasoning, we are in the domain not of theoretical reasoning but practical judgment... To say that an answer cannot be derived theoretically is not to say that judgments need be arbitrary... We shall need to make complex and debatable empirical and utilitarian judgments... In the face of great empirical complexity... [we need to] find reasonable answers. The result may well be a complex system with several layers of democratic government, each operating with a somewhat different agenda.[11]

It was precisely this type of institutional framework that was arrived at in Dayton after a series of 'complex and debatable empirical and utilitarian judgments'.

The wisdom of that judgment has been the subject of heated debate ever since. Some critics have forcefully emphasized the double standards inherent in the international community condoning and even sanctioning the partition of Yugoslavia and then insisting that BiH must be kept whole as a showcase of tolerance and coexistence.[12] Others have reminded us of a popular saying in the former Yugoslavia, roughly translatable as: 'Without BiH there can be no Yugoslavia, and without Yugoslavia there can be no BiH.' For practical purposes, the Dayton settlement ran the risk of satisfying none of the three Bosnian peoples – the Serbs and Croats by denying them the right to either govern themselves in sovereign jurisdictions or to merge with their neighbouring kin-states, the Bosnian Muslims (or Bosniacs) by creating such a decentralized state that it became doubtful whether the 'state', even if juridically existent, could have any meaningful empirical reality. As one sceptic noted, 'BiH is now the only state in the world composed of both a republic and a federation'.[13]

From its inception this improbable state – or rather the settlement that led to its creation[14] – evoked calls for radical revision. One of the most persistent voices for intrusive state-building by the international community with the strategic objective of 'integrating' BiH was the International Crisis Group (ICG), a policy advocacy group based in Brussels. The ICG paid lip-service to 'Dayton' but in fact advocated strategies and tactics which if implemented would lead to the superseding of the Dayton settlement, whose pillars are group rights and autonomy, by a unitary[15] and even centralized state.[16] In other words, the ICG's preferred approach amounted to a radical and subversive critique of the fundamentals of the Dayton state. The ICG agenda had influential Bosnian proponents. The best known is the politician Haris Silajdžić who, while serving as co-chair of the BiH Council of Ministers in January 2000, published a 'memorandum on change'. This memorandum called for 'preserving and strengthening all relevant positive elements' of Dayton but also for 'some reconstruction'. In fact, the memorandum went on to argue that it had become 'essential to *urgently* and *radically* reconstruct those elements which are non-integrative, ineffective and even partly counterproductive' (my emphasis). In particular, the memorandum complained that 'the state institutions of BiH function more like international conferences than organs of state', and demanded that the international community act to eliminate aspects of the political structure 'that favour nationally exclusivist political options'. The document also called for steps to 'bring about rapid, mass returns of refugees and displaced persons'.[17]

The core motive behind this memorandum – which of course never acquired the infamy of the Serbian Academy of Arts and Sciences' 1986 declaration in Belgrade – became clear in the autumn of 2000 when Silajdžić's, Party for BiH (SBiH) campaigned in Bosnian elections on the slogan 'Bosnia Without Entities'.[18] Stripping away the inessentials, the memorandum was at its core a demand for the liquidation of Republika Srpska (RS). The 'multiethnic' and apparently 'civic' vision of integration in post-war BiH is an attention-seeking device for some sectarian Bosniac political elements who want to appear 'liberal' to Westerners – distinguishing them both from ethno-nationalists in their own group and from the incorrigibly nationalist 'enemy' group(s) – and the preserve of either naïve or motivated Westerners who do not, and perhaps do not wish to, understand the historical context and institutional antecedents of the present Bosnian state.

By the late 1990s, the ICG's reports, while often well researched and informative, had acquired a monotonous, predictable quality, filled with prescriptions for international action that looked like a radical interventionist's fantasy. In autumn 2001, Wolfgang Petritsch implied the irrelevance of this revisionist perspective when he told a Sarajevo magazine that 'the Dayton peace agreement is an international, binding agreement. There are no question marks hanging over it.'[19] This was just as well, because opinion surveys conducted in 2003 by the UN Development Programme suggested that 'a state of citizens' – something close to the ostensibly civic, integrationist formula – was supported by only 52 per cent of Bosniacs, 17 per cent of BiH Croats and 9 per cent of BiH Serbs.[20] In other words, this was an idea overwhelmingly rejected by two of the three Bosnian communities, and favoured by barely half of the third (and numerically largest) community. After the failure of the Yugoslav idea and the second

Yugoslav state,[21] and the 43 months of bitter violence in BiH that resulted, a unitary state based on a common Bosnian national identity is simply unrealizable, at least for the present and foreseeable future. But it would also be anti-democratic – against the wishes of the vast majority of Bosnians. By late 2003 the ICG effectively closed down its Sarajevo office and shifted its attention to other more current and presumably compelling crisis spots.

The other alternative to the unwieldy Dayton compromise – the partition of BiH into three sovereign ethno-national statelets or the incorporation of the Serb and Croat statelets as units of Serbia-Montenegro and Croatia respectively, leaving a Bosnian Muslim rump state – has largely faded from public view and debate over the past decade. This has happened mostly because it has been clear since Dayton that the international community is unanimous in ruling out partition.

When I was writing *Bosnia after Dayton*, during 2001, it was already clear to me that the Dayton settlement, integrationist urgings and partitionist cravings notwithstanding, would, probably with some rationalizing reforms, provide the long-term political framework for the country. Close to Dayton's tenth anniversary, we can legitimately ask whether this framework provides the basis for a viable multi-national democracy in BiH. My answer is a cautious affirmative.

The Consociational Confederation

The Bosnian state is a consociational confederation. Consociationalism is an empirical model of government developed by the political scientist Arend Lijphart and other scholars as an institutional prescription for plural and divided societies which gives primacy to collectivities rather than individual citizens. Its underlying ethos and policymaking procedures are oriented to broadly based agreement across groups, in contrast to the majoritarian mechanism conventionally used in non-consociational democracies.[22]

Consociationalism is built into all levels of the Bosnian state established by Dayton, from the tripartitite collective state presidency to the municipal tier of government.[23] In addition, the Bosnian state is *confederal* in character. In a confederation, 'self-rule' is so extensive that the federating units, rather than the federal government, are the dominant layer of government. In other words, confederations emphasize self-rule at the expense of shared rule. The Bosnian state is such a confederal union, between its two political entities – a radically autonomous RS and a Federation of BiH (FBiH) in which most competencies are devolved to the ten cantons (eight of which have clear Bosniac or Croat majority populations). Segmental autonomy, one of the pillars of a consociational structure, can take a variety of forms, both territorial and non-territorial. In the Bosnian case, its primary manifestation is ethno-territorial autonomy.

The Bosnian settlement, however, has two major international dimensions, both of which are missing from the 'classic' formulations of the consociational approach. First, it is the result of an internationally brokered peace treaty, negotiated under American stewardship, rather than a pact reached in the domestic domain. This meant that the role of the international community would be paramount in its implementation. The Dayton agreement is also international in that it is a *regional* treaty. It was signed by the then leaders of Serbia and Croatia in addition to the then Bosnian Muslim leader, underlining the regional roots and causes of the conflict that tore Bosnia apart. More important in substantive terms, the Dayton settlement authorized both BiH entities to establish and develop special relationships with neighbouring states – effectively Serbia-Montenegro and Croatia – and permitted Bosnian citizens to hold concurrent citizenship of those neighbouring states. In other words, the confederal element of the Bosnian settlement transcends BiH's borders – it is a suprastate, regional settlement based on porous internal *and* external borders. If the road to recovery for the region of former Yugoslavia (to some extent barring Slovenia) – which faces common problems of post-communist democratization and economic reform – lies in renewing ruptured links through cross-border cooperation, this is unambiguously a *good* thing. BiH is, as it was before the war, a demographic microcosm of what was Yugoslavia and could in some ways be a pivot of such a renewed regionalism across much of the former Yugoslav space.

In both these international features – especially the latter – the Dayton accord is similar to ongoing or attempted consociational settlements in other deeply divided societies, such as Northern Ireland, Cyprus and Lebanon. This type of settlement has numerous critics. Three of the most powerful criticisms are:

- The entrenchment, indeed reification of collective ethno-national identities.
- The reliance on segmental elites to make the system work, and the likelihood that in the aftermath of protracted enmity and/or severe violent conflict, such elites will lack the will and/or the capacity required.
- The argument that consociational frameworks work in moderately divided societies, such as Switzerland or Belgium, where there is an overarching national identity and no recent history of violent conflict, but not in deeply divided societies such as Bosnia or Northern Ireland.

These are substantive and legitimate points. But counter-arguments exist. The communitarian basis of such settlements is not due to some sort of identity fetishism, but is a response to difficult situations where ethno-national faultlines are the dominant cleavage in society and politics. Elite cooperation, cutting across segmental divides, is indeed a tall order in post-conflict contexts, but two caveats are in order. First, a striking characteristic of peacebuilding and stabilization processes in societies like Northern Ireland and Bosnia is the degree of international community involvement. Sworn enemies, if left to themselves, may not be willing and able to cooperate, but a judicious mixture of international inducement and compellance may just work to elicit the grudging pragmatism necessary from them. Second, the passage of time may have a moderating effect on even the most bitterly-held animosities. These two factors combined can produce such unprecedented developments as power-sharing in government between the Democratic Unionist Party and Sinn Fein in Northern Ireland.

Finally, it is true that consociational, confederal settlements have difficult prospects in deeply divided societies. Yet there is a paradox here. Although Lebanon's

National Pact broke down in the mid-1970s, the post-civil war settlement turned out to be a renovated version of the same framework. Even though independent Cyprus's experiment with consociationalism lasted barely four years, from 1960 to 1963, before collapsing amid discord and strife, the Annan Plan followed the same principles, built on a confederal foundation. It is almost universally recognized that the Good Friday pact, whatever its flaws, represents the only feasible path to uneasy, democratic coexistence in Northern Ireland. The complex Dayton compromise is modelled on the confederal, consociational structure of socialist Yugoslavia during the 1970s and 1980s – not an auspicious legacy. Yet in post-Yugoslavia and post-war Bosnia, where 'nation-building' integration is a fantasy, at once hopelessly naïve and mindlessly arrogant, and partition and segregation equally not a possibility, this paradigm is the only way forward.

It is in recognition of this reality that the major reform to BiH's governmental structure since the end of the war – enacted at the behest of the international community in April 2002 – has further extended and deepened the Dayton paradigm of group-based rights. This reform has given Serbs guaranteed rights and representation in the FBiH and non-Serbs the same in the RS. As a result the RS now has Bosniac and Croat vice-presidents and, more significantly, up to 50 per cent of RS government ministers have to be non-Serbs (five Bosniac, three Croat). An upper chamber of the RS legislature has parity representation of the three communities. Serbs are guaranteed reciprocal rights in Federation institutions, including parity representation in the upper chamber of that entity's legislature and access to ministerial and deputy ministerial portfolios in the executive. As Petritsch, who shepherded the reform as High Representative, puts it: 'One cannot and should not get rid of the ethnic paradigm.'[24] Of course, much of this reform can be derided as either symbolic or superficial window dressing. But this levelling of the institutional structure of rights and representation across BiH still represents a step in the right direction, especially in the context of substantial minority returns (on which more below).

Further incremental, rationalizing reforms to BiH's institutional framework are possible during the Dayton state's second decade. In *Bosnia after Dayton*, I emphasized the difficulties in the Bosnian context of implementing schemes aimed at encouraging cross-ethnic integration through the deliberate design of electoral systems, of the kind favoured by the political scientist Donald Horowitz.[25] I am convinced of the soundness of this, and believe that the current electoral system of proportional representation through party/coalition lists (list PR) is the appropriate choice for BiH. Nonetheless, it is conceivable that elements of the integration through electoral engineering approach, based on multiple preferential voting and/or ethnic vote distribution requirements for certain executive posts at various levels of government, can be introduced with some success, albeit in a very limited way, in the foreseeable future. This should not be ruled out as permanently infeasible – times change and conditions can change with time. Similarly, the proposal presented in early 2004 by the European Stability Initiative (ESI), a specialist think-tank, for the cantonization of BiH – whereby the Federation tier of government would be abolished and the RS would become the largest and most populous of 12 cantons comprising a federal state – is worthy of serious debate.

> [The] proposal is to progressively abolish the Federation, and with it the constitutional status of the entities. The result would be a simplified, three-layered federal state with twelve autonomous units: the ten cantons of the current Federation, Republika Srpska and the District of Brčko. This would represent a fundamental change to the structure of the state, turning it into a normal, European federal system with central, regional and municipal governments.[26]

Reform on these lines may have the beneficial side-effect of solving the Dayton state's major residual problem – the disaffection of BiH Croats with the Federation arrangement that precipitated a rebellion in 2001. A Balkan Switzerland would still be a far cry, but the proposal is well argued and most important, feasible. In fact, it may not even represent an immensely 'fundamental' change, just an important rationalizing reform of the status quo that would facilitate the process of BiH's integration into trans-European institutions. A gradual strengthening of the 'shared rule' component of federalism is feasible in BiH – indeed, it is already underway – and would create a more symmetrical, balanced and workable federal state. But such a gradual change in the balance between self-rule and shared rule would have limits, above all because the competitive party system in BiH is segmented along ethno-national cleavages and no significant party with a cross-national base of support exists in the country. Bosnia will still remain an explicitly multi-national state based on group rights and self-rule for its three major peoples.

The notion that a (con)federal, consociational structure of government is an inherent obstacle to Bosnia's journey to Europe – or more precisely to the European Union (EU), since Bosnia is culturally and geographically already in Europe – is sadly misguided and entirely unfounded. One of the EU's new members is the still-divided island of Cyprus. Cyprus's situation is somewhat complicated, because although membership applies in principle to the whole island, in practical terms it is currently valid for the Greek-Cypriot south only – the Turkish-Cypriot north is effectively excluded pending a final settlement. Had the Annan Plan passed the popular referendum in both jurisdictions, this would not have been the case. The entire island would have acceded as one country in principle and in practice to the EU, as a very decentralized confederal republic of two 'constituent states' whose government is based on consociational principles. The Dayton compromise did contain certain elements that needed revision in order to meet basic criteria for membership eligibility in trans-European institutions – for example, the superseding of multiple armies from the civil war period by an umbrella Bosnian army. But there is no imperative whatsoever to throw the baby out with the bathwater.[27]

Bosnia's situation and future are precarious. But that is not because – at least not primarily because – of the institutional structure of the Bosnian state and the principles that underpin that structure. It is due to other factors: the dire condition of the economy and mass unemployment; the emigration of highly educated and qualified citizens that began in 1992 and continued after the war; the extremely poor quality of post-secondary education that, coupled with poor job prospects, encourages emigration by bright young people who want to make something of their life; and the extremely low calibre of the political class, which is ineffective more because of incompetence than inter-ethnic wrangling. Bosnia is so fragile because of these factors, not because of some original sin visited on it in Dayton, Ohio in November 1995.

Liberal Internationalism or Liberal Imperialism?

The line between liberal internationalism and liberal imperialism is admittedly thin and in the case of Bosnia since Dayton, the distinction probably lies in the eyes of the beholder. Yet arguments that in their critical zeal invoke historical analogies between international engagement in post-Dayton BiH and colonialism – such as Britain's imperial rule over India, which was occasionally sought to be justified with recourse to ideas of a 'liberal' civilizing mission – run the risk of substituting caricature for critique (they also risk trivializing the brutality and avarice of British colonial rule in India).[28] Such arguments have two basic shortcomings. First, they do not seem to adequately acknowledge the *context* of internationally-led state-building and democratization in BiH after 1995. That context has involved the onerous, thankless task of building a state and a democracy in a deeply divided fragment of a 'former' country which underwent institutional and social meltdown, and in the more or less chaotic aftermath of a messy end to overlapping civil wars across much of former Yugoslavia and within BiH. If the international community in post-1995 BiH has perceived and presented itself as the upholders of law, order, reason and morality in a manner reminiscent of 'liberal' imperialist powers of a previous era it is because of this context, where local political elites have frequently been no better than gangsters and local publics have emerged severely traumatized and shell-shocked from the bloody implosion of the regime and society they knew. This is the context that at least partly explains the dilemma Petritsch encountered – although he felt uncomfortable about 'imposing' democracy and the rule of law, he also felt compelled to continuously intervene. Indeed, the more convincing critical analogy with the authoritarian, controlling aspects of the international mission in BiH does not need to travel either to India or back to the nineteenth century. The better analogy is with the communist regime in the second Yugoslavia (1945–91), which constantly sought to cover up its transparency and accountability deficits by assuming a high moral and ideological pedestal. BiH had possibly the most conservative variant of this regime among the republics of former Yugoslavia.[29]

The second shortcoming is that in focusing its attack on the most intrusive and authoritarian aspects of international activity – specifically the wide-ranging powers of intervention in the political process vested in the High Representative's person and office after December 1997 – such arguments could, inadvertently or otherwise, give an unbalanced and incomplete picture of the international role in BiH after Dayton. The viceregal powers of the High Representative to dismiss elected public officials and party leaders, impose legislation by decree and ban media deemed offensive are justly controversial, and I made the point several years ago that although 'a policy of selective sanctions may have been unavoidable, given the venal, gangster-like disposition of many Bosnian power-brokers...[this] is probably not consistent with the longer-term aim of fostering genuine pluralism and rule of law in BiH'.[30] A debate on these powers and when and how they are applied, with what explanation and consequence, has therefore long been overdue (see Richard Caplan, this volume).

It ought to be noted, however, that there are at least some cases where use of extraordinary powers has had effects that can be regarded as beneficial. In November 1999, for example, the High Representative summarily sacked 22 municipal and cantonal officials from all three communities for 'obstructing' implementation of the Dayton accords. One of them was Stipe Marić, the hardline Croat mayor of the Mostar South-West municipality, which constitutes the heart of urban Mostar. Marić's removal helped unblock returns by evicted Bosniacs and Serbs to this part of the city. In fact, I would argue that the most serious error of international strategy in BiH has been not the exercise of decree powers from up 'high', but the misguided and unproductive quest for 'non-nationalist' or 'non-extremist' collaborators among the Bosnian political class. This led to international sponsorship of Milorad Dodik's government in the RS from 1998 to 2000 and of the 'Alliance for Change', mostly in the Federation although state-wide as well, from 2000 to 2002. The behaviour and performance of these Bosnian surrogates proved to be disappointing in the extreme, and they were voted out by the electorate as a result.

Yet the international presence in BiH has been about more than authoritarian meddling. Virtually all developments in BiH since the end of the war that contribute to a slightly better present for its citizens and open up better prospects – however tenuous – for their future have been due to international effort, often very intensive and protracted. Examples include the Central Bank, opened in 1998, which issued the Bosnian currency and eliminated the absurd and unviable situation in monetary and financial affairs prevalent until then, and the Election Law enacted in 2001 which facilitated BiH's membership in the Council of Europe. But the most notable achievement of international engagement has been in the returns by wartime refugees and displaced persons, particularly the return of 'minority' expellees' to their homes in areas dominated by members of another community. The most progressive – and ambitious – clause of Dayton was its guarantee that all who wished to return would be enabled to do so. But that was just a promise, and the scale of the problem was enormous – 1.2 million refugees and 1.1 million internally displaced people, of a pre-war population of 4.4 million.

After sluggish minority returns, especially to the RS, between 1996 and 1999, minority returns accelerated in 2000 and peaked in 2001 and 2002 as security conditions and perceptions improved across most of the country, falling off again in 2003 and 2004 as the pool of returnees approached saturation point. By 31 August 2004 minority returns totalled 445,735 people across the country, a significant figure for a country whose population is approximately 3.5 million. Of these, 156,731 persons – overwhelmingly Bosniac – had returned to the impoverished terrain of the RS.[31] This level of minority return in the decade since Dayton – almost half a million people – would not have materialized without energetic implementation of the international community's Property Law Implementation Plan (PLIP), the sustained efforts on the ground of its multi-agency Reconstruction and Return Task Force (RRTF), the reform of local policing supervised until end-2002 by the UN International Police Task Force (IPTF) and the security cover provided until end-2004 by the Stabilization Force (SFOR). Of course, the figures of registered minority returns could be somewhat inflated and probably are, given that some returnees come back only temporarily to repossess and then sell their houses and apartments, and it needs to be remembered that elderly people, who will not live much longer, are disproportionately represented among such returnees. Nonetheless, the international commitment to the *right* of return, which has resulted in substantial minority returns in difficult circumstances, sets a positive and rare example. The robust defence of the principle of return and its vigorous enforcement at the cusp of the twentieth- and twenty-first centuries is an exceptionally encouraging development given the grim history of the twentieth century, when mass expulsions on ethno-national grounds occurred repeatedly and irreversibly. The Palestinians of 1948, the Hindus, Muslims and Sikhs of the Indian subcontinent in 1947, and the central and east European Germans in 1945–46 never had the opportunity afforded to Bosnians 50 years later. But Bosnians should not be begrudged that opportunity.

Conclusion

On 23 July 2004 a reconstructed replica of the famed *stari most* or 'old bridge' across the Neretva river in Mostar,[32] which was destroyed in November 1993 during heavy fighting in the town, was ceremonially inaugurated amid much fanfare. A galaxy of notables from the Yugoslav successor-states and the international community graced the occasion, which was covered live by major international broadcast media and featured on the front pages of many of the world's leading newspapers the next morning. The local reaction to this international jamboree was circumspect. Cutting across communities, many Mostaris agreed that the new structure somehow lacked the grace and splendour of the sixteenth-century original. The event also evoked reactions ranging from indifference to sullen hostility among most of the city's Croats, who are concentrated in west Mostar.[33] However, even Mostar's Bosniacs, who dominate the *stari grad* or 'old town' where the bridge lies, who identify the most with the city's Ottoman heritage, and who welcomed the reconstruction of the bridge destroyed by BiH Croat forces during the civil war, had little time or patience for the orchestrated shenanigans of the international community who descended in droves on their town. Indeed:

> Local Bosniacs poured scorn on the international obsession with the bridge's alleged wider meaning, such as the one voiced by the international community's High Representative Paddy Ashdown, who said [in his speech] that the bridge is a cornerstone of Bosnia's reconstruction as a multiethnic society. As if that was not enough, Bosnia could, according to Ashdown,

become a bridge between Islamic countries and Europe, helping the two worlds overcome misguided and stereotyped views of each other... 'That may be too much reconciliation for one bridge', said a local Bosniac.[34]

Grandiloquent declamations by grandees are a predictable if tiresome feature of such occasions. Yet it is important to contradict false perceptions and expectations which – especially when disseminated by an apparently authoritative source – receive wide currency. The new old bridge in Mostar, far from heralding Bosnia's multiethnic resurrection, makes little difference to inter-community relations in the town, and Bosnia is not a laboratory for addressing and healing global schisms either. The words of BiH's first international High Representative are far better judged: 'The peace agreement balances the reality of division with structures of cooperation and integration, and is based on the hope that over time the imperative of integration in the country and the region will be the dominant factor.'[35]

A decade after Dayton, the Bosnian state has made progress towards becoming a minimally functional multi-national democracy. To the extent that fears of state failure still loom, it is not because of the political-institutional framework but because of severe social problems arising from impoverishment and unemployment, emigration and organized crime. The international intervention to build and stabilize a Bosnian state and a Bosnian democracy is unfinished, much like a building under construction whose main decorative feature is unsightly scaffolding. That international intervention will never entirely live down the 'liberal imperialist' taint – and justifiably so. But at the same time it would be inaccurate and unfair to reduce the entire enterprise to 'liberal imperialism'. Both 'liberal internationalism' and 'liberal imperialism' are fashionable labels. They and their respective partisans – the missionaries and the doomsayers – should be treated with caution.

A decade from now, Bosnia will still be an interesting saga and puzzle for all students of state-building under international auspices and of democratization in a deeply divided society. The promised land – the EU – remains frustratingly distant. Yet as a EU Police Mission (EUPM) monitors the Bosnian police in the wake of the UN's exit, a lean EU Force (EUFOR) provides the security guarantee, and the euro widely circulates as a parallel currency to the Bosnian convertible mark, a beginning has been made. It is probable at the very least that the cyclical pattern, familiar since the late nineteenth century, of violent conflict every one or two generations in Bosnia and its wider region has finally been consigned to history. The departure has taken place; the arrival is another matter.

NOTES

1. J.S. Mill, *Considerations on Representative Government*, New York: Liberal Arts Press, 1958 [1861], pp.230, 232–3.
2. Wolfgang Petritsch, 'The Fate of Bosnia and Hercegovina', interview with C. Solioz, 2003. Provided to this author as part of personal communication.
3. For an explanation of the institutional architecture of the Dayton settlement see S. Bose, *Bosnia after Dayton: Nationalist Partition and International Intervention*, New York: Oxford University Press, 2002, ch.5. For an analysis of how the Dayton settlement was reached see ch.2.

4. J. Linz, A. Stepan and R. Gunther, 'Democratic Transition and Consolidation in Southern Europe, with Reflections on Latin America and Eastern Europe', in P.N. Diamandouros and H. Puhle (eds), *The Politics of Democratic Consolidation: Southern Europe in Comparative Perspective*, Baltimore: Johns Hopkins University Press, 1995, p.122.

5. A. Przeworski, *Sustainable Democracy*, Cambridge: Cambridge University Press, 1995, p.21.

6. J. Linz and A. Stepan, "Political Identities and Electoral Sequences: Spain, the Soviet Union and Yugoslavia", *Daedalus*, Vol.121, No.2, 1992, p.123.

7. Rogers Brubaker has usefully conceptualized this sort of post-communist conflict as a triadic one between new nationalizing states, their national minorities, and the external national homelands of those minorities. See R. Brubaker, *Nationalism Reframed: Nationhood and the National Question in the New Europe*, Cambridge: Cambridge University Press, 1996, ch.3.

8. C. Bildt, *Peace Journey: The Struggle for Peace in Bosnia*, London: Weidenfeld & Nicholson, 1998, p.392.

9. F. Whelan, 'Democratic Theory and the Boundary Problem', in J. R. Pennock and J. Chapman (eds), *Liberal Democracy: NOMOS XXV*, New York, New York University Press, 1983, pp.13–47.

10. R.A. Dahl, *Democracy and its Critics*, New Haven: Yale University Press, 1989, p.207. For a persuasive explanation of why popular referenda provide no solutions to disputed sovereignty see Dahl, 'Democracy, Majority Rule and Gorbachev's Referendum', *Dissent*, Vol.38, No.4, 1991, pp.491–6. In Bosnia, such a referendum, held on 29 February and 1 March 1992, proved to be the catalyst to the outbreak of civil war.

11. R.A. Dahl, *Democracy, Liberty and Equality*, Oslo: Norwegian University Press, 1986, pp.124–5.

12. R.M. Hayden, 'Schindler's Fate: Genocide, Ethnic Cleansing and Population Transfers,' *Slavic Review*, Vol.55, No.4, 1996, pp.727–48, P. Radan, 'Yugoslavia's Internal Borders as International Borders: A Question of Appropriateness', *East European Quarterly*, Vol.33, No.2, 1999, pp.137–55; Radan, 'The Badinter Arbitration Commission and the Partition of Yugoslavia', *Nationalities Papers*, No. 25, 1997, pp.537–57.

13. G.N. Bardos, 'The Bosnian Cold War: Politics, Society and International Engagement after Dayton', *The Harriman Review*, Vol. 11, No. 3, 1999, p.2.

14. The best-known insider account of the making of the Dayton accords is R. Holbrooke, *To End A War*, New York: Random House, 1998.

15. Note that 'unitary' should not be confused or conflated with 'united', as it frequently is. A unitary state is one based on a single conception of national identity. The Bosnian state established by Dayton is an explicitly multi-national state which recognizes and institutionally accommodates multiple national identities.

16. The International Crisis Group's output on Bosnia was prolific. For representative samples see *Is Dayton Failing? Bosnia Four Years after the Peace Agreement*, Balkans Report, No.80, 28 October 1999, at www.crisisweb.org/home/index.cfm?id=1524&l=1 and *Breaking the Mould: Electoral Reform in Bosnia & Herzegovina*, Balkans Report, No.56, 4 March 1999, at www.icg.org/home/index.cfm?id=1502&l=6.

17. Haris Silajdžić, 'Memorandum on Change: The Dayton Peace Accord – A Treaty that is Not Being Implemented', statement released in Sarajevo, 25 Jan. 2000.

18. While the segregationist Serb Radical Party (SRS) was banned in BiH at this time for its 'anti-Dayton stance' no sanctions were imposed on the SBiH. Just before the November 2000 elections Richard Holbrooke appeared in Bosnia and called for the proscription of the Serb Democratic Party (SDS), the largest party in the RS.

19. Interview in *Walter* magazine, 5 Sep. 2001.

20. Cited in F. Bieber, 'Ethnic Structure, Inequality and Governance of the Public Sector in Bosnia & Hezegovina', study prepared for the UN Research Institute for Social Development, 2003, mimeo, p.101.

21. For a good selection of essays on the Yugoslav idea in the nineteenth and twentieth centuries see D. Djokić, *Yugoslavism: Histories of a Failed Idea, 1918–1992*, London: Hurst, 2002.

22. See A. Lijphart, *Democracies: Patterns of Majoritarian and Consensus Government in Twenty-One Countries*, New Haven: Yale University Press, 1984, chs 1, 2.

23. See Bose, *Bosnia after Dayton* (n.3 above), especially chs 2, 5.

24. Petritsch, (n.2 above).

25. See D. Horowitz, *A Democratic South Africa? Constitutional Engineering in a Divided Society*, Berkeley: University of California Press, 1991, ch.5, and Bose, *Bosnia after Dayton* (n.3 above) ch.5.

26. European Stability Initiative, 'Making Federalism Work: A Radical Proposal for Practical Reform', Berlin, Brussels and Sarajevo: ESI, 8 Jan. 2004, at www.esiweb.org/docs/showdocument.php?document_ID=48.

27. For a study of the linkages between post-communist democratization and EU accession in Poland, Hungary, the Czech Republic, Romania, Bulgaria and Slovakia see M.A. Vachudova, *Europe Undivided: Democracy, Leverage and Integration after Communism*, Oxford: Oxford University Press, 2005.
28. G. Knaus and F. Martin, 'Travails of the European Raj: Lessons from Bosnia and Herzegovina', *Journal of Democracy*, Vol.14, No.3, 2003, pp.60–74, at www.journalofdemocracy.org/articles/ KnausandMartin.pdf.
29. For a survey of this history see N. Andjelic, *Bosnia-Herzegovina: The End of a Legacy*, London: Frank Cass, 2003, chs. 1, 2.
30. Bose, *Bosnia after Dayton* (n.3 above), p.277.
31. 'Total Minority Returns In/To BiH from 1996 to 31 August 2004', accessed 29 Nov. 2004, at www.unhcr.ba.
32. For a fine illustrated history of this city see *Mostar: From its Beginnings to 1992*, Mostar: Mutevelić, 2004. On Mostar during and after the 1992–95 war see Bose, *Bosnia after Dayton* (n.3 above), ch. 3.
33. Author's personal interviews and observations in Mostar, July 2004.
34. 'Mostar: The Bridge over the Neretva', *Transitions Online*, 26 July 2004.
35. Bildt (n.8 above), p.392.

From Dayton to Europe

DAVID CHANDLER

There is a consensus about Dayton – that is repeated so often it is virtually a mantra of international officials – that the 1995 peace agreement was a treaty 'designed to end a war, not to build a state'.[1] Commentators regularly argue that Dayton was negotiated by the nationalist parties, whose leaders caused the war in the first place, and that it therefore secured the power of these ethnically-based political parties.[2] Essentially, therefore the political process since Dayton has been seen as 'the continuation of war by other means', in an inversion of Clausewitz's doctrine.[3] The domestic political process in BiH is seen as illegitimate and fundamentally flawed. It is alleged that the numerous annexes and small print of the Dayton agreement have tied the hands of the international community and created a complex set of political institutions which stymie the building of a strong centralized state and continue to enable ethnically-based political parties to dominate the policy-making process. Dayton and, by implication, the Bosnian voters and their representatives, in this reading, bear the responsibility for the weakness and lack of legitimacy of central state institutions and the failure of the state-building aspirations of BiH's international benefactors.

This essay seeks to establish that this consensus is based on a myth and that the Dayton agreement has, in fact, facilitated external regulation, rather than restricting it. The framework created at Dayton was an extremely flexible one, which has enabled international actors, unaccountable to the people of BiH, to shape and reshape the agenda of post-war transition. Dayton's flexibility has been the key factor enabling external powers to permanently postpone any transition to

Bosnian 'ownership'. The only transition which has taken place has been from the ad hoc policy-ownership of self-selected members of the Peace Implementation Council (PIC) to direct regulatory control under the aegis of the European Union (EU). This transition has been brought about through informal and unaccountable mechanisms of external regulation, and has been imposed 'from above' without any debate or genuine involvement of the people or elected representatives of BiH. In sum, the flexibility of external mechanisms of regulation has been a central factor in 'sucking-out' the capacity of BiH's political institutions and undermining the legitimacy of the Bosnian state.[4]

The following section briefly considers the disputed origins of the Dayton agreement, after which the post-Dayton developments are briefly analysed in two stages. The first period is 1995–99, during which time the powers of the PIC High Representative were extended, but with little clear policy direction or end point for the ad hoc international administration. The second period, 2000–2005, saw a gradual transformation of external regulative mechanisms under the leadership of the EU, which laid a comprehensive framework for European 'ownership' of the post-Dayton process. Throughout both these periods, Bosnian input or ownership of the policy-making process has been little more than rhetorical. Dayton has provided the framework in which the external process of managing the post-Dayton peace has been transformed beyond recognition, while the population of BiH and their elected representatives have been marginalized from the political process and the elected bodies bypassed by the creation of new ad hoc mechanisms of direct and indirect EU interference.

Origins

Post-Dayton BiH is fundamentally distinct from the formal protectorates of Kosovo and East Timor, which involved the direct oversight of the United Nations under UN Security Council resolutions 1244 and 1272.[5] BiH is an independent sovereign state and member of the United Nations. As William Bain correctly notes, Dayton did not establish a formal protectorate relationship; instead Dayton is 'legitimated by the principle of consent'.[6] Rather than an external imposition, Dayton formally appears to be a treaty made by the local powers – BiH and its neighbours, Croatia and the rump former Federal Republic of Yugoslavia (FRY). It was not by UN Security Council resolution but by the coercive fiction of 'local consent' that international actors were invited to oversee Dayton and to install the temporary post-conflict administrative mechanism of the Office of High Representative (OHR). This was an office only 'consistent with relevant United Nations Security Council resolutions', not formally run by or directly accountable to the UN.[7]

The parties who consented to the agreement and had formal 'ownership' of it were coerced into signing it and had little say over the content of the 'agreement'. Dayton was in essence a US-managed process and the agreement was initialled on 21 November 1995 at the Dayton air force base in Ohio.[8] The European powers resented being sidelined by the US and lobbied Washington for UN involvement in overseeing the implementation of the peace agreement. The US refused, and the Europeans responded with the idea of establishing a Peace Implementation Council. This could, first, help to provide some sense of international legitimacy in the absence of UN involvement and, secondly, and more importantly from the European perspective, ensure that Washington included the Europeans and others in the policy-process.

The PIC was a legal figment, designed to cohere the international management of the Dayton process, but *without* the restrictive ties of international law.[9] Dame Pauline Neville Jones, former Political Director of the UK Foreign and Commonwealth Office and leader of the British delegation to the Dayton peace conference, was instrumental in the establishment of the PIC. As she later described it: 'Everybody knew that this was a phoney. Everyone also knew that we had to find something.'[10] On 8–9 December the first PIC conference was held at Lancaster House in London; prior to this, 'all the agencies had been drilled' and 'everyone knew their lines', and a detailed transitional programme for BiH was established.[11] On 14 December the Dayton peace agreement was formally signed in Paris.

The Dayton process was based on the arbitrary and ad hoc use of international power to establish a unique regime of post-conflict external regulation, one without previous historical precedent. The lack of international legal accountability explains the ad hoc and flexible nature of the powers of the High Representative. Prior to the negotiations in Dayton, Ohio, the US envisaged control of both military and civilian implementation of post-war BiH and planned a very powerful role for the High Representative. During Dayton, the European governments made high-level *démarches* insisting that the civilian role was emphasized and requesting that the High Representative be a European. The US partly conceded, but, in so doing, sought to reduce the significance of the High Representative position.[12] Once agreement was reached, it was understood that the High Representative would always be a European, although one chief deputy was likely to be German and one American.[13]

The Europeans had to fight their corner by stealth for more influence for the High Representative. The definition of the role and authority of the High Representative was intentionally left ambiguous. The Europeans wanted to have more influence but could not openly state this in the formalizing of the Dayton annexes in the run-up to the PIC conference, otherwise the US would have stonewalled. As Dame Pauline Neville Jones relates, the key victory for the Europeans was to manage to insert a role of 'coordination and facilitation' for the High Representative.[14] Once the job was secured, the Europeans subsequently undertook a lot of 'underpinning', allocating tasks to strengthen the position. The main concern of the US was safeguarding the autonomy of NATO security operations; for this reason the – now European-led – High Representative was prevented from developing any meaningful mechanism to coordinate relations between the civilian and military implementation of the agreement. However, as the security aspects of Dayton implementation became less important, the Europeans took on greater responsibilities and the High Representative's power incrementally increased.

It should be noted that the Dayton process was an ambiguous, ad hoc and unaccountable one from the outset. At the time of its establishment, the Peace Implementation Council – tasked with overseeing the implementation of

Dayton – had no international legal standing. According to Dame Pauline Neville Jones, the PIC 'was working in a legal vacuum'.[15] It was only after the event that the PIC was recognized in a UN Security Council resolution of 15 December, which cast retrospective legitimacy on the proceedings.[16]

The Dayton peace agreement was unlike any other peace treaty of modern times, not merely because it was imposed by powers formally external to the conflict, but because of the far-reaching powers given to international actors, which extended well beyond military matters to cover the most basic aspects of government and state. The majority of annexes to the Dayton agreement were not related to the ending of hostilities, traditionally the role of a peace agreement, but to the political project of state-building in BiH, of 'reconstructing a society'.[17]

Reconstructing Bosnian society was undertaken in the same interventionist spirit as Dayton itself. Carl Bildt, the first international High Representative for the new state, described the Dayton Agreement as 'by far the most ambitious peace agreement in modern history'.[18] It was 'ambitious' because, under the guise of a negotiated peace settlement, it sought to build a state – a state which was not a product of popular consensus or popular involvement and was seen by many Bosnians as an external imposition. The marginalization of the people of BiH from their own political system by external powers was summed up in Bildt's observations on the new constitution (Annex 4 of the Dayton agreement)[19]: 'No-one thought it wise to submit the constitution to any sort of parliamentary or other similar proceeding. It was to be a constitution by international decree.'[20]

Although often presented as a peace agreement rather than a framework for the reconstruction of BiH, the civilian annexes comprised five-sixths of the Dayton accords and involved a wide range of activities in which international actors, coordinated by the OHR, were mandated to temporarily play key coordinating roles.[21] For this reason, the state-level elections, to be held within nine months of the signing ceremony, were initially seen to be crucial for restoring ownership over the new state to its citizens. Under the Dayton agreement there was to be a year of internationally supervised transition, during which there would be elections and the establishment of the political institutions of the new state, which were to be elected and directly accountable to the people.[22]

1995–99: Strengthening the High Representative

The planned year of internationally supervised transition to self-governing democracy was due to end with the election of state and entity bodies in September 1996, symbolizing 'the democratic birth of the country'.[23] Although these bodies were elected under internationally supervised and ratified elections, the transitional international administration was prolonged for a further two-year 'consolidation period' and then, in December 1997, extended indefinitely. The extension of the time-limits for international withdrawal and the creation of new mandates for international agencies, coordinated by the PIC, was justified initially by the ambiguous wording of the Dayton agreement itself but later by increasingly subjective 'interpretations' of the mandate by the High Representative, including innovative reference to the 'spirit of Dayton'.[24]

The Dayton agreement provides little guidance for understanding the extension of international mandates or the mechanisms of international administration over the new state. This is because the agreement was ostensibly a treaty between the regional parties and not formally a treaty between the international agencies and the government of BiH. The Dayton agreement was rigid where it concerned the limits to BiH self-rule but extremely flexible in relation to the powers which international actors could exercise over this nominally independent state. As Paul Szasz notes, the Dayton agreement was 'merely a part of total arrangements to bring peace to Bosnia'.[25] It is worth quoting at length the international constitutional lawyer closely involved in the development of Dayton:

> Explicitly mentioned or merely implied by those texts are a host of other agreements or arrangements, which are to be concluded...by or within the numerous international organisations assigned various roles by these texts, and which may take the form of bilateral or multilateral executive agreements, resolutions of the [United Nations] Security Council or decisions of NATO, the OSCE...and other organisations... [E]vidently the parties to the GFA [General Framework Agreement] and the ancillary agreements could not bind these external actors...nor, of course, are these external actors precluded from taking steps not foreseen in these texts.[26]

This flexibility has been exemplified by the extension of the OHR's powers. The High Representative has explained this process as one which has no fixed limits: 'if you read Dayton very carefully... Annex 10 even gives me the possibility to interpret my own authorities and powers'.[27] The pattern of ad hoc and arbitrary extensions of international regulatory authority was initially set by the PIC itself as it rewrote its own powers and those of the High Representative at successive PIC meetings. The most important of these were the initial strategic six-monthly review conferences: at Florence, in June 1996; Paris, in November 1996; Sintra, in May 1997; and Bonn, in December 1997.

At the Sintra meeting, in May 1997, a new package of measures to ensure co-operation with the High Representative was announced, including the capacity to pursue deadlines announced by the PIC and enact measures in the case of non-compliance.[28] These measures included visa restrictions on travel abroad for 'obstructive' BiH representatives as well as economic sanctions targeted at a local level and the capacity to curtail or suspend any media network or programmes which contravened 'either the spirit or letter' of the Dayton agreement.[29] At the Bonn PIC summit, in December 1997, these measures were extended to give the High Representative the power to directly impose legislation, giving international officials both executive and legislative control over the formally independent state. The OHR was now mandated to enact 'interim measures' against the wishes of elected state, entity, cantonal and municipal elected bodies. These decrees were to remain in place until formally assented to by the respective level of government. The 'Bonn powers' also enabled the High Representative to dismiss elected representatives and government officials held to be obstructing the OHR's task of implementing the Dayton agreement.[30]

It should also be highlighted that the extended mandates, laid down at Bonn, were qualitatively different from earlier extensions to the OHR's powers: the new mandates granted by the PIC, to itself, for the purpose of overseeing BiH, were also made indefinite.[31] International withdrawal and the ceding of sovereignty and policy-making powers to BiH institutions was now to be dependent on an ill-defined set of 'benchmarks' to be determined by the PIC at a time of its own choosing.[32] Since December 1997, successive High Representatives have grasped the opportunities unaccountable power has provided, using them to impose legislative measures against the will of elected bodies and to sack hundreds of BiH public officials, from members of the Presidency and entity prime ministers down to municipal civil servants.[33]

By 1999, the PIC and the OHR had accumulated an array of powers unimaginable in 1995 when the Dayton agreement was signed. Yet, despite the new mandates and the indefinite extension of the power to impose legislation and to dismiss non-compliant officials, the international state-builders seemed to be running out of ideas. The international bureaucracy increasingly appeared to be running the country with little purpose or legitimacy. The war over Kosovo, and the more interventionist approach of the EU to the region which followed, finally provided the international administrators with a new source of legitimacy.[34] This legitimacy was to come not from any new attempt to involve or engage with the people of BiH, but from the promise of guiding the small and economically impoverished state to the pot of gold that was held to come with EU membership.

2000–2005: The Transition to EU 'Ownership'

Prior to 2000, the EU had been closely involved in the work of the OHR, for example, at its June 1998 Council meeting declaring the establishment of an EU/BiH Task Force, with the aim of increasing cooperation and assisting in policy-making in the crucial areas of judicial reform, education, media, good governance and economic reform.[35] However, despite an increasingly direct EU input into policy-making, the EU played a subordinate and supporting role within the PIC Dayton framework rather than dictating its own terms. The PIC Declaration from the December 1998 Madrid meeting, for example, stated that Dayton implementation was the priority and that it was BiH's 'performance in implementing its Dayton obligations' that would dictate 'the pace of integration into European structures'.[36] The EU's 'close involvement' in BiH politics was formally limited to the 'civilian implementation of the Dayton agreement'.

From 2000 onwards this relationship was to be reversed. The flexibility of the Dayton framework was to be fully revealed as the mechanisms of regulation shifted informally from the PIC to the EU and, without the need for any formal consultation of the people of BiH, Dayton gradually was to become subordinate to the requirements for eventual EU membership. Even more remarkable, the 'temporary' powers of international policy-imposition under the OHR were to be transferred to the EU itself, operating on its own behalf. In effect, the EU would be mandated to negotiate with itself in determining every aspect of policy-making in Bosnia.

In March 2000 the EU announced a Road Map as a first step for BiH in the Stabilization and Association Process (SAP). This document established 18 key conditions which BiH had to fulfil in order to start the preparation of a Feasibility Study which would then form the basis of negotiations for a Stabilization and Association Agreement. These conditions covered far-reaching policy reforms concerning elections, the civil service, state institutions, border services, the judiciary, trade regulations, foreign direct investment, property laws and public broadcasting.[37]

This shift in perspective, away from international regulation under the increasingly strained legitimacy of the High Representative's 'interpretation' of the Dayton agreement, towards regulation legitimized by the requirements necessary for the EU accession process was confirmed by the PIC at the May 2000 meeting in Brussels.[38] As Carl Bildt noted at the meeting, in his capacity as the Special Envoy of the UN Secretary-General to the Balkans: 'the discussion has moved away from the exit strategies of the international community from Bosnia towards, instead, the entry strategies of Bosnia into the international community in general and Europe in particular'.[39]

Since May 2000, the main objectives of EU assistance have not been couched in terms of supporting Dayton but in the much more inclusive terminology of support for BiH within in the framework of the SAP.[40] More importantly, the framework used by the PIC and the OHR has increasingly been shaped by the EU Road Map and subsequent EU strategies of engagement rather than by Dayton itself. In fact, too strong an attachment to the Dayton settlement, through the defence of entity rights and 'vital interests' protections for BiH's constituent peoples, has been interpreted as a barrier to legislative progress towards EU integration.[41]

At the Zagreb summit of EU and regional top officials, in November 2000, the BiH leaders fully committed themselves to meeting the Road Map conditions, and the Zagreb Declaration has subsequently been used by the OHR to bring EU requirements under his mandate of regulation and coordination.[42] Following the Zagreb Declaration, the EU established a Community programme of Assistance for Reconstruction, Development and Stabilization (CARDS) and a programme of EU technical assistance for BiH. In 2001, the European Commission adopted a Country Strategy for BiH which covers the period 2002–2006 and provides a framework for EU assistance. Since 2001, assistance of more than €240 million has been committed under the CARDS Programme, supporting BiH's participation in the Stabilization and Association Process. The EU also increasingly deployed conditionality in the granting of macro-economic support in return for recommended economic and political reforms.[43]

The transfer of power to the EU more directly can be seen in the OHR's 2002 reform of the Council of Ministers with the post of chairman of the Council no longer subject to eight-month rotation but held for the whole of the legislative period and becoming a central administrative role, involving responsibility for the work of the Directorate for European Integrations (DEI) – established under the same edict and charged with the task of preparing a strategy of European integration.[44]

The DEI has, in effect, become the key executive body of BiH, supported in its operational structuring and institutional linkages by funding directly from the European Commission. The DEI is the main partner to the European Commission in the SAP and has been tasked with 'special responsibilities', including negotiating and supervising the implementation of agreements made with the EU. Based on the centrality of the EU accession process, the Chairman of the Council of Ministers (CoM) has been granted a high level of executive authority, becoming the de facto BiH prime minister.[45] The Chairman has the task of coordinating strategies and policies among state institutions and between entity governments and of ensuring the harmonization of BiH laws with the *acquis communautaire* of the EU. His office has the assistance of EU advisors to draft new laws compliant with the *acquis* and to conduct the compliance check of all BiH proposed legislation.

The strengthening of executive power through the new institution of the DEI has been an integral part of the transition to more direct EU involvement, which has necessitated the 'rebranding' of the 'anomalous' Bonn powers of the High Representative. The EU has stated the problem in these terms:

> They certainly raise justified questions about BiH's ability to sustain a SAA [Stabilization and Association Agreement]. Nevertheless, while the 'Bonn Powers' are certainly anomalous among EU partner states, their existence in BiH need not automatically exclude that country from moving towards SAA negotiations. To make this case, BiH needs to give evidence that the powers are generally declining in relevance and that their use occurs ever less within core SAA areas.[46]

Interestingly, the use of the Bonn Powers to impose legislation by edict is not necessarily seen as problematic for BiH's closer integration into the EU. There is a clear danger of 'double standards' in the EU's turning a blind eye to the lack of democracy in BiH. For this reason, the November 2003 SAP progress report seeks to downplay the undermining of democratic processes involved in the use of High Representative edicts. The EU suggests that this is often merely a matter of imposing 'soft decisions', alleging that the OHR steps in merely to follow up policies already agreed in advance. Closer informal EU cooperation with the DEI and the Chairman of the CoM means that 'agreements' can then be imposed on governments at entity level without this appearing to be a 'hard' exercise of coercive power. The EU, in fact, wishes to conflate external diktat with freely-negotiated agreement in stating that: 'Current evidence suggests…that the "push" of the Bonn Powers is gradually being replaced by the "pull" of European institutions.'[47]

This process of alleging a basis of 'policy agreement' which is then imposed through 'soft decisions' could be seen in the OHR's establishment of special reform commissions, involving appointed BiH nationals and chaired by an international representative. These commissions have helped provide a veneer of 'agreement' without going through a formally accountable political process. They have been used for policy issues where the OHR faces clear popular opposition, for example, on indirect taxation, defence, intelligence services and on Mostar city administration. Three of the four commission's findings have then been imposed by edict.[48] In the case of the Mostar commission, the major administrative reforms were imposed despite a marked lack of any 'agreement' by BiH participants (see Florian Bieber, this volume).[49] The dishonesty of the process was highlighted by the use of agreement on minor issues to argue that the imposition of the major reforms was merely the use of 'soft' power, clarifying reforms on which there was largely agreement.[50]

At the EU Thessalonica summit, in June 2003, additional instruments to enhance EU regulation in BiH were developed. These included a Joint Declaration on Political Dialogue aimed at reinforcing the convergence of positions on foreign policy questions to reach alignment with the EU Common Foreign and Security Policy (CFSP).[51] The most important EU initiative, however, was the development of a new European Partnership, established to 'enrich' and 'intensify' the SAP, setting out BiH's political, economic and other priorities.[52] The Partnership priorities are divided into short-term, for 1 to 2 years, and medium-term, of 3 to 4 years, and include over 50 areas where policy-reforms are required to meet EU demands for 'harmonization', from the reorganization of political institutions and public administration to privatization and sensitive economic programmes to remove 'labour rigidities', 'implement bankruptcy legislation' and 'lower the ratio between government expenditure and GDP'.[53]

The priorities of the Partnership are based on the EU's political and strategic priorities in the light of their assessments of the BiH government's Annual Reports. However, it should be noted that there is no relationship of accountability or Bosnian 'ownership' involved in this priority-setting process. The Partnership policy-guidelines only involve 'informal consultations' with BiH representatives.[54] The BiH government is then 'expected to respond to the European Integration Partnership by preparing and implementing Action Plans, with a timetable and details of how they intend to address the Partnership's priorities'.[55] The EU provides security, funds the international assistance, and runs the policy programmes for Bosnia; if this is a 'partnership' it is a highly unequal one.[56]

The increased intensity of EU engagement with the BiH policy-making process has necessitated the reinforcement of the meetings of the EU/BiH Consultative Task Force, to assist in the Annual Reports and annual Action Plans. The EU has also established a Coordination Board for Economic Development and EU Integration in order to develop medium- to long-term economic strategy and direct the BiH Council of Ministers in the formulation of a Poverty Reduction Strategy Paper in negotiation with the World Bank.[57] In order to ensure that the DEI can cope with the huge amount of directives flying from Brussels to Sarajevo, the EU will be seconding civil servants from EU member states to work as advisers as well as providing targeted technical assistance and institution-building support under CARDS.[58]

While the real transition to European Union ownership has been largely operating at the informal level, this has also begun to be reflected in formal changes, such as in the EU Police Mission taking over from the UN Mission to Bosnia at the end of 2002 and the assumption of EU responsibility for a follow-on mission (EUFOR) to take over the broader security tasks from the NATO SFOR force in December 2004.[59] The ending of the UN International Police Task Force (IPTF) mandate is illustrative in this regard as it did not result in any greater 'ownership' for the Bosnian authorities. Under the EU, in the first ever civilian crisis management deployment under the European CFSP,[60] the mandate of the mission is no less authoritative than that of the UN IPTF. It establishes 'a broad approach with activities addressing the whole range of Rule of Law aspects, including institution-building programmes and police activities' and is designed not merely to support Dayton implementation but also to support the EU's institution-building under the CARDS regulations and the SAP more broadly.[61] The Head of Mission reports to the EU's Special Representative Lord Ashdown, who reports to the Secretary General/High Representative for CFSP, thus ensuring a 'unified chain of command' – a chain of command which does not involve any BiH input or accountability.[62]

Lord Ashdown was named as the first EU Special Representative in BiH in March 2002, taking up his duties when he assumed the position of the High Representative that May.[63] The creation of Ashdown's 'double-hatted' position as both EU and PIC representative marked a clear signal of transitional intent. As far as Ashdown understood his position, it was clear that he was to be the last High Representative.[64] By this he did not understand that 'ownership' was to be given to Bosnian institutions but rather that his role would be taken over by new mechanisms of the EU.

This move reflects other formal organizational changes. In 2002, the PIC was 'streamlined' providing a clearer European co-ordinating role. A Board of Principals was established as the main co-ordinating body, chaired by the EU Special Representative and meeting weekly in Sarajevo.[65] In real terms it would seem that the OHR is already more dependent on the EU than the PIC, and in 2003 the EU provided over half of the OHR's operating budget.[66] The so far largely informal process of EU regulation will become a contractual one once BiH signs up to a formal Stabilization and Association Agreement (SAA).

The SAA is an international agreement that has precedence over any other laws of the country. After being signed, the agreement becomes enforceable when it has been ratified by the BiH government, European Parliament and the national parliaments of EU members. Following this BiH will be legally obligated to undertake certain activities in SAA areas within strict time limits. Through the negotiation of the SAA the EU Special Representative and the executive policy-making institution of the DEI will maintain full regulatory control over the post-Dayton process.

Conclusion

By 2005 the EU was routinely involved in every level of BiH policy preparation and implementation, and annual BiH government work plans were being drawn up to meet the comprehensive SAP requirements. There can be little doubt that there has been a transition from the ad hoc, unaccountable, and largely unfocused, rule of the PIC. Yet this transition has not been one towards Bosnian ownership. Even the EU recognizes that 'BiH "ownership" of reform remains limited' with international initiative, input and pressure guiding the process of transition.[67] As far as the engagement of the people of BiH or their elected representatives is concerned, little has changed over the ten years since the Dayton agreement. The BiH public have been excluded from the transition process and while there is general support for EU membership there has been little public discussion of the costs and benefits involved.

Rather than state-building, it would appear that ten years of international regulation under the framework established by the Dayton agreement have done little either to build the capacity of the BiH state or to legitimate it in the eyes of the population. The powers and the authority of the state have been subsumed by external actors, sucking out the life from the elected bodies which were initially to have taken over government responsibilities following a year's transitional period.

Today, BiH is administered directly through the ad hoc mechanisms institutionalized under the powers of the EU Special Representative, and policy-making is essentially the preserve of Brussels, implemented with the assistance of the EU-funded and advised Directorate for European Integrations. The policy input allowed for Bosnian representatives is purely consultative, through hand-picked and internationally managed special commissions. Those commentators who wish to argue that the external administrators have been constrained by Dayton, or who wish to blame the fragility of Bosnia's domestic governing bodies on the 'immaturity' of the people of Bosnia and their elected representatives, unfortunately tend to ignore this overarching framework of external regulation.

NOTES

1. Lord Paddy Ashdown, 'International Humanitarian Law, Justice and Reconciliation in a Changing World', The Eighth Hauser Lecture on International Humanitarian Law, New York, 3 Mar 2004, at www.nyuhr.org/docs/lordpaddyashdown.pdf. See also B. Denitch's view that Dayton was a 'terrible peace to end a terrible war', 'Postscript', in *Ethnic Nationalism: The Tragic Death of Yugoslavia* (revised ed.), Minneapolis: University of Minnesota Press, 1996.
2. See for example, M. Kaldor, 'One Year After Dayton', in *Dayton Continued in Bosnia Herzegovina (1)*, The Hague: Helsinki Citizens' Assembly Publication Series 11, 1997, pp.28–30.
3. Ashdown (see n.1 above).
4. On 'capacity sucking out' see, for example, F. Fukuyama, *State Building: Governance and World Order in the Twenty-First Century*, London: Profile Books, 2004, p.139 ff; also M. Ignatieff, *Empire Lite: Nation-Building in Bosnia, Kosovo and Afghanistan*, London: Vintage, 2003, pp.98–101.
5. UN Security Council Res. 1244, 'On the Situation Relating to Kosovo', 10 June 1999, at http://daccess-ods.un.org/TMP/5321889.html; UN Security Council Res. 1272, 'On the Situation in East Timor', 25 Oct 1999, at http://ods-dds-ny.un.org/doc/UNDOC/GEN/N99/312/77/PDF/N9931277.pdf?OpenElement.
6. W. Bain, *Between Anarchy and Society: Trusteeship and the Obligations of Power*, Oxford: Oxford University Press, 2003, p.150.
7. S. Chesterman, *You, the People: The United Nations, Transitional Administration, and State-Building*, Oxford: Oxford University Press, 2004, p.76.

8. See R. Holbrooke, *To End a War: Sarajevo to Dayton: The Inside Story*, New York: Random House, 1998.
9. The PIC comprises 55 countries and agencies that were involved in Dayton implementation, by assisting it financially, providing troops, or directly running operations in BiH. The London Conference established a Steering Board as the executive arm of the PIC, involving Canada, France, Germany, Italy, Japan, Russia, United Kingdom, United States, the Presidency of the European Union, the European Commission, and the Organization of the Islamic Conference, which is represented by Turkey. Since the London Conference, the PIC has come together at the ministerial level five times to review progress and define the goals of peace implementation: in June 1996 in Florence; in December 1996 in London; in December 1997 in Bonn; in December 1998 in Madrid, and in May 2000 in Brussels (for further information see 'OHR General Information', at www.ohr.int/ohr-info/gen-info/#pic).
10. Dame Pauline Neville Jones, keynote speech, 'Rethinking the Dissolution of Yugoslavia' conference, Senate House, Centre for South-East European Studies, School of Slavonic and East European Studies/University College London, 18 June 2004.
11. Ibid.; for the conclusions of the PIC conference, which were to form the annexes to the Dayton agreement, see 'Conclusions of the Peace Implementation Conference held at Lancaster House, London', 8 Dec. 1995, at www.ohr.int/pic/default.asp?content_id=5168.
12. See C. Bildt, *Peace Journey: The Struggle for Peace in Bosnia*, London: Weidenfeld & Nicolson, 1998, ch. 9.
13. E. Cousens and C. Cater, *Towards Peace in Bosnia: Implementing the Dayton Accords*, Boulder, CO: International Peace Academy/Lynne Reinner, 2001, p.46.
14. See the Dayton General Framework Agreement for Peace, Annex 10: 'Agreement on Civilian Implementation', at www.ohr.int/dpa/default.asp?content_id=366.
15. Interview with the author, London, 18 June 2004.
16. UN Security Council Resolution 1031, 'On Implementation of the Peace Agreement for Bosnia and Herzegovina and Transfer of Authority from the UN Protection Force to the Multinational Implementation Force (IFOR)', 15 Dec. 1995, at http://ods-dds-ny.un.org/doc/UNDOC/GEN/N95/405/26/PDF/N9540526.pdf?OpenElement.
17. Bildt, 'The Important Lessons of Bosnia', *Financial Times*, 3 April 1996, at www.ohr.int/articles/a960403a.htm.
18. Bildt, 'Response to Henry Kissinger's Article in the Washington Post of 8 Sept. entitled, "In the Eye of a Hurricane", OHR Article by the High Representative', 14 Sept. 1996, at www.ohr.int/articles/a960914a.htm.
19. General Framework Agreement (n.14 above), Annex 4, 'Constitution of Bosnia and Herzegovina', at www.ohr.int/dpa/default.asp?content_id=372.
20. Bildt, (see n.12 above), p.139.
21. J. Gow, 'A Region of Eternal Conflict? The Balkans – Semantics and Security', in W. Park and G.W. Rees (eds), *Rethinking Security in Post-Cold War Europe*, London: Longman, 1998, p.169.
22. For more details on the Dayton agreement and annexes see D. Chandler, *Bosnia: Faking Democracy after Dayton*, London: Pluto Press, 1999, pp.43–51.
23. 'PIC Chairman's Conclusions of the Peace Implementation Council', Florence, 13–14 June 1996, §27, at www.ohr.int/docu/d960613.htm.
24. Under the Dayton agreement, Annex 10, Article 5, the High Representative has the 'final authority in theater regarding interpretation of this Agreement' (see n.14 above).
25. P. Szasz, 'Current Developments: The Protection of Human Rights through the Dayton/Paris Peace Agreement on Bosnia', *American Journal of International Law*, Vol.90, 1996, p.304.
26. Ibid.
27. Carlos Westendorp, 'Interview', *Slobodna Bosna*, 30 Nov. 1997, at www.ohr.int/press/i971130a.htm.
28. PIC Communique: Political Declaration from Ministerial Meeting of the Steering Board of the Peace Implementation Council, Sintra, 30 May 1997, §92, at www.ohr.int/docu/d970530a.htm.
29. Ibid., §35, 36 & 70.
30. 'PIC Bonn Conclusions: Bosnia and Herzegovina 1998: Self-Sustaining Structures', Bonn, 10 Dec. 1997, XI, §2, at www.ohr.int/pic/default.asp?content_id=5182.
31. Ibid, XI, §1.
32. See, for example, 'PIC Declaration of the Ministerial Meeting of the Steering Board of the Peace Implementation Council', Luxembourg, 9 June 1998, §108, at www.ohr.int/pic/default.asp?content_id=5188.

33. The archive of the High Representative's 'interim measures', at www.ohr.int/decisions/archive.asp. The archive of decisions to remove officials or to suspend them from office can be found at www.ohr.int/decisions/removalssdec/archive.asp.
34. See I. Kemp and W. van Meurs, 'Europe Beyond EU Enlargement', in W. van Meurs (ed.), *Prospects and Risks Beyond EU Enlargement: Southeastern Europe: Weak States and Strong International Support*, Opladen: Leske & Budrich, 2003, pp.63–4.
35. PIC Declaration, *Annex: The Peace Implementation Agenda, Reinforcing Peace in Bosnia and Herzegovina – The Way Ahead*, Madrid, 16 Dec. 1998, Section VI: Bosnia and Herzegovina within Europe, at www.ohr.int/pic/default.asp?content_id=5191.
36. Ibid.
37. The full text of the EU 'Road Map' is reproduced in *Europa South-East Monitor*, Issue 11, May 2000, at www.ceps.be/files/ESF/Monitor11.php.
38. See *Annex to the PIC Declaration: Required Actions*, Brussels, 24 May 2000, at www.ohr.int/print/?content_id=5201.
39. Bildt, 'Is the Peace a Success?', Remarks to the Peace Implementation Council, Brussels, 23 May 2000, at www.bildt.net/index.asp?artid=176.
40. European Commission, 'The EU's Relations with Bosnia and Herzegovina', June 2003, at http://europa.eu.int/comm/external_relations/see/bosnie_herze/index.htm.
41. European Commission, 'Report from the Commission to the Council on the preparedness of Bosnia and Herzegovina to negotiate a Stabilization and Association Agreement with the European Union', COM(2003) 692 final, Brussels, 18 Nov. 2003, §B.1.1, at http://europa.eu.int/comm/external_relations/see/docs/com03_692_en.pdf.
42. 'Zagreb Summit, Final Declaration', 24 Nov. 2000, at: http://faq. macedonia.org/politics/eu/zagreb.summit.pdf; see also Petritsch, 'Disappointing Progress of Bosnia and Herzegovina on the Path to Closer European Integration', Press Release, Office of the High Representative, 28 June 2001, at www.ohr.int/print/?content_id=4469.
43. European Commission, 'Commission Staff Working Paper: Bosnia and Herzegovina Stabilization and Association Report 2004', SEC(2004) 375, Brussels, no date, §3.2, at http://europa.eu.int/comm/external_relations/see/sap/rep3/cr_bih.pdf.
44. Law on the Council of Ministers of Bosnia and Herzegovina, Office of the High Representative, 3 Dec. 2002, at www.ohr.int/decisions/statemattersdec/default.asp?content_id=28609.
45. In fact, Ashdown now refers to him in this way, see International Crisis Group, 'Thessaloniki and after II: The EU and Bosnia', *Balkans Briefing*, Sarajevo/Brussels, 20 June 2003; see also, European Commission, 'Report from the Commission to the Council' (see n.41 above), §B.1.1.3.
46. Ibid., §B.1.1.5.
47. Ibid.
48. The exception is the Defence Reform Commission, see European Commission, 'Commission Staff Working Paper' (n.43 above), §2.2.
49. See Commission for Reforming the City of Mostar, 'Recommendations of the Commission Report of the Chairman', 15 Dec. 2003, at www.ohr.int/archive/report-mostar/pdf/Reforming%20Mostar-Report%20(EN).pdf; 'Decision Enacting the Statute of the City of Mostar', Office of the High Representative, 28 Jan. 2004, at www.ohr.int/decisions/mohncantdec/default.asp?content_id=31707.
50. V. Perry, 'Quotas, Bridges, and Guarantees: The Politics and Process of Reforming Mostar', paper presented at the Institute for Strengthening Democracy in Bosnia and Herzegovina, Seventh International Seminar, Democracy and Human Rights in Multiethnic Societies, Konjic, Bosnia, 12–17 July 2004.
51. European Commission, 'Report from the Commission to the Council' (n.41 above), §B.3.1.
52. European Commission, 'Council Decision on the principles, priorities and conditions contained in the European Partnership with Bosnia and Herzegovina', COM(2004) yyy final, Brussels, no date, at http://europa.eu.int/comm/external_relations/see/sap/rep3/part_bih.pdf.
53. These restrictive economic policies are sensitive as they would mean declining social protection in a state where half the population are already, according to the EU, 'at or near the poverty line', see European Commission, 'Report from the Commission to the Council' (n.41 above), §C.
54. European Commission, 'Communication from the Commission to the Council and the European Parliament: The Western Balkans and European Integration', COM(2003) 285 final, Brussels, 21 May 2003, §2, at http://europa.eu.int/comm/external_relations/see/2003.pdf.
55. Ibid.
56. For further information on the SAP process in the region see Chandler, 'Governance: The Unequal Partnership', in Meurs (ed.) (n.34 above), pp.79–98.
57. European Commission, 'Report from the Commission to the Council' (n.41 above), §B.3.7.1.

58. European Commission, 'Communication from the Commission to the Council' (n.54 above), §2.
59. European Commission, 'Commission Staff Working Paper' (n.43 above), §2.2.
60. 'Mission Statement', European Union Police Mission, at www.eupm.org/mission/ms.htm.
61. 'Council Joint Action of 11 March 2002 on the European Police Mission' (2002/210/CFSP), *Official Journal of the European Communities*, Council of Europe, §3, at http://www.eupm.org/mission/bt/council1.pdf.
62. Ibid., §7.
63. Further information on the EU Special Representative, at www.eusrbih.org/.
64. Interview with the author, Vienna, 5 July 2002.
65. 'OHR General Information' The weekly meeting are attended by: OHR, SFOR, OSCE, EUPM, UNHCR, European Commission, the World Bank, the IMF and the UNDP.
66. European Commission, 'Commission Staff Working Paper' (n.41 above), §5. Its budget in 2004 was €21.1 million. Contributions to the OHR budget broke down as follows: EU 53 per cent, USA 22 per cent, Japan 10 per cent, Russia 4 per cent, Canada 3 per cent, Organisation of the Islamic Conference 2.5 per cent, others 5.5 per cent (see 'OHR General Information', (n.9 above)).
67. European Commission, 'Commission Staff Working Paper' (n.41 above), §2.3.

Economic Reform and the Transformation of the Payment Bureaux

DOMINIK ZAUM

In the light of the apparent close relationship between economic conditions and the outbreak of conflict, economic reforms have been a central element of most peacebuilding missions since the end of the cold war.[1] Bosnia and Herzegovina (BiH) has been no exception in this context. The dissolution of Yugoslavia and its collapse into civil war were preceded by a protracted economic crisis from the 1970s onwards, which arguably increased divisions between as well as within the republics.[2] Even though economic liberalization was hardly discussed at Dayton and appears only at the margins of the General Framework Agreement for Peace (GFAP),[3] the first Peace Implementation Council (PIC) in London at the beginning of December 1995 committed BiH to the establishment of a free market economy.[4] At subsequent meetings, the PIC and the PIC Steering Board not only confirmed this commitment, but increasingly made requests for specific reforms towards this end, such as transforming the payment bureaux, initiating privatization or reforming the labour laws,[5] increasing the pressure on a Bosnian political elite frequently unwilling to engage in such reforms.

This essay analyses one of the key economic reforms pursued by the international community in BiH: the transformation of the payment bureaux. The payment bureaux were a central part of the socialist Yugoslav payment system, run centrally by the Office of Social Bookkeeping in Belgrade, which aimed to maintain a degree of central control over a highly decentralized socialist economy characterized by social ownership and self-management.[6] After the collapse of Yugoslavia, the payment service in BiH split into three different bureaux, one controlled by each ethnic group. The international community, in particular USAID, which led the reform of the payment system, viewed the payment bureaux not only as an obstacle to the development of a free market economy, but also as a source of corruption and illegitimate finance for the parties who controlled them. Consequently, transforming them had two aims: first, to further economic liberalization; and second, to weaken parallel structures challenging the political authority of the state institutions.

The analysis of the payment system reform provides insights not only into the policy aims and the normative framework underlying the statebuilding activities of the international community in BiH,[7] but also into the political instruments available to the international community. The remainder of the essay is divided into three parts. The first part will analyse the international community's involvement in the reform of the payment system, looking at the initiation of the reform, the drafting of the key legislation, and the implementation of the reform. The second part will assess the aims of international economic policymaking in BiH, economic liberalization on the one hand, and broader institution-building goals on the other. The third part will, by way of a conclusion, briefly discuss the effectiveness of the policy instruments used to further the international community's aims, and explore some of the problems for state-building raised by the analysis.

Dismantling the Payment Bureaux

Initiation of Payment System Reform

The importance of a functioning payment system for the transition to a market economy has for some time been recognized by international organizations involved in economic reform in emerging economies.[8] As Robert Lisfield and Fernando Montes-Negret have argued, an efficient payment system is essential to promote economic activity, in particular trade and commerce, it reduces transaction costs, is crucial for the development of capital markets and sophisticated financial instruments, and contributes to the establishment of free-market structures.[9] In BiH, the payment system had been monopolized by the state-controlled payment bureaux, a legacy of the Social Bookkeeping Service of the former Yugoslavia. During the war, the Social Bookkeeping Service, run from Belgrade, split into three payment bureaux in BiH, one controlled by each of the three ethnic groups.[10]

An extensive inquiry by USAID into the functioning of the three payment bureaux discerned six basic functions: the operation of the payment system; tax collection and distribution; accounting services for business and government; cash management; statistics collection; and lending functions.[11] These functions gave the payment bureaux a central role in controlling economic activity in BiH. All transactions larger than KM 99 had to be conducted through the payment bureaux.[12] In addition, companies had to deposit all their cash with their payment bureaux in the evening; payroll, taxes and customs duties had to be processed through them; and companies could only withdraw up to KM

1,000 per day.[13] The fee structure for transactions was opaque,[14] and both local businesses and the international community suspected that the payment bureaux were used to channel money to the political parties who controlled them.[15] Furthermore, the inefficient payment system promoted illegal and underground economic activity, resulting in extensive revenue losses for the governments. The total costs of the payment bureaux for the economy of BiH, including among other things excess labour costs for businesses, forgone economic growth, and forgone interest income, have been estimated to have been between KM 255 million and KM 311 million in 1997.[16]

For all these reasons, the Macroeconomic Assistance Programme initiated by USAID in 1998 identified the payment bureaux as the major obstacle to economic development in BiH, and as an effective tool for political control of businesses by the dominant parties, lacking transparency and public accountability.[17] As a result, USAID pushed for the dismantling of the payment bureaux and the reform of the payment system, and for this to be included in the declaration of the 1998 Madrid PIC, which set 31 December 2000 as the deadline for the reform.[18] Later, the dismantling of the payment bureaux was also included as a condition in the EU Roadmap, a list of economic and institutional reforms that BiH had to complete before the opening of negotiations for a Stabilization and Association Agreement with the EU.

Drafting of the Legislation

The dismantling of the payment bureaux has been one of the largest economic reform projects the international community addressed in BiH. In total, it necessitated more than 30 laws regulating not only the new payment system, but also the transfer of the other functions of the payment bureaux to different institutions, and the creation of new institutions, such as treasuries on the state, entity and cantonal level. Because of this complexity, the analysis here will concentrate on two core aspects of the reform: first, the two central laws regulating the transfer of payment functions from the payment bureaux: the Laws on the Internal Payments System and the Laws on Payment Transactions; and, second, the transfer of government responsibilities to government institutions, using the transfer of taxation functions from the payment bureaux to the Federation Tax Administration as an example.

The international community started to work on the reform early in 1999, as mandated by the Madrid PIC. In February 1999 the 'International Advisory Group for Payment Bureaus and Payment System Transformation' (IAG) was established, to 'assist and advise authorities in both entities on the dismantlement [sic] and elimination of the payment bureaux and to provide technical assistance to the institutions that will take over the functions currently performed by the Payment Bureaux'.[19] The membership of the IAG consisted of representatives from USAID, CAFAO (the European Commission funded Customs and Fiscal Assistance Office), OHR, the EC, the World Bank, the IMF, and six advisers from the US Treasury. The meetings of the IAG were chaired by USAID and co-chaired by the World Bank and the IMF. The IAG established eight working groups: Tax, Customs, Statistics, Payment Systems, Public Revenues,

Privatization, Legal, and Coordination, addressing the different issues arising from the dismantling of the payment bureaux.[20] These working groups consisted of members of the IAG and representatives from the relevant entity ministries and institutions, thus including local institutions from an early stage of the law-making process. The large number of working groups, and the wide range of issues they addressed, is an indication of the wide range of issues to which the reform pertained.

The legal working group started with the drafting of the necessary legislation early in 1999. In conjunction with this, the IAG initiated a functional analysis of the payment bureaux and developed a 'blueprint' for the reform that was discussed with the prime ministers of the two entities in February 1999.[21] The functional analysis was prepared jointly by members of USAID, CAFAO, and the World Bank under the leadership of USAID, and was presented to the IAG in May 1999.[22] Here, as in the earlier USAID Report, *Payment Bureaux in Bosnia and Herzegovina: Obstacles to Development and a Strategy for Orderly Transformation*, a detailed strategy for the implementation of the desired reforms was outlined, based on analytical work previously conducted for the IMF and the World Bank.[23] With regard to the focus of this analysis, the report outlined a schedule for drafting and passing the Laws on Internal Payments Systems and the Laws on Payments Transaction, and for the transfer of responsibilities to the Tax Administrations.[24]

The Internal Payments System Laws for the Republika Srpska (RS) and the Federation (FBiH) regulate payment operations in terms of which bodies are authorized to perform them, and which operations can be conducted. They also define the nature of different accounts and of payments through them, and regulate which records and statistics the authorized payment organizations (such as banks and post offices) are required and allowed to collect. These laws were crucial for the process of reforming the payments system. First, they established which organizations would be part of the reformed payment system, and outlined their functions within it. Second, the laws were important for the transition towards the new payment system, as they regulated the functions of the payment bureaux until they were fully dismantled, and established governing boards responsible for implementing the reform of the payment bureaux, thus enhancing the accountability and transparency of these institutions.[25] The adoption of the laws would therefore end the monopoly position of the payment bureaux over domestic payments, and establish an accountable governance structure through the governing board. As the laws were key to the whole reform, the IAG wanted to address them immediately. The original USAID plan aimed at amending the FBiH law by March 1999, and the RS law by May 1999.[26] In the Functional Analysis the IAG envisaged that both entities would have completed the necessary legislation by July 1999.[27] In the end, neither deadline was met.

In the RS in particular, resistance to the reform was very high, as politicians preferred to maintain political control over financial flows. The payment bureau had been part of the entity-owned RS Development Bank, and before it could be dismantled, the two had to be separated. This was supposed to be completed by May 1999, but only in March 2000 did the RS government finish this separation.[28] Drafting of the RS law began in August 1999, and was mostly carried out by the US Treasury and the IAG legal working group, together with RS officials. The drafting process dragged on until October 2000, due to resistance and foot-dragging by the RS government. When a final draft was produced in October 2000 and passed on to the government, the crushing defeat of the governing coalition in the RS in the elections on 11 November 2000 meant that there was no authoritative government in place to discuss the draft and pass it on to the RS National Assembly. As a result the law was never adopted. When the deadline for the payment system reform approached, the law was imposed by the High Representative on 20 December 2000.[29] Some important provisions, in particular the creation of the governing board, had been fulfilled earlier by RS governmental decree in the absence of a law regulating it,[30] after the international community strongly pressured the RS government during frequent visits from international officials, who made it clear that no matter how much the government would try to delay the process, the payment bureaux would be dismantled by the end of 2000. The governing board was at first supposed to consist of three members, appointed by the RS government and the Banking Agency.[31] After June 1999, the membership was increased to five members, including an international official: the governor of the BiH Central Bank.[32]

In FBiH, the amendments to the law had been prepared jointly by the BiH Central Bank, US Treasury and the IAG legal working group by March 1999, and presented to the government for adoption.[33] However, the FBiH government only adopted them, under international pressure, on 3 June 1999, and then submitted the proposal to both houses of the FBiH parliament for urgent procedure.[34] The House of Representatives passed the law on 1 July 1999, and the House of Peoples, after some delay, on 16 September 1999.[35] Similarly, the appointment of members of the governing board, essential for the reform to proceed, dragged on after the law had been adopted by the government. Of its five members, two were to be appointed by the Federation Prime Minister, two by the Minister of Finance (in both cases one Bosniac and one Croat), the fifth member was the international governor of the Central Bank. By the end of July, only one member had been appointed, and it took until September for the new board to be established.[36]

Three features characterized the policymaking process described above:

- The main concern of the two sets of laws discussed is the delineation of state authority over economic activities, attempting to reconcile between the 'need for governance' and the 'need to restrict government'. They limit the rights of the state (and therefore of the groups controlling the state institutions) to interfere with economic life. In the decentralized, socially owned economy of the pre-war Yugoslavia, the payment bureaux had been an essential instrument of state control to manage the economy. The dismantling of the payment bureaux reduced political control over financial flows and credit, and limited state involvement in the economy. However, it also identified a role for the state in governing the economy, and therefore assigned certain functions to state institutions, such as the administration and collection of taxes, as analysed below.

- While representatives of the international community frequently emphasized the importance of the reforms for the international community and for the development of a market economy in BiH,[37] the entity governments resisted the reform. In the eyes of the international community, this was mainly due to the fear of losing personal benefits through the reform.[38]

- Even though local institutions had been involved in the drafting from the beginning, the process was almost completely driven by the political will of the international community, against resistance from the Bosnian political class. The international community initiated the reforms after USAID had identified the payment bureaux in BiH as the major obstacle to economic development. It also provided the necessary analysis and financial verification for the legislation. Almost all of the drafting and redrafting work was conducted by the IAG, in particular by the US Treasury and the IAG Legal Team, with officials from the entity ministries, especially the Ministries of Finance, participating in the working groups. The IAG was careful to harmonize the two entity laws as much as possible, often against resistance from local governments, and when the High Representative imposed the laws in the RS, they were identical to the ones adopted in the Federation.

Implementing Reform

Passing the two laws in the entities established the framework within which the payment bureaux could be dismantled and their assets and tasks transferred to other institutions. The plans for these transfers were drawn up by different IAG working groups, who analysed and determined requirements in terms of additional legislation, human resources, and IT support in order to ensure a smooth transfer. This process ran parallel to the passing of the core legal framework discussed above, especially once the entity authorities started to delay the passing of the legislation. The analysis of the transfer of functions to the Federation Tax Administration (FTA), organized and carried out by the IAG Tax Working Group, illustrates this part of the process of dismantling the payment bureaux.

The work plan for transferring the relevant functions from the payment bureaux to the FTA stretched the transition over one year, from December 1999 to December 2000.[39] It involved legislative changes, organizational changes, and the provision of equipment and training of personnel. The functions that had to be transferred to the FTA were predominantly tax payment functions: the calculation of payroll, enterprise and turnover taxes, and the verification and control of payment of payroll taxes.[40] The task of transferring these functions involved four aspects: the amendment of three laws (Wage Tax Law, Law on Contributions, and the Law on Tax Administration); the amendment of supplementary regulations for applying these laws; the assessment of the needs of the FTA and provision of support in terms of IT infrastructure and employee training, and establishment of procedures for cooperation between commercial banks and the FTA – to ensure information and data flow now that commercial banks would hold the relevant information about accounts the payment bureaux previously held; and finally, the design of new tax forms.

The amendments to the Wage Tax Law and the Law on Contributions were drafted by the Tax Working Group, composed of two US Treasury members and a representative of the OHR, in December 1999.[41] The amendments to the Law on Tax Administration were drafted by the FTA by June 2000. After the drafting procedure, the IAG Legal Survey Team, consisting of a US Treasury official and two Bosnian lawyers employed by the USAID Macroeconomic Reform Project[42] reviewed and coordinated the drafts, first with officials from the FTA and then with the FBiH Ministry of Finance, which forwarded the drafts to the government. The amendments to both laws were to be passed by 30 June 2000 according to the Tax Working Group action plan. Though the FTA and the IAG had agreed on a draft and forwarded it to the FBiH Ministry of Finance by Spring 2000, the Ministry failed to discuss the draft with the Tax Working Group and to pass it on to the government for discussion. As a result, both laws were imposed by the High Representative on 20 December 2000.[43]

The deadline set out within the action plan for the passing of the amendments to the Law on Tax Administration was 30 July 2000. The law was discussed and unanimously approved by the FBiH government on 20 July 2000,[44] and forwarded to both houses of the legislature for urgent procedure. The law was part of a larger package of legislation on economic reform that the IMF and World Bank urged the FBiH government to pass, communicated in two letters to the government: a letter from the IMF outlining the tasks of the responsible ministers for economic reform on 6 July 2000,[45] and a letter from the World Bank related to the Second Credit for the Public Funding of Structural Adjustment (PFSAC II) and its implementation progress, discussed by the government on 20 July 2000.[46] It was reiterated by the representatives of IMF and World Bank during a meeting with FBiH Prime Minister Edhem Bičakčić on 28 July 2000.[47] Under strong pressure from the international community – both informal and verbal in the meetings with the government, and formally through the condition-alities attached to the PFSAC II – both the FBiH House of People and House of Representatives passed the law in extraordinary sessions, dealing almost exclusively with the economic measures requested by the IMF and World Bank, on 31 July 2000 and 2 August 2000 respectively.[48]

The Madrid PIC declaration had set 31 December 2000 as the deadline for the dismantling of the payment bureaux, the transfer of its functions to the appropriate agencies, and the establishment of the new payments system. The whole reform was only finished in time because the High Representative imposed six laws on 20 December, several of which have been discussed above, so that they would be in effect on 1 January 2001.[49] The payments system began to operate on 5 January 2001, and after a brief adjustment period has led to major improvements in the financial sector, in particular in the FBiH, where implementation has been more consistent and where several well-established foreign banks have entered the market introducing new financial services, like ATMs and credit cards. In the RS, where implementation of the laws by the entity government was half-hearted at best, such success was much more limited.[50]

The reform of the payment system can be regarded a success on two accounts. First, the reform was beneficial for the BiH economy, leading to improvements in the financial sector in BiH. Second, it was successful from the perspective of weakening parallel structures controlling and exploiting institutions of economic governance for their own benefit. A range of factors have contributed to the success of the reform of the payment system. First, the reform did not just establish new institutions but also provided resources for equipment and training, to strengthen their capacity. Second, the international community closely coordinated its efforts through the IAG. As a result, it could effectively draw on the resources and expertise of the different agencies involved, and could coordinate its responses to the FBiH and RS governments. Third, the international community used a range of elements of its political authority to promote the reform. Thus, it provided expert advice, put pressure on the governments informally through visits and conversations, or formally through conditionalities attached to further aid, and finally used the Bonn powers to impose the legislation. However, with the exception of the Wage Tax Law and the Law on Contributions, the impositions only occurred after the parliamentary crisis and the looming elections made it unlikely that the law would be passed in time for the reforms to finish within the deadline set by the PIC.

However, the payment system reform also revealed some of the problems of policymaking by the international community in BiH. Even though the FBiH and RS administrations were involved in the drafting process from an early date, in the end the whole process was predominantly driven by the international community, which conducted the majority of the drafting work and did not accept substantial changes to the draft. Thus, despite local participation, there was little local ownership of the reform process. Such lack of local ownership is indicative of an approach to policymaking by states and international organizations involved in state-building missions that perceives the problems of state-building to be technical, rather than political. As technical issues, they can best be addressed by experts, provided by the international community, and do not require political consultation or debate, as the ends of the policy are not in question. The problems this can pose for the state-building efforts of the international community are discussed in more detail below.

The Aims of Economic Reform

The international community advanced two reasons for the dissolution of the payment bureaux. First, their removal was necessary for the establishment of an effective payment system, to move BiH towards the establishment of a free market economy. Second, the payment bureaux were seen as a source of corruption, and their dissolution considered necessary to weaken parallel structures, and consequently strengthen legitimate state institutions and the rule of law. This section explores the content and implications of these two purposes of payment system reform.

Economic Liberalization

The establishment of a free market economy is a central part of the normative framework underlying the state-building activities of the international community. The concern with establishing markets seems, on the one hand, pragmatic. Thus, market economies are generally considered to be more effective in ensuring economic growth than socialist planned economies. As Roland Paris has observed:

> Although debates continue over the appropriate balance between the market and the state in economic development, there is a near-universal agreement today that non-market economic policies (that is, those that do not give the market the primary role in allocating scarce resources) are too inefficient to generate sustained economic growth.[51]

On the other hand, the commitment to free markets is also normative, promoting a particular view of the role of the state in the management of the economy. The international community considered it '*inappropriate* to have payments system, Central Bank, private-sector banking, and possibly statistics and information functions under the control of the [Ministry of Finance]'.[52]

Consequently, the reform of the payment system limited the authority of the state over the economy by removing the payments system, the Central Bank, private sector banking, and statistics and information functions from the control of parallel structures and the entity governments. This normative aspect of the commitment to market liberalization and the limitation of the state's role in the economy – promoting it not just because of its consequences for economic development, but because it is considered to be the *appropriate* way of organizing economic life – is further underlined by recent research into the effects of market liberalization on building peace and stability in post-conflict environments, which has raised the question whether market liberalization in some cases might deepen the divisions between different groups (see also Michael Pugh, this volume).[53]

The aim of establishing a free market economy also conforms with BiH's envisaged integration into European structures, which require it to be a market economy. However there is another logic informing economic reform efforts in BiH, including the payment system reform, and that is the strengthening of legitimate state institutions. In contrast to the establishment of a market economy, which aims at limiting the role of the state, this aims at strengthening particular state institutions, raising an interesting tension in the economic reform efforts of the international community in BiH.

Weakening Parallel Structures

The international community in BiH has frequently used economic policy to further particular political goals. Thus, the Economic Task Force, chaired by the OHR, has frequently linked the disbursement of aid to political conditionalities.[54] By dismantling the payment bureaux, the international community hoped to weaken parallel structures that challenged the authority of legitimate state institutions, to reduce corruption and to strengthen the rule of law.

Without the payment bureaux, the parties controlling them would lose not only an important source of income but also a tool for controlling BiH's economy.

This aspect of the reform is indicative of a broader strategy of strengthening public institutions necessary for the existence of a self-sustaining peace in BiH. This strategy was first comprehensively formulated at the Brussels PIC in May 2000, but parts of it were already foreshadowed in the Peace Implementation Agenda of the Madrid PIC in December 1998. As Marcus Cox has argued, at Brussels the PIC for the first time identified a number of institutions necessary for the long-term sustainability of the state and established deadlines by which these institutions should be in place.[55] Strengthening these institutions not only entailed the establishment of the relevant legal framework and the strengthening of institutional capacity, but necessarily also involved attempts to dismantle parallel institutions.

The use of economic reforms to promote political integration and centralization seems appealing as they can be justified on economic grounds and can be presented as a technical, rather than a political issue – similar to the functional integration of coal and steel production in Europe after the Second World War.[56] Thus, not only the payment system reform but a range of other economic policies have aimed at strengthening the state-level institutions in BiH, for example the establishment of state-level regulatory bodies such as the Telecommunications Regulatory Agency[57] and the State Regulatory Commission for Electric Energy.[58] One example was the introduction of state-level indirect taxation, considered by the international community to be essential to adequately fund the growing number of state-level institutions[59] and to break their dependence on fiscal transfers from the entities. When the law was adopted on 29 December 2003, under extensive pressure from the international community,[60] the High Representative hailed the reform as 'one of OHR's major achievements... transferring competency from the entity to the state level.'[61]

Conclusion

The reform of the payment system has been a successful reform in the context of state-building in BiH, both by enhancing the development of the financial sector and by weakening the influence of parallel structures over the economy. It entails a range of lessons, especially with regards to the methods of policy-making by international administrations. In particular four aspects of the process seem to have contributed to its success:

• *The high degree of coordination the international organizations achieved through the IAG.* As a result, they did not expose any policy differences that could have been used by local elites resisting the reform to obstruct the process, as happened, for example, in the case of the civil service reform.[62] Instead, all organizations involved, in particular USAID, the OHR, the World Bank, and the IMF, presented the same message to the entity governments: the payment bureaux will have to be dismantled by December 2000.

- *The effective use of international authority.* The close coordination also meant that the international community could effectively use its authority to promote the reform, using different policy instruments at the disposal of different organizations. While USAID could provide technical advice and resources for training and infrastructure, the World Bank could use conditionalities, and the OHR, in the last instance, could use its authority to impose parts of the legislation. The united position and close coordination made the demands issued by its representatives much more credible.
- *The availability of sufficient resources.* In addition to establishing the necessary legal basis for the new institutions, USAID in particular provided the technical support to the new institutions, including the provision of IT equipment, training and the drafting of internal operating procedures. Without this support, the institutions would have remained little more than empty shells, lacking the capacity to fulfil the functions assigned to them.
- *The responsible use of the Bonn powers.* Despite the strong resistance to the reform of the payment bureaux, the power to impose legislation was only used sparingly. Imposition was used only as a last resort, when the laws for different reasons failed to proceed through the domestic law-making process. Furthermore, the imposition established institutional structures that were sustainable, due to the continued capacity-building support given to them.

However, independent of whether the dismantling of the payment bureaux successfully furthered the ends pursued by the international community, the question remains whether this style of policy-making is the appropriate way of pursuing institutional reforms in a post-conflict country. By treating state-building as a technical, rather than political enterprise, the international community has compromised local ownership of the development of Bosnian political and administrative institutions, raising three major problems:

- *The lack of ownership.* This might compromise the sustainability of these institutions. Building institutions requires political choices, affecting the distribution of resources and power, and involving the weighing of different political concerns against each other. Consequently, new institutions will benefit some groups more than others, and if local elites do not participate in the decision-making process, they are unlikely to accept them, as the implementation problems of financial sector reforms in the RS suggest.[63]
- *The failure to develop local capacity.* This is implied by the lack of local ownership and lack of local responsibility and conjures the possibility of the dependency of BiH on the international community to develop and implement public policy.[64]
- *The lack of accountability.* The international community is fundamentally unaccountable to those over whom it exercises political authority, failing to live up to the most basic good governance criteria which it professes to promote (see Richard Caplan, this volume). It thus sets a very bad

example of governance to local political elites. The way the international community engages in state-building in BiH might therefore undermine one of the principal goals which it pursues: the establishment of democratic, self-sustaining institutions of government in BiH.

Ten years after the Dayton conference, the situation in BiH has changed beyond recognition. The country has been comprehensively disarmed; and political institutions, legitimized by elections considered free and fair by international observers, have been established, though remain weak. Economic and social issues, rather than problems of peace and security, are the foremost concern of most Bosnians.[65] As the problems facing the country have changed, so should the methods used by the international community in BiH: away from executive decision-making and the imposition of particular institutions – short-cutting the domestic law-making process – and towards a more co-operative approach, emphasizing local ownership and a limited, accountable use of the Bonn powers. This would force the Bosnian political class to take responsibility for their decisions.

NOTES

1. P. Collier, *Economic Causes of Civil Conflict and Their Implications for Policy*, Washington DC: World Bank, 2000. For a discussion of post-conflict state-building policies by international administrations, see R. Caplan, *A New Trusteeship? The International Administration of War-torn Territories*, Adelphi Paper 341, Oxford: Oxford University Press, 2002; S. Chesterman, *You, the People: The United Nations, Transitional Administration, and State-Building*, Oxford: Oxford University Press, 2004.
2. S. Woodward, *Balkan Tragedy: Chaos and Dissolution after the Cold War*, Washington DC: Brookings Institution Press, 1995.
3. None of the GFAP annexes addresses issues of economic reconstruction or development. However, the Preamble of the Constitution of BiH, which is part of the GFAP, commits BiH to the promotion of a market economy.
4. PIC, *Conclusion of the Peace Implementation Conference Held at Lancaster House*, London, 8–9 Dec. 1995, Art.43.
5. PIC, *Declaration of the Peace Implementation Council*, Madrid, 16 Sept. 1998, Section IV.18.
6. On socialist self-management and the concept of socially owned property, see D.D. Milenkovich, *Plan and Market in Yugoslav Economic Thought*, New Haven: Yale University Press, 1971; S.L. Woodward, *Socialist Unemployment: The Political Economy of Yugoslavia 1945–1990*, Princeton: Princeton University Press, 1995; M. Uvalic, 'Privatization in the Yugoslav Successor States: Converting Self-Management into Property Rights', in M. Uvalic and D. Vaughan-Whitehead (eds), *Privatization Surprises in Transition Economies*, Cheltenham: Edward Elgar, 1997, pp.267–300.
7. On the normative framework underlying the international statebuilding efforts in BiH, see D. Zaum, 'The Paradox of Sovereignty: International Involvement in Civil Service Reform in Bosnia and Herzegovina', *International Peacekeeping*, Vol.10, No.3, 2003, pp.102–20.
8. For example D.B. Humphrey, *Payment Systems: Principles, Practice, and Improvements*, World Bank Technical Paper, No.260, Washington DC: World Bank, 1995; R. Lisfield and F. Montes-Negret, *Modernising Payment Systems in Emerging Economies*, World Bank Policy Research Working Paper, No.1336, Washington DC: World Bank, 1994.
9. Lisfield and Montes-Negret (n.8 above), pp.7–8. See also D.B. Humphrey and S. Sato, *Transforming Payment Systems: Meeting the Needs of Emerging Market Economies*, World Bank Discussion Paper, No.291, Washington DC: World Bank, 1995.
10. European Stability Initiative, *Reshaping International Priorities in Bosnia and Herzegovina, Part I: Bosnian Power Structures*, Berlin: ESI, 14 Oct. 1999, p.5, at www.esiweb.org/docs/showdocument.php?document_ID=4; International Crisis Group, *Why Will No-one Invest in Bosnia and Herzegovina? An Overview of Impediments to Investment and Self-sustaining*

Growth in the Post-Dayton Era, ICG Balkans Report, No.64, Sarajevo: ICG, 1999, p.10. The payment bureaux were known as ZPP in the Bosniac, ZAP in the Croat, and SPP in the Serb areas.
11. USAID, *Payment Bureaus in Bosnia and Herzegovina: Obstacles to Development and a Strategy for Orderly Transformation*, Sarajevo: USAID, 1999, pp.8–14.
12. KM = Konvertibilna Marka, the currency of BiH; 1KM = approximately € 0.5.
13. USAID (n.11 above), pp.30-31.
14. USAID (n.11 above), p.40.
15. ICG (n.10 above), p.43. M. Pugh, 'Postwar Political Economy in Bosnia and Herzegovina: The Spoils of Peace', *Global Governance*, Vol.8, No.4, 2002, p.471; interview with OHR official, Sarajevo, 25 Sept. 2001.
16. USAID (n.11 above), pp.57–8.
17. Ibid., p.20; author's interview with a USAID official, Sarajevo, 28 Sept. 2001.
18. PIC (n.5 above), Section IV.18.
19. OHR, *Economic Newsletter*, Vol.2, No.2, Sarajevo: OHR, March 1999.
20. USAID, *BiH Economic Update 2000 – 3rd Quarter*, Sarajevo: USAID, 2000, p.37.
21. OHR (n.19 above).
22. USAID, *Transformation of Payment Bureaus in Bosnia and Herzegovina: Functional Analysis and Strategic Implementation Plan*, Sarajevo: USAID, 1999.
23. USAID (n.11 above), p.4.
24. Ibid., pp.61–2; USAID (see n.22 above), pp.45–51.
25. The Laws on Internal Payments System is identical in both entities. For the provisions of the laws, see OHR, *Decision Imposing the Law on Internal Payments System of the Republika Srpska*, Sarajevo: OHR, 20 December 2000.
26. USAID (n.11 above), p.61.
27. USAID (n.22 above), p.50.
28. USAID (n.20 above), p.36-7.
29. Author's interview with an OHR official, Sarajevo, 25 Sept. 2001, and further conversation on 13 Dec. 2001; see also OHR (n.25 above).
30. OHR, *Economic Newsletter*, Vol.2, No.5, Sarajevo: OHR, June 1999.
31. OHR, *Economic Newsletter*, Vol.2, No.3, Sarajevo: OHR, April 1999.
32. This brought the RS law in line with the provisions of the law drafted in the Federation. OHR (n.31 above); see also OHR (n.25 above).
33. OHR (n.31 above).
34. OHR (n.30 above). Under urgent procedure, which has to be approved by both Houses, laws skip the drafting stage in parliamentary committees.
35. OHR, *Economic Newsletter*, Vol.2, No.6, Sarajevo: OHR, July 1999; OHR, *Economic Newsletter*, Vol.2, No.7, Sarajevo: OHR, Aug. 1999; OHR, *Economic Newsletter*, Vol.2, No.8, Sarajevo: OHR, Sept. 1999.
36. OHR, *Economic Newsletter*, Vol.2, No.7 (n.35 above).
37. C. Patten, 'Speech to the Peace Implementation Council', Brussels, 23 May 2000; W. Petritsch, 'Address by the High Representative for BiH to the OSCE Permanent Council', Vienna, 19 Nov. 2000; W. Petritsch, 'Chatham House Speech', London, 18 Feb. 2000; W. Petritsch, 'Speech to the Club of Three', Brussels, 29 June 2000; PIC, *Declaration of the Peace Implementation Council*, Brussels: PIC, 23/24 May 2000, Annex: Required Actions; PIC Steering Board, *Communiqué by the PIC Steering Board*, Brussels: PIC Steering Board, 8 Feb. 2000; PIC Steering Board, *Communiqué by the PIC Steering Board*, Sarajevo: PIC Steering Board, 4 April 2000; PIC Steering Board, *Communiqué by the PIC Steering Board*, Brussels: PIC Steering Board, 27 Sept. 2000; C. Westendorp, 'Speech at the Fifth Donors' Pledging Conference for Bosnia and Herzegovina', Brussels, 20 May 1999.
38. Author's interview with OHR official, Sarajevo, 25 Sept. 2001; author's interview with World Bank official, Sarajevo, 24 Sept. 2001; see also USAID (n.11 above), p.10.
39. IAG Tax Working Group, *Work Plan for Transferring Functions from the Payment Bureaus to the Federation Tax Administration*, undated internal document provided by USAID, Sarajevo.
40. USAID (see n.22 above), pp.19-24.
41. Communication with USAID official (email), 19 December 2001.
42. Ibid.
43. OHR, *Decision amending the Law on Wage Tax*, Sarajevo: OHR, 20 Dec. 2000; OHR, *Second Decision amending the Law on Contributions*, Sarajevo: OHR, 20 Dec. 2000.
44. Government of the Federation of BiH, 'Minutes, 49th Session of the Federation of BiH government', 20 July 2000. Unofficial translation on file with the author.

45. Government of the Federation of BiH, 'Agenda, 47th Session of the Government of the Federation of BiH', 6 July 2000. Unofficial translation on file with the author.
46. Government of the Federation of BiH, 'Agenda. 49th Session of the Government of the Federation of BiH', 20 July 2000. Unofficial translation on file with the author.
47. ONASA, 'E. Bicakcic Meeting with US Ambassador, Heads of IMF, WB', Sarajevo, 28 July 2000.
48. ONASA, 'Extraordinary Session of FBiH Parliamentary House of Peoples', Sarajevo, 31 July 2000; ONASA, 'Federation House of Reps Passes Law on Labor', Sarajevo, 2 Aug. 2000.
49. In addition to the laws discussed, the *Law on Financial Operations in the Republika Srpska* was imposed by the High Representative on 20 Dec. 2000.
50. ICG, *Bosnia's Precarious Economy: Still Not Open for Business*, Balkans Report, No.115, Sarajevo: International Crisis Group, 7 Aug. 2001, pp.27–35, Vol.4, No.2, Sarajevo: OHR, April 2001; European Commission, Economic Reform Monitor – Supplement C: Economic Situation and Economic Reform in Central and Eastern Europe, No.3, Oct. 2001, Brussels: EC, 2001, p.10.
51. R. Paris, *At War's End: Building Peace after Civil Conflict*, Cambridge: Cambridge University Press, 2004, p.199.
52. USAID (n.11 above), p.27. (emphasis added.)
53. Paris (n.51 above), on BiH, see pp.97–107 in particular.
54. S. Woodward, Z. Hertic, and A. Sapcamin, 'Bosnia and Hercegovina', in S. Foreman and S. Patrick (eds), *Good Intentions: Pledges of Aid for Postconflict Recovery*, Boulder, CO: Lynne Rienner, 2000.
55. M. Cox, *State Building and Post-Conflict Reconstruction: Lessons from Bosnia*, Geneva: Centre for Applied Studies in International Negotiation, Jan. 2001, p.15.
56. European Stability Initiative, *Taking on the Commanding Heights: Integration of Network Industries as a Tool of Peace Building. A Proposal for the Peace Implementation Council*, Berlin: ESI, 3 May 2000, at www.esiweb.org/docs/showdocument.php?document_ID=9.
57. OHR, *Decision Imposing the Telecommunications Law of BiH*, Sarajevo: OHR, 11 Sept. 1998.
58. OHR, *Economic Newsletter*, Vol.5, No.1, Sarajevo: OHR, May 2002, Section 4.
59. PIC Steering Board, *Communiqué by the PIC Steering Board*, Brussels: PIC Steering Board, 1 April 2004.
60. OHR, *Economic Newsletter*, Vol.6, No.4, Sarajevo: OHR, Sept. 2003, p.3.
61. OHR, '25th Report by the High Representative for Implementation of the Peace Agreement to the Secretary-General of the United Nations', Sarajevo: OHR, 3 March 2004, Section IV.8.
62. Zaum (n.7 above)
63. ICG (n.50 above).
64. European Stability Initiative, *Governance and Democracy in Bosnia and Herzegovina – Post-Industrial Society and the Authoritarian Temptation*, Berlin/Sarajevo: ESI, 2004, at www.esiweb.org/docs/showdocument.php?document_ID=63.
65. A World Bank study in 2002 found that unemployment and poverty were the most important concerns of the BiH population. See World Bank, *Bosnia and Herzegovina: Local Level Institutions and Social Capital Study, Vol.1 (Draft)*, Sarajevo: World Bank, June 2002, p.20.

Police Reform: Peacebuilding through 'Democratic Policing'?

GEMMA COLLANTES CELADOR

In the 1990s, police reform has become an essential pre-requisite for the success of post-conflict peacebuilding missions. In most, if not all, war-torn societies (from intra-state conflicts) the police were, prior to and/or during the conflict period, politically biased, militarized, corrupt, ethnically (or group) divided, disrespectful of human rights and inefficient at ensuring the security of all citizens. The promotion of good governance, lasting peace and development depends, to a large extent, on breaking this history of police bias, intimidation and brutality. Therefore it is now an accepted idea and policy goal – within the international community – that the post-conflict reconstruction and rehabilitation of war-torn societies must entail from an early stage the reform and restructuring, or even the complete re-establishment, of local police forces according to the norm of 'democratic policing'.[1]

Bosnia and Herzegovina (BiH) is one of the many examples that confirm this trend.[2] One of the goals of the Dayton Peace Accords was to ensure that Bosnian police forces operated in accordance with the best international policing standards, including respect for internationally-recognized human rights and fundamental freedoms. There is an overwhelming consensus among the international actors active in BiH, both governmental and non-governmental, on the important role that police reform plays in the restoration of lasting peace. In the words of High Representative Paddy Ashdown: 'Professional police forces, operating within the law, and at the service of the citizen, are a hallmark of any decent, peaceful, civilized community. This is what the people of this country [BiH] deserve and what they demand.'[3]

This essay provides an assessment of the international-led police reform efforts in BiH. More particularly, it suggests that the UN Mission in Bosnia and Herzegovina (UNMIBH), and its International Police Task Force (IPTF), have undoubtedly made a positive contribution to the political and economic reconstruction, and social rehabilitation, of post-war BiH. Nevertheless, in many significant respects their efforts to reform and restructure the Bosnian police forces failed to make the progress which the UN and other international actors expected. The article focuses on the evaluation of two UN programmes – the minority police recruitment policy and the certification process for all Bosnian police officers – which were developed with the aim of contributing to the broader peacebuilding agenda in BiH. The UN minority police recruitment policy was designed to help in the refugee return process, whereas the certification of police officers was designed to assist in the reconciliation process. Under these programmes, BiH police reform became part of what Annika Hansen describes as 'a major state building exercise' as police reform became central to the externally-managed 'process of changing the dynamic of a society'.[4] Although much this essay discusses the UN period (end 1995–end 2002), the analysis will also include some remarks on the post-2002 phase, and the EU Police Mission (EUPM).

The Restoration of Law and Order

In June 1996 the UN Secretary-General reported: 'Among the most difficult tasks in the peace process is to assuage the intense and widespread fear and desire for retribution resulting from a vicious conflict in which civilians were the principal targets and victims.'[5] Incidents of detention without charge or trial, ill-treatment, threats, violence or obstruction aimed at preventing people from returning to their homes or causing others to flee were reported in many areas of BiH in the initial post-conflict phase. These events represented a continuation of ethnic cleansing in the disputed territories. The common feature of every such instance was that members of minority communities were most at risk since they had the least sympathy from the authorities and thus, the least physical protection from the police. In many instances the police were also the perpetrators of those acts. The flourishing of lasting peace in a post-conflict society depends, first of all, on popular legitimacy.[6] It could therefore be argued that in the immediate phase of peace implementation the Bosnian police forces continued to be a threat, rather than an asset, to the building of peace.

Commenting on the security situation in 2004, the European Commission Functional Review of the Bosnian police forces specified that the level of ordinary crime (excluding organized crime, corruption and terrorism) was lower in BiH than in the EU and candidate states.[7] Ashdown agreed with this conclusion: 'BiH is not a dangerous country. The streets of Sarajevo are safer than the streets of London. But it is a country in the grip of corruption and organised crime.'[8] However, a similar evaluation of the situation cannot be applied to the specific situation of minority returnees. Human rights organizations, some journalists and other critics defend the claim that BiH still suffers from what the International Crisis Group (ICG) has described as a 'persistent if low-level campaign of violence against returnees'.[9] To this picture one can also add the continuation, although at a lesser level than in the immediate post-conflict phase, of 'crimes against culture'.[10] This type of crime involves not physical but rather psychological damage and conveys the implicit message that minorities are not welcome, leading to the latter living in fear and, thus, jeopardizing the reconciliation process.

It could be argued that the persistence of ethnically-motivated crime is, to a certain degree, inevitable because, as Graham Day puts it, 'there will always be raw, powerfully raw, edges in society where revenge, not justice, is the motivating key, the motivating factor'.[11] Therefore, from the point of view of this article, what matters is what action the police are taking to tackle this problem. Reports from several international and regional organizations, and governments, show that, in some areas of BiH, local police investigators are still highly politicized and fail to treat these cases adequately.[12] It should therefore come as no surprise that the 2003 European Commission Feasibility Study for BiH identified the reinforcement of returnee security as a EUPM priority.[13] The same message was conveyed at a public consultation roundtable organized by the Police Restructuring Commission in October 2004 in Sarajevo, and attended by members of NGOs and professional organizations. Among the issues raised by participants was that the 'police needed to do more to ensure the security of minority returnees'.[14]

This section has highlighted that the police's role in restoring law and order in BiH still remains unsatisfactory. However, this is by no means an indication that progress has not been made since late 1995. Indeed the situation today is no longer characterized by the high levels of crime and political violence that developed during the first few years of peace implementation. At the same time, despite nine years of police reform efforts by the international community, the persistence of nationalist attitudes in some areas of the country means that some Bosnian citizens still do not enjoy complete physical security or 'a sense of security' due to their ethnicity. Although the police no longer engage directly in human rights violations of the kind witnessed during the war and in the immediate post-conflict phase, there are still instances where they prove unable or unwilling to make redress in this situation.

The UN Minority Recruitment Policy

The international community believes that for BiH to recover completely from the war and become a 'normal' state and society, the effects of the ethnic cleansing campaign that took place during the war and in the immediate post-conflict phase need to be redressed.[15] The UNMIBH and IPTF tried to contribute to the refugee return process by creating ethnically-integrated police forces. The deployment of minority police officers as a magnet for minority returns to pre-war areas was a central part of a core programme (police restructuring) in the UNMIBH/IPTF 2000–02 Implementation Plan.[16] The UN asserted that the return of minority police officers to pre-war areas would act as a 'confidence-building measure' for refugees and internally displaced persons (IDPs) wanting to go back. The presence of minority police officers would ensure the security of minority returnees, or at least would lead to the perception of security among this group. However, the UN expected the minority police programme to achieve a lot more than just ensuring the security of minority returnees.[17]

One of the defining characteristics of the 'democratic policing' paradigm is the creation of multi-party or multi-ethnic police forces that represent the society they serve in an impartial and professional manner. As Graham Day puts it, 'it has to be recognized that the emphasis on minority recruitment is not an end in itself but an essential first step in breaking down structural barriers to a professional non-ethnically prejudiced local police service'.[18] The UN worked under the assumption that by making police officers from different ethnic groups go through the same training, both inside and outside the police academies, an *esprit de corps* would gradually develop. Police officers would no longer see the world through the mindset of membership of a particular ethnic group but would adopt the 'master identity' of a police officer, representing the interests of the Bosnian state.[19]

The end result would be that police officers of different ethnicities would work side by side and, in doing so, would learn to treat all citizens equally. This internal transformation of the police institution would set an example to both the majority group and the minority returnees in any given area of BiH. It would show them that, despite the atrocities committed in the name of ethnicity during the war, it was possible to live and work together peacefully. This model would, in theory, create a virtuous circle, ultimately leading to more minority returns to pre-war areas as well as building confidence in the peace settlement among the majority and minority groups in any area. This virtuous circle has been described by David Bayley as the police's contribution to creating 'bonds of citizenship'. He acknowledges that the police cannot eradicate hatred arising from social diversity but asserts that, by being fair, effective and open in their actions, they can contribute to creating an environment that lessens the likelihood that hatred will result in interpersonal violence.[20]

Implicit in the UN policy was the assumption that the police, as the most visible daily manifestation of the state and the rule of law in civilians' lives, could advance this sense of confidence to the people upon whom the success of the Dayton Peace Accords depends.[21] A case in point is Mostar, where the Bosniac and Croat police forces were reunified in the belief that this would, in turn, lead to greater toleration and reconciliation. Indeed, at the ceremony to mark the completion of the merger process, the then Mayor, Neven Tomić, stated that the creation of a single city police force would lead to the general reunification of Mostar.[22]

The success of the UN minority police recruitment policy is debatable.[23] The UN assessments, carried out at the end of 2002, show that the Brčko District, the State Border Service and the court police had genuinely multi-ethnic police forces. However, the entity and cantonal police forces, which represent the main bulk of police forces in BiH, had not met their mandatory minority quotas, particularly at middle and senior management levels.[24] Although the EUPM has identified minority recruitment as one of its goals, the situation in 2004 is still very similar to that in 2002.[25] Reasons for this failure in both entities include differences in salary, Book of Rule regulations, housing and schooling conditions, and the pressure from their own ethnic group not to accept the job. Some of these factors also explain why in some municipalities, where the ethnic quotas have been met, the majority of police officers have chosen not to live locally and instead commute from areas where their ethnic group is in the majority.[26] Therefore, despite meeting the minority quotas, these examples would still constitute a failure of the UN minority recruitment policy on its own terms. By not living in the areas that they police, these police officers were not setting the 'right' example for would-be minority returnees to those areas. Instead, it could be argued that they send the opposite message, and their actions may even discourage others from returning to those pre-war areas.

Moreover, even if the UN police quotas had been met all over BiH, it could still be argued that the UN policy of 'minority police first, minority returnees later' would probably have only a limited impact on the refugee return process. Trends in the refugee return process show that minority returnees' decisions to return depend on a variety of 'practical assessments of their conditions of life' which are influenced by a number of institutional, demographic, geopolitical and economic obstacles, in addition to the level of personal security.[27] As a Serb returnee to the Nisici village, near Sarajevo, expressed it:

> It is not likely that anyone else will return here. We have everyday problems with the electric power and water. Roads are bad. There is no job to find and that is our greatest problem. Bosniacs do not touch us, but it is felt that we are not welcome. They tell us to return for any document a few times in the municipal building. Only those who have no other solution return here.[28]

Within this context, it is very difficult to envisage how multi-ethnic police forces could attract minority returnees to pre-war areas. It is often argued that the reform of the judiciary and the prison system, political parties, and the like should come at the same time as the police. What the example of the refugee return process in BiH illustrates is that in some instances the net should be cast even wider. The idea that the police can help create 'bonds of citizenship' cannot be applied to post-conflict areas where other institutions and services that are key to people's basic lives – such as employment, education and health care – are absent.

The UN emphasis on recruiting minority police officers has also led to a number of problems that cast a shadow over the merits of this approach to multi-ethnicity. Arguably the emphasis on strict ethnic quotas could prove counterproductive for the development of a professional and efficient police force in BiH. The recruitment of minority police officers by ethnic quota is to a certain extent incompatible with the promotion of merit-based, professional forces. The concerns expressed are not merely that the quality of police recruits could fall, but that – by favouring positive discrimination at the expense of meritocracy, particularly with regard to the allocation of senior level police positions – further tensions could be generated within the police force between officers of different ethnicities.

The end result could therefore be a strengthening of ethnic identities. In which case, members of ethnic minorities in the police forces would have nothing to gain, and much to lose, from positive discrimination measures of this kind. In BiH there have been a high number of cases where minority police officers have faced antagonism and discrimination in their contacts with work colleagues from the majority group.[29] Such hostility is partly due to the loss of jobs by police officers from the majority group in order to fulfil the minority quotas. For example, in the Republika Srpska (RS) about 1,500–2,000 Serb police officers would have to be dismissed in order to reach the 20 per cent quota of minority officers which the UN determined to be the minimum level for the RS.[30] In many instances, vacancies remain unfilled because no officers of the right ethnicity (Croat and Bosniac in the RS, Croat or Bosniac in different parts of the FBiH, or Serb in FBiH) can be found.[31]

The value of strict ethnic quotas is even more difficult to accept when one takes into account the opposition to setting strict ethnic quotas – when it came to the reform of the BiH state-level civil service – from the OHR, the Council of Europe's Venice Commission and other international actors. The reasons given, in this case, were that it would constrain the development of meritocracy, and thus professionalism and effective governance, within Bosnian society and also that it would be in violation of European anti-discrimination legislation.[32] Completely abandoning the multi-ethnic ideal in the police forces is not a viable possibility: this would send out a negative message and impact particularly badly on minority returnees in some parts of BiH. However, as a EUPM police officer privately suggested, the international community could perhaps afford to relax the ethnic quotas, starting with lower numbers of places for minority police officers and then gradually increasing that number as and when the number of minority returnees increased.[33] This would at least get around the problems of empty positions, which is having a negative impact on the effectiveness of police work.

The hostility and harassment suffered by minority police officers, when working side-by-side with colleagues of the majority group, also undermines the UN belief that through common training and daily contact an *esprit de corps* would take root amongst officers, leading them to substitute their ethnic identity with their occupational identity. Drawing from the available literature on police studies, it is possible to argue that – without change in the broader social context – the theory that strong group identities can be subsumed by an overriding, apolitical, professional police identity remains unproven. Even in multi-cultural countries in the developed world, with established regimes, there are few examples where this state of affairs has been attained. Ellis Cashmore's study of the benefits of recruiting more ethnic minority police officers and enhancing cultural diversity training for the police in the UK in the late 1990s is illustrative. He describes these initiatives as 'pernicious in that they contrive to give the appearance of progress, while actually achieving little'.[34]

The UN Certification Process

In the former Yugoslavia the police ensured political conformity, stability and order on behalf of Tito's multi-national, but single party, regime. They often resorted to repressive measures to fulfil this duty. During the war the Bosnian nationalist parties used the police to assert their control; the police were actively engaged in smuggling, gun running, black marketeering and other criminal activities as well as in the commission of war crimes in the name of ethnic cleansing. Many officers engaged in these crimes remained in the police ranks after the signing of the Dayton accords, permitting or in some cases participating in the violation of citizens' rights during the first few years of peace implementation.[35] Moreover, both during and immediately after the war the police forces were filled with individuals who had never served before and were certainly not qualified to join. These included many soldiers who, following the Dayton settlement, 'swapped their camouflage-type uniforms for blue ones and joined the police forces'.[36] The internal situation of the police forces was a great threat to peacebuilding in BiH. The UNMIBH/IPTF, and the international community more generally, soon realized that one of the first steps in the reconciliation process between peoples, communities and the Bosnian state was redeeming the image of the police and using the institution to set a 'model' for society by abiding by the new rules. Identifying and bringing to account those police officers that committed atrocities during the war, or were in violation of the Dayton Peace Accords, would send a positive message to the population.[37]

In April 1996, the Federation (FBiH) authorities signed the *Bonn-Petersberg Agreement on Restructuring the Police Federation of Bosnia and Herzegovina* with the UNMIBH/IPTF and, at the end of 1998, the RS ratified a similar agreement. These accords gave the UN mission the authority to reorganize the police forces in both entities.[38] Furthermore, in December 1996, the UN Security Council passed Resolution 1088 which provided UNMIBH/IPTF with the power to investigate or assist with investigations into human rights abuses by law enforcement personnel, as well as to report on the efforts of the BiH authorities to cooperate in this regard with the UN mission.[39] These powers were used to carry out a country-wide process of screening all Bosnian police forces, known as the 'certification process'.[40] Those who did not meet the UNMIBH/IPTF standards were 'de-authorized', that is, precluded from holding any position within any law enforcement agency in BiH in the future, including jobs of an administrative nature. The criteria used for selection included educational credentials, IPTF training, compliance with the property legislation, absence of war crime convictions by the International Criminal Tribunal for the former Yugoslavia (ICTY) or domestic courts, and the commission of no human rights violations or other so-called 'serious breaches of duty or law' prior to or during the screening process.[41] Police officers could also fail to pass this vetting process for committing a number of minor offences. What made them 'minor' was the fact that they resulted from inadequate skills or negligence – for example, sleeping on duty or not showing up for work.[42]

There was a substantial reduction in police numbers, particularly in the preliminary stages when, prior to the registration phase, local authorities were
asked to produce lists with the names of all police officers under their authority.[43]
According to UN data, of the 44,000 police personnel (including administrative
staff) present at the end of the war, only 15,786 were certified.[44] However,
these figures could be misleading. There are claims that the Bosnian police
forces still have among their ranks officers with war crimes or other criminal
records. This could be due to the politicization of the process by the local authorities, the underperformance of some IPTF officers when carrying out their
duties, lack of time, the quality of some of the sources of information used, or
the restricted categories of police staff that could be screened.[45]

The certification process only represented a non-prosecutorial sanction that
had to be supplemented by domestic criminal codes and laws on internal
affairs. Local law enforcement agencies were obliged to comply with
UNMIBH/IPTF's recommendations on the selection and removal of police officers. They were also required, when necessary, to take appropriate measures of
redress, including dismissal, and the initiation or continuation of disciplinary proceedings or of internal or criminal investigation.[46] UNMIBH/IPTF did not have
the resources to carry out criminal proceedings itself. It also hoped that by designing certification in this manner it would encourage local ownership of the reconciliation process.[47] However, given the existing evidence, it is difficult to accept
that the Bosnian police forces are now much more accountable than before the
start of the certification process. In many cases, neither disciplinary nor criminal
proceedings have been initiated by the local authorities against police officers
de-authorised for criminal or 'serious violations of duty or law' and, for those
who have been subjected to disciplinary or criminal proceedings, the punishments
have not always been appropriate for the severity of the acts committed.

The accountability measures introduced by the UN, in the form of the
certification process, have not led to higher levels of popular trust and confidence
in the police and thus in the Bosnian state.[48] A survey carried out by the NATO
Stabilization Force (SFOR) in early 2003 concluded that 19 per cent of respondents had 'a lot of confidence' in the ability of the Bosnian police to deal
with problems, 36 per cent had 'some confidence', and 36 per cent 'little or no
confidence'.[49] Ashdown asserted, in mid-December 2004, that:

> More than half of those who had themselves been a victim of crime were
> unsatisfied with the police response. Over 80 percent in both the RS and
> the Federation believe that criminals get away with their crimes and 87
> percent feel that politicians should do more to make the police more effec-
> tive. They know what most of the professionals in this room know: That the
> fight between the police and the criminals is not a fair fight. That the deck is
> stacked in favour of lawbreakers, not law enforcers. That the system doesn't
> work.[50]

Some of the plausible explanations for the low public stock with which the
police are held and the alleged continuing abuses of police power, particularly
regarding the ubiquitous use of traffic 'fines',[51] is the mismatch between the

expectations and the resources and conditions of work for these state-sector employees. As one of the Bosnian police officers interviewed for this study put it, the working conditions of police officers do not allow them to follow a 'respectable life'.[52] In the words of a member of the local NGO community, 'the police can contribute very little to other sectors of society...it is the most frustrated sector in society right now'.[53] According to Ashdown, the Police Restructuring Commission recognizes that 'morale in the police service has never been lower and that reform also means better salaries, benefits, training, and career prospects'.[54] The improved salaries and benefits proposed by the Police Restructuring Commission would go a long way towards improving the current situation. Nevertheless, it remains to be seen if they will succeed in tackling the core of the problem, the low public esteem and lack of respect in which the police are held.

An EUPM official described the problem as the 'over-democratization' of the Bosnian police forces, to such an extent that their monopoly over the use of force has been taken away completely.[55] Following events like the de-certification of 19 members of the Sarajevo Canton Special Forces in 2002, many citizens and police officers have come to the conclusion that criminals 'can hurt the police even without firing a single bullet'.[56] Indeed some police officers blame the certification process for the fact that 'nobody takes them seriously now'.[57] This lack of respect reached a peak point towards the end of UNMIBH/IPTF's mandate when there were over 15 cases of citizens' assaults against police officers.

Consequently, there are officers who have decided that it is better to do nothing than to act and risk verbal or physical harassment from a citizen or, even worse, losing their job.[58] This outcome is not that unusual in the case of externally-managed police reorganizations. In the case of Haiti, for instance, the interim police force was demoralized, ineffective and afraid of the people they were supposed to serve.[59] In a US National Bureau of Economic Research paper, Canice Prendergast revealed similar behavioural patterns in the Los Angeles Police Department during the mid- to late-1990s.[60] Increasing levels of external civilian oversight led to a number of scandals and a subsequent increase in complaints against individual police officers. Faced with this situation, officers had the choice of continuing to pursue cases aggressively, at the risk of inciting public complaints, or doing nothing and having the Los Angeles police blamed collectively for rising crime levels. The second option was chosen, leading to a drop in pro-active policing, and thus in arrest levels, while gang-related crime rose. Prendergast's conclusion was therefore that overzealous civilian oversight might be counterproductive to the development of a culture of accountability within the police.

Conclusion

The UN arrived in BiH at the end of 1995 with the goal of making the police 'part of the solution, not part of the problem'.[61] This essay has argued that, although the police are no longer part of the problem, they still cannot be regarded as part of the solution. Compared with the war and the immediate post-conflict phase, the police are no longer perpetrating or condoning large-scale violations of human rights. There are, nevertheless, occasions where they are failing to deal effectively with cases involving minority returnee victims. However, the contribution of the UN minority recruitment programme and the UN certification process to the return of refugees and IDPs to pre-war areas and the reconciliation process respectively, have not measured up to the claims forwarded by the UN and other international actors. In both these cases, the lack of a well-thought-out UN strategy, practical problems during implementation, and the persistence of nationalist attitudes in some areas of BiH account for some of the failures. However, both examples also raise a question over the theory that the police can be changed before society changes.

Socially-engineering the police according to 'democratic policing' precepts may help to assist in the difficult task of transforming a society, but it cannot work in isolation from a broad range of other social mechanisms. If anything, the attempts to use the police as a 'transmission mechanism'[62] of the values that the international community wants the whole of BiH to adopt has led to the undermining of the basic functions of the police to the point that the institution is now in a parlous state. It remains to be seen whether the EUPM and OHR will be able to help the Bosnian police forces overcome the current impasse.

ACKNOWLEDGEMENTS

I would like to thank Jenny Mathers, Patrick Finney, Wolfango Piccoli, Melanie Wagner and the editor of this volume, David Chandler, for their valuable feedback and encouragement. Constructive comments were also provided by the participants at various conferences where earlier versions were presented. I would also like to extend my gratitude to all the international and Bosnian officials that found the time to talk to me, as well as to the University of Wales, Aberystwyth, and the University Association for Contemporary European Studies (UACES) for their financial support.

NOTES

1. The concept of 'democratic policing' represents the idea that the police are a service, not a force, with the primary focus on the security of the individual rather than the state. Its defining characteristics are 'responsiveness' to the needs of individuals, and 'accountability' for its actions to the public it serves. D. Bayley, *Democratising the Police Abroad: What to Do and How to Do It*, Washington DC: US Department of Justice, 2001, pp.11–5, at www.ncjrs.org/pdffiles1/nij/188742.pdf.
2. For an overview of other international-led police reform missions see A. Hansen, 'From Congo to Kosovo: Civilian Police in Peace Operations', *Adelphi Paper*, No.343, 2002, pp.15–32.
3. Paddy Ashdown, 'HR/EUSR Speech at the EUPM Inaugural Ceremony', OHR Press Office, Sarajevo, 16 Jan. 2003, at www.ohr.int/ohr-dept/presso/presssp/default.asp?content_id=28917.
4. A. Hansen, 'Strengthening Indigenous Police Capacity and the Rule of Law in the Balkans', in M. Pugh and W.P.S. Sidhu (eds), *The United Nations and Regional Security*, Boulder, CO: Lynne Rienner, 2003, p.175.
5. *Report of the Secretary-General Pursuant to Resolution 1035 (1995)*, UN Doc. No.S/1996/460, 21 June 1996, §33, at www.un.org/Docs/secgood3.htm.
6. M. Kaldor, 'Security Structures in Bosnia and Herzegovina', in G. Cawthra and R. Luckham (eds), *Governing Insecurity: Democratic Control of Military and Security Establishments in Transitional Democracies*, London: Zed Books, 2003, p.205.
7. European Commission, *Financial, Organisational and Administrative Assessment of the BiH Police Forces and the State Border Service*, Sarajevo, 30 June 2004, p.6, at www.mpr.gov.ba.

This document is the first review to be completed in preparation for the drafting of the BiH Strategy for the reform of public administration. A total of nine systemic and sectoral reviews of public administration in BiH were planned for 2004. The basis of these functional reviews is the Memorandum of Understanding signed between representatives of the BiH authorities and the European Commission on 19 November 2003 in Sarajevo.

8. 'Press Conference: High Representative to Give Police Restructuring Commission its Mandate, 2/7/04', OHR International Press Briefings, Sarajevo, 5 July 2004, at www.ohr.int/ohr-dept/presso/pressb/default.asp?content_id = 32884.

9. International Crisis Group, *The Continuing Challenge of Refugee Return in Bosnia and Herzegovina*, Balkans Report, No.137, 2002, p.18, at www.crisisweb.org/home/index.cfm?id = 1473& l = 1; see also B. Ivanisević, 'Legacy of War: Minority Returns in the Balkans', in Human Rights Watch, *World Report 2004: Human Rights and Armed Conflict*, 2004, p.357, at http://hrw.org/wr2k4/download/wr2k4.pdf.

10. According to Graham Day there are three types of crimes in a post-conflict situation: crimes against the person (e.g. assault, rape, murder); crimes against property (e.g. looting, burning houses); and crimes against culture (e.g. attacks against historical sites, religious symbols). G. Day, 'Policekeeping: Challenges of Law and Order in Peace Operations', presentation given at the US Institute of Peace, Washington DC, 29 March 2001, at www.usip.org/events/2002/2001fellows_presents.html#audio.

11. Ibid.

12. International Crisis Group (n.9 above), p.18; UN High Commissioner for Refugees, *UNHCR's Position on Categories of Persons from Bosnia and Herzegovina in Continued Need of International Protection*, Sarajevo, 2001, at www.unhcr.ba/publications/Position.PDF; US Department of State, *Bosnia and Herzegovina – Country Reports on Human Rights Practices 2003*, Washington, DC: Bureau of Democracy, Human Rights and Labour, 2004, at www.state.gov/g/drl/rls/hrrpt/2003/27829pf.htm.

13. European Commission, *Report from the Commission to the Council on the Preparedness of Bosnia and Herzegovina to negotiate a Stabilization and Association Agreement with the European Union*, Document No.COM (2003)692 final, 2003, p.26, at www.delbih.cec.eu.int/en/index.htm.

14. 'Roundtable Discussion on the Police as a Service to the Community', EUPM website, www.eupm.org/News/Latest%20Events.htm. The Police Restructuring Commission was created by Ashdown in July 2004 with the mandate to develop proposals for a single police system that is effective and efficient in serving the citizens and free from political interference. The commission is composed of Bosnian political and police representatives and the EUPM Commissioner, and chaired by Wilfred Martens, former Prime Minister of Belgium. The Commission also draws on the OHR and the European Commission for technical assistance.

15. Confidential interview by the author with EU official, Brussels, May 2003.

16. Some measures were initiated before 2000, such as the negotiation and introduction of procedures for selection and recruitment.

17. Confidential interview by the author with UNMIBH official, Sarajevo, July 2002.

18. G. Day, 'The Training Dimension of the UN Mission in Bosnia and Herzegovina (UNMIBH)', *International Peacekeeping*, Vol.7, No.2, 2000, p.159.

19. John Braithwaite defines 'master identity' as that identity that 'overrides all other statuses in determining how people will respond'. Cited in L. Sherman, 'Consent of the Governed: Police, Democracy, and Diversity', in M. Amir and S. Einstein (eds), *Policing, Security and Democracy: Theory and Practice*, Huntsville, TX: Office of International Criminal Justice, 2001, p.24. A similar logic has guided police reform efforts in FYROM. See, for example, C.F. Wehrschuetz, 'The Long March of the former Yugoslav Republic of Macedonia', *OSCE Newsletter*, Vol.IX, No.3, March 2002, p.3, at www.osce.org/publications/newsletter/2002-03/nl032002.pdf.

20. D. Bayley, 'Policing Hate: What Can Be Done?', *Policing and Society*, Vol.12, No.2, 2002, pp.83–91.

21. Confidential interview by the author with UNDP official, New York, April 2003.

22. Z. Jukić, 'Bosnia: Mostar Police Reunited', Institute for War and Peace Reporting, *Balkan Crisis Report*, No.319, 20 Feb. 2002, at www.iwpr.net.

23. This was one of the conclusions which emerged from a number of confidential interviews by the author with UNMIBH and OHR officials, Sarajevo and Banja Luka, summers of 2002 and 2003.

24. Strict ethnic quotas were set in the RS in accordance with the 1997 Municipal Elections results, and in the FBiH according to the 1991 census. The ethnic quotas in the FBiH were calculated per canton. UNMIBH/IPTF internal documents, July–Nov. 2002.

25. Confidential interviews by the author with EUPM officials, Sarajevo, July and August 2003.

26. International Crisis Group, *Policing the Police in Bosnia: a Further Reform Agenda*, Balkans Report, No.130, 10 May 2002, pp.40–44, at www.crisisweb.org/home/index.cfm?id=1500&l=1.
27. Confidential interview by the author with UNHCR official, Sarajevo, July 2003.
28. *Vesti* [Belgrade], 19 Oct. 2003. Translated and reproduced in *Tuzla Night Owl* [Tuzla], 20 Oct. 2003, at: www.tfeagle.army.mil/tfeno. See also G. Toal and C. Dahlman, 'The Effort to Reverse Ethnic Cleansing in Bosnia-Herzegovina: The Limits of Returns', *Eurasian Geography and Economics*, Vol.45, No.6, 2004, pp.439–64.
29. Confidential interview by the author with UNMIBH official, Sarajevo, July 2002; see also Day (n.18 above), p.159.
30. D. Orsini, 'Security-sector Restructuring in Bosnia-Herzegovina: Addressing the Division?', *Conflict, Security and Development*, Vol.3, No.1 (2003), p.88.
31. Confidential interviews by the author with EUPM officials, Sarajevo and Travnik, July and August 2003.
32. D. Zaum, 'The Paradox of Sovereignty: International Involvement in Civil Service Reform in Bosnia and Herzegovina', *International Peacekeeping*, Vol.10, No.3, 2003, pp.102–20.
33. Confidential interview by the author with EUPM official, Travnik, July 2003.
34. E. Cashmore, 'Behind the Window Dressing: Ethnic Minority Police Perspectives on Cultural Diversity', *Journal of Ethnic and Migration Studies*, Vol.28, No.2, 2002, p.327.
35. International Crisis Group (n.26 above), p.22; G.L. Naarden, 'Non-prosecutorial Sanctions for Grave Violations of International Humanitarian Law: Wartime Conduct of Bosnian Police Officials', *The American Journal of International Law*, Vol.97, No.2, 2003, pp.342–52.
36. Confidential interview by the author with OHR official, Sarajevo, August 2003.
37. The credibility of the UN was also at stake. If nothing was done, the Bosnian population would probably question and lose trust in the contribution that UNMIBH/IPTF was trying to make to the post-conflict reconstruction and rehabilitation of their country. This issue is beyond the scope of this article and therefore it will not be elaborated further.
38. An OHR Supervisor Order allowed for a similar police restructuring agreement in Brčko in October 1997.
39. OHR, *Bosnia and Herzegovina: Essential Texts*, 3rd rev. edn, Sarajevo, 2000, p.542, §28.
40. The certification process became one of the core programmes in the UN Implementation Plan 2000–02.
41. A 'serious violation of duty or law' included, but was not limited to, human rights violations or failure to properly investigate human rights violations; violations of the Criminal Code, the Criminal Procedure Code or disciplinary rules; violations of IPTF policies or non-cooperation with IPTF; violations of the responsibilities and obligations under the DPA; and ordering a subordinate to commit any such acts, or failing to intervene when such acts were committed. UNMIBH/IPTF internal document, Feb. 2001.
42. Ibid.
43. Confidential interview by the author with OHR official, Sarajevo, August 2003. The certification process was divided into three phases: registration, provisional authorisation and final certification.
44. *Report of the Secretary-General on the United Nations Mission in Bosnia and Herzegovina*, UN Document No.S/2002/1314, 2002, §11, at www.un.org/Docs/sc/reports/2002/sgrep02.htm.
45. Confidential interviews by the author with EUPM, OHR and Bosnian civil society officials in various locations of BiH, August 2003.
46. UNMIBH/IPTF internal document, May 2002.
47. Confidential interview by the author with OHR official, Sarajevo, August 2003.
48. This is one of the conclusions that came out from confidential interviews with UNMIBH, OHR and EUPM officials as well as Bosnian police officers in various locations in BiH, summers of 2002 and 2003.
49. Confidential interview by the author with EUPM official, Sarajevo, July 2003.
50. 'High Representative Calls on PRC to Eradicate Politics from Police Reform', OHR Press Release, 13 December 2004, at www.ohr.int/ohr-dept/presso/pressr/default.asp?content_id = 33717.
51. Evidence from the field points to the fact that, whereas in the majority of cases finding a second job is the usual practice to supplement the salary as a police officer, some traffic police officers resort to the so-called traffic 'fines'. That is, penalizing drivers financially for traffic infractions that have not taken place or that might be less important than the police officer claims.
52. Confidential interview, Travnik, July 2003. This police officer was alluding here to the police officers' low salaries that are often paid late, sometimes up to four months late.
53. Confidential interview, Sarajevo, July 2003.

54. OHR Press Release (see n.50 above).
55. Confidential interview, Sarajevo, August 2003.
56. A. Kebo, 'Police as a Hostage', *Oslobodjenje* [Sarajevo]. Translated and reproduced in *Bosnia Daily* [Sarajevo], No.560, 14 Aug. 2003. In 2002, 19 members of a special police unit in Sarajevo were de-certified following a raid that led to the capture of some high-profile criminals. They were de-certified because it was claimed that the officers had used disproportionate force against the criminals during the raid. This decision led to public outrage. In the words of Amra Kebo, the above-mentioned journalist: 'Not all of them exceeded their authority. But all of them lost their jobs, humiliated and embarrassed… International representatives had an opportunity to correct obvious mistakes, but did not want to talk amiss to each other. Who is controlling the controllers?' Following the end of the UN mission, domestic courts, including the Human Rights Chamber of BiH, have begun to challenge the legality of these and other dismissals. In August 2003, 15 Doboj policemen were temporarily suspended in Teslić over their use of weapons against drug dealers. According to the newspaper *Dnevni Avaz*. 29 Nov. 2003, 'journalists mostly asked if this means that the "Sarajevo case" is repeating [sic], would this encourage drug dealers, and what would be the motive for policemen to fight crime in the future'. Translated and reproduced in *Tuzla Night Owl* [Tuzla], 30 Nov. 2003, at www.tfeagle.army.mil/tfeno.
57. Confidential interview by the author with a member of the donor community, Sarajevo, August 2003.
58. Confidential interview by the author with EUPM official, Sarajevo, August 2003.
59. E. Mobekk, 'International Involvement in Restructuring and Creating Security Forces: the Case of Haiti', *Small Wars and Insurgencies*, Vol.12, No.3, 2001, pp.97–114.
60. Cited in A. Hills, *Border Control Services and Security Sector Reform*, DCAF Working Paper Series, No.37, 2001, pp.21–2, at www.dcaf.ch.
61. Paddy Ashdown, 'From Dayton to Brussels', *Reporter*, 12 May 2004, as reported by the OHR Press Office, at www.ohr.int/ohr-dept/presso/pressa/default.asp?content_id=32492.
62. This term has been borrowed from R. Paris, 'International Peacebuilding and the "Mission Civilisatrice"', *Review of International Studies*, Vol.28, No.4, 2002, pp.637–56.

The Return of Refugees and Internally Displaced Persons: From Coercion to Sustainability?

DANIELA HEIMERL

The basic dilemma...is the structural tension between the necessity for massive, intensive and multifaceted external 'interference', on one hand, and the economic and political dependence as well as deficits in democratisation and regional ownership that this very interference generates in the weak states of an unstable region, on the other.
Iris Kempe and Wim van Meurs, 'Europe beyond EU Enlargement'[1]

The 1991 Bosnia and Herzegovina (BiH) census counted a total population of 4.3 million people. Slightly over half of the population (approximately 2.3 million) left their homes during the 43 months of the war and soon afterwards. Of these, about 1.3 million people became refugees, dispersed throughout 25 host countries, including neighbouring states of the former Yugoslavia, Europe, the United States, Canada and Australia. About one million remained in BiH as internally displaced persons (IDPs).[2] At the start of 1996, out of the approximately three million people remaining in BiH, 80 per cent or 2.4 million were affected by the war. The demographic impact of the fighting, in what had also been a war against BiH as a multi-ethnic place of coexistence and tolerance,[3] was dramatic: there was no municipality in the country where the pre-war ethnic composition remained intact.

The forced ethnic migrations, triggered by the conflict and linked to the disintegration of the federal structures of the Yugoslav state, provoked the worst refugee crisis Europe had faced since the Second World War.[4] By early 1996, Germany was host to the largest number of refugees from BiH (345,000), followed by Croatia (288,000), Serbia and Montenegro (254,000), and many other countries were host to tens of thousands of refugees – Austria (80,000), Sweden (61,500), Switzerland (26,700), Slovenia (33,400), the Netherlands (23,000), Denmark (23,000), the United Kingdom (13,000) and Norway (12,000). Bosniacs constituted the largest number of refugees (610,000), followed by BiH Croats (307,000), BiH Serbs (253,000) and others (23,000). More than half of the refugees (some 620,000) originated from territories now in the Republika Srpska (RS) and 598,000 fled from the Federation (FBiH).[5]

This essay seeks to examine the policy of international community representatives in BiH through highlighting the distinction between the initial post-war period, where there was little coercive international intervention, and the post-Bonn era of direct intervention. In the former period, people returned to areas where they were members of the majority ethnicity, and where returns took place, refugee return consolidated the ethnically homogenizing trends of the war. In the following period, the international community focused on prioritizing minority returns with the intention of fulfilling the Dayton aspiration of a return to the status quo ante of 1991. The essay then goes on to consider the reasons for this much more interventionist practice in relation to refugee return and to assess the successes and limitations of this approach.

The Evolution of International Return Policy

The international community's policy intervention with regard to the treatment of the refugee and IDP question developed in response to the experience of return movements and the changing international context. During 1996–97, the return movements provoked an ethnic consolidation. This was followed by a shift in international policy, between 1997 and 2000, which aimed to re-establish the pre-war situation. The desire to 're-mix' the country's three separated communities was central to the state-building political agenda, and from 2000 onwards a breakthrough with regard to the minority return could be clearly distinguished.

1996–97: Ethnic Consolidation

The authors of the Dayton peace accords (DPA) placed a particularly high priority on the return of refugees and IDPs to their pre-war homes, hoping that such return would reverse the territorial, political and ethnic partition of the country. The 'Agreement on Refugees and Displaced Persons', Annex 7 of the Dayton agreement, provided a right to return unique in international law – which conventionally terms 'return' as repatriation to one's home country.[6] For post-war BiH, return was stated to mean the right of all refugees and displaced persons freely to return to their homes of origin (Annex 7, Article 1, 1). This right of 'domicile return' meant that refugees and IDPs could return to their home dwelling and property occupied prior to the outbreak of war in 1991.[7] Article 2 clarified the novel and exacting standards demanded of the post-war Bosnian authorities to: 'ensure that refugees and displaced persons are permitted to return in safety, without risk of harassment, intimidation, persecution, or discrimination, particularly on account of their ethnic origin, religious belief, or political opinion'.[8]

In practice, return and return-related reconstruction was handled, from the outset, by international agencies with non-political mandates, in particular the UN High Commissioner for Refugees (UNHCR) and the World Bank. They focused on the easier task of majority return, returning refugees and IDPs to areas controlled by their own ethnic group. The greatest year for return movements was 1996 when more than 250,000 refugee and IDP returns were recorded, declining through 1997 and 1998. These returns occurred almost exclusively to areas where the returnees were part of the majority group. 'This is what is most do-able and safest, given the conditions on the ground', the former UN High Commissioner for Refugees, Mrs. Ogata, stated in December 1996.[9] There were no high-level political interventions to promote minority returns. Indeed, as then Senior Deputy High Representative Michael Steiner explained, at the end of 1996: 'There was no political support in the "big capitals" to push for minority returns. The capitals had other priorities and this was not one of them. For them Annex 7 was rhetorical.'[10]

Annex 7 – while, in theory, creating a framework that could reverse ethnic cleansing and bring the country back to the demographic character and property relations which existed in 1991 – depended, at first, on an awkward division of power between the international community and local political institutions. The strategy of the international community was based on the proposition that returns could be agreed with the entity authorities (created through the displacement movements) using a mix of bribes, threats and other leverage available. This was informed by the general assumption that the role of the international community in BiH was merely to help the local authorities implement the DPA.

Thus, the international community, represented by the international agencies, allowed the local authorities the power to choose the homes to be reconstructed and to identify the pre-war occupants entitled to reconstructed flats. Thus, local authorities throughout the country continued demographic engineering, focusing on creating incentives for their own IDPs to settle permanently where it benefited their respective ethnic agendas. Entity, canton and, most often, municipal authorities achieved this through the distribution of building plots, construction materials, business premises and commercial real estate to displaced persons. In fact, few if any Bosnian authorities were prepared to promote inward minority returns and most were ready to actively resist this, using means ranging from the violent to the bureaucratic.

Reliance on the main nationalist parties and ethnic oligarchs – who had been confirmed in power in their respective territories by the first post-war elections in September 1996 – as partners to implement the DPA and to promote returns without discrimination was a doomed undertaking. Taking their orders from the top, many municipality and canton officials, of all ethnic groups, actively obstructed returns, pursuing parallel policies of ethnic exclusivity and attempting to preserve their monopoly on power.

Against this background, a number of schemes designed to get the process of minority return under way met with failure.[11] These included targeting special areas for return; pilot projects within the Federation; the 'Open Cities' initiative;[12] shelter programs – intended to kick-start the repair and reconstruction effort until larger reconstruction projects could be initiated; repairing housing; organizing assessment visits; blacklisting obstructionist municipalities; and resettling the zone of separation – land along the Inter-Entity Boundary Line between the RS and FBiH.

The separation of the communities – which was obtained by violence and then perpetuated by political and territorial separation under the DPA – was indirectly strengthened by international policy which enabled the consolidation of these divisions during the first two years after the war. As a consequence, at the start of 1998, overwhelming ethnic majorities existed in most of BiH, with only a handful of areas containing minority populations greater than 10 per cent (about 13 per cent in Tuzla and Sarajevo cantons). At the same time, the return of refugees contributed significantly to the IDP problem, inflating their ranks and worsening the situation of those already displaced.

International policy had worked on the assumption that the majority of refugees and IDPs would want to return voluntarily to their pre-war homes. However, many refugees and IDPs did not share this aspiration in the short- or in the medium-term, and many did not aspire to return at all. Hundreds of thousands of refugees had been granted permanent status in their host countries. Others, being forced to leave their host country, started procedures to emigrate to third countries, and many who returned to Bosnia applied for emigration visas. Though there were strong indications that refugees and IDPs were, in the main, interested in return, when people expressed their wish not to return, this was often discounted as not being a genuine opinion but one influenced by intimidation and manipulation by nationalist politicians.

Slow progress in the number of minority returnees was considered narrowly as evidence of the failure of the human rights situation to improve. However, the barriers to return were often social and economic, and not solely concerning security (see Gemma Collantes Celador, this volume). The question of refugee return cannot be understood in such narrow, deterministic terms. Patterns of social inclusion – family and kinship support, neighbourhood and local community links, circles of friends and other social networks, such as those of the workplace – were disrupted. New patterns of exclusion emerged – with problems of unemployment, poverty and homelessness and with new status hierarchies, based on ethnicity, religion, war-time standing in the community and new socio-economic factors. Thus the decision whether to return was not a simple matter. Each individual's decision was, and is, made for a different balance of reasons.[13]

Refugees and IDPs faced a host of obstacles to domicile return. To follow the intricacies of return in BiH, the distinction between 'minority' and 'majority' return, however, is essential. Majority returnees face the normal run of problems in a post-war situation. Some conditions – such as severely depleted housing stock, war-time property laws and a devastated economy – plagued all returnees. But a particular burden was often imposed on people seeking to return to areas where they would be in the minority, where they would be confronted with all the diverse forms of discrimination that go along with being seen as the 'other' in a political environment still driven by virulent nationalism – for example, beatings of the newly arrived, the voluntary destruction of re-built houses just before the owners returned, a lack of work or schooling opportunities, administrative harassment, problems accessing social services, obtaining valid identity papers, or the provision of water and power utilities. Indeed, the political factors often played out in socio-economic terms. While minority returnees were subject to violence and intimidation, they were also victims of socio-economic discrimination at virtually every level.

1997–2000: Prioritizing Minority Return

After the initial return movement from 1996 to 1997, the process seemed to be at an end. At the start of 1998, most of the remaining refugees and IDPs, almost 1.5 million people, would have been in the minority if they had returned to their original homes. In late 1997, there was a policy shift towards much more direct international intervention in promoting the Dayton Annex 7 aim of a population return to the status quo ante of 1991. The Bonn Peace Implementation Council called upon the High Representative to use his 'full authority to facilitate the resolution of difficulties by making binding decisions...[and to] take actions against persons holding public office or officials...found by the High Representative to be in violation of legal commitments made under the Peace Agreement or the terms for its implementation'.[14] With the coercive mechanisms in place, the international community now decided that it was time to prioritize the thorny question of minority return.

Led by the Office of the High Representative (OHR), international agencies showed a new resolve in countering violent opposition to minority returns. The OHR had previously established the Reconstruction and Return Task Force (RRTF) in January 1997 as a forum for coordination and as a management mechanism spearheading returns at the local level.[15] The Bonn PIC measures strengthened the RRTF by granting it additional resources and appointing a deputy High Representative to lead it. It was to pursue a coercive, as distinct from a humanitarian or voluntary approach to minority returns.

Two reasons are often forwarded to explain the change of focus of the international community. First, the voluntary return movement had institutionalized the ethnic divisions of the war rather than challenging them, as had been previously hoped. The international focus on the right of return, and the right to vote in the municipality in which citizens had lived in 1991, had been specifically designed to challenge the ethnical homogeneity of the entities. However, the success of the nationalist parties in the September 1996 elections demonstrated that substantial return had merely strengthened the hold of nationalist elites. It was felt that this could only be broken by forcing the issue of minority return. There was an element of self-interest at stake here, with a growing awareness among leaders of the Contact Group, that unless they radically changed their policy, there would be no progress in creating conditions for the withdrawal of the NATO-led forces.

Second, despite political obstructionism within BiH, host countries were determined to repatriate Bosnian refugees. In late 1996, Western European states, starting with Germany, which had been host to the largest number of refugees, began proceedings to send Bosnian refugees back.[16] German policy was to encourage voluntary repatriation by a variety of means, including incentive packages and repatriation assistance. The threat of a new wave of repatriations put added pressure on the international agencies. The UNHCR warned that up to 200,000 refugees might return from abroad, mostly Bosniacs from Germany whose homes were originally located on territory now within the RS.[17] It noted that unless there was a 'major break-through in minority return movements', this repatriation would result in relocation to majority areas, consolidating ethnic separation and making it more difficult for minority groups to return if their homes were occupied by 'relocatees'. It appeared certain that unless action was taken, this new flow of returning refugees would continue the unwelcome trend of returns consolidating ethnic divisions.

It was clear that the ambitious aim of return to the pre-war status quo was not shared unanimously by the humanitarian agencies. 'Hostile relocation', the deliberate placement of groups of people in housing belonging to other ethnic groups to secure control over territory and prevent minority return, was certainly part of the political programme of the nationalist parties. However, many humanitarian agencies maintained that relocation could also be part of the solution to the refugee problem, providing an important component in the search for durable solutions for refugees and IDPs who were not ready or willing to accept domicile return. This was also suggested because of agencies' concern that, without such relocations, the normalization of the country might be held hostage indefinitely to an unattainable agenda.

The increased return movement appears to have been triggered by several factors, including refugee impatience, increased international community willingness to use the powers vested in the OHR to remove obstructionist officials and implement property laws, the legislation facilitating return being finally in place and beginning to be implemented, a change in the psychology of the majority and minority populations, and changes in regime in Croatia and the Federal Republic of Yugoslavia.

The 1999 action plan of the Reconstruction and Return Task Force (RRTF) represented the most determined effort thus far to implement a policy of mass return in BiH.[18] Focusing on three factors necessary for a breakthrough in minority return – space, security and sustainability – the plan was based on a new methodology to support minority returns. The High Representative's imposition of new property laws,[19] as well as the RRTF's emphasis on the rule of law, succeeded in turning what was formerly a highly politicized issue into a simple question of technical adherence to the law. In an effort to open up the housing stock, evictions from refugee property took place throughout the country. Using the Property Law Implementation Program (PLIP), the primary focus shifted from tolerating excuses for non-implementation by local officials to emphasis upon following the letter of the law, as expressed in the RRTF document 'Non-negotiable Principles in the Context of the Property Law Implementation'. Officials were dismissed who refused to implement the new property laws. The Property Implementation Plan provided for an international officer to monitor implementation of the law and to encourage local authorities to resolve outstanding cases in each of Bosnia's municipalities. The International Police Task Force (IPTF) exercised its supervisory powers over local police forces to ensure that evictions took place as ordered. Double Occupancy Commissions, composed of local and international officials, worked to prioritize evictions of people with multiple dwellings. This combination of legal and political pressure yielded results. Thus, the PLIP altered the perceptions of the refugees and IDPs. They could no longer assume either that their former homes were lost to them, or that they could themselves occupy somebody else's property indefinitely. As a result, a major psychological barrier had been breached.

Refugees and IDPs were also indispensable actors themselves. It is vital to note that by far the majority of minority returns were individual, voluntary and spontaneous, which meant that they returned on their own initiative, without international assistance or approval from the local authorities. High-profile organized repatriation by the international community only made up for a minor proportion of return movements (see further, Roberto Belloni, this volume).

Most returns were to rural areas. But there was also progress in Sarajevo. The 1998 Sarajevo Declaration succeeded in encouraging the return of 20,000 non-Bosniacs. This had an effect throughout the country: returnees from RS and Croat-majority regions, in coming back to Sarajevo, then freed up the housing they had illegally occupied in their majority areas, which allowed increased return to these areas and created the momentum for a 'virtuous circle' of nation-wide minority returns.[20]

2000–2003: Minority Returns Peak

By the end of 2000, the international community had established the basis for large-scale minority return. In its 2001 World Report, Human Rights Watch underlined a 'breakthrough in one of the most serious of Bosnia-Herzegovina's human rights issues: the return of the refugees and displaced persons'.[21] Thus, it was not until four years after the war that significant levels of minority returns were recorded. For the first time since the signing of Dayton, refugees and IDPs returned in relatively large numbers to areas where they would be part of an ethnic minority. Although the numbers were comparatively modest, their political significance was important, indicating that local politicians were losing their capacity to resist the demands of refugees and IDPs. These movements against the grain of both the war and nationalist propaganda appeared in the last quarter of 1999 and grew steadily in 2000, when UNHCR figures registered an increase of more than 50 per cent on 1999. A significant turnaround seemed to have occurred. The figures of the UNHCR for the years 2000 and 2001 seemed indeed to reflect an evolution of the perception of the two entities by potential minority return candidates. In 2001 and 2002, the numbers of the minority returns peaked.

In September 2004, the UNHCR announced that over one million people uprooted by the 1992–95 war had returned to their pre-war properties, including 440,147 former refugees and 560,326 IDPs.[22] This represented, in fact, just slightly more than half of the population forced to flee their homes. Nearly 75 per cent of the returnees went back to the Federation and 25 per cent to the RS.

An estimated 20,000 have returned to the Brčko district which is administered autonomously. A relatively high proportion, just under half of the total, returned to areas in which they are in a minority, including many to the places that saw some of the worst atrocities during the war. It should be noted though that the situation remains volatile in many parts of the country and that a challenge remains to consolidate the returns that have taken place to make them sustainable.

This said, it would appear that the exacting conditions of Annex 7 will never be completely satisfied. The years of 2003–2004 have been marked by a sharp decline in the overall rate of returns, the process winding down in most areas. Refugees are still numerous in neighbouring countries, with about 100,000 in Serbia and Montenegro and Croatia: the regional issue has been part of the refugee dilemma from the start and it is evident that the criss-cross pattern of refugee exodus cannot be reversed without a solution on a regional scale. Unless there is a regional repatriation, the return process in BiH is partially blocked. There are also the 500,000 refugees, which have been granted asylum, regularized a permanent residency or adopted a new citizenship elsewhere and the 50,000 currently living in Western Europe without a durable solution for their future. The number of IDPs within BiH is an estimated 313,000.[23]

However, numbers alone do not tell the full story of the return process. If the overall goal of return is not only to reverse ethnic cleansing but also to help re-create a genuinely multi-ethnic society, it is necessary to explore the quality of that return. The intention behind the extensive intervention to implement Annex 7 of the Dayton accords was intended to achieve more than simply ensuring that refugees and IDPs could reclaim their property. It was ambitiously intended to create the conditions that would give minority returnees a chance of surviving and prospering in their former communities. The relatively poor record of return – both quantitatively and qualitatively – suggests that the original thinking behind this strategy may have been mistaken. It is this that is considered in the following section.

The Limitations to Imposed Return

Despite enormous international efforts to promote domicile return, getting uprooted persons physically back home is only half the task of re-creating a functioning multi-ethnic society. The other half involves fostering the conditions in which returnees and especially minority returnees can survive and reintegrate themselves into their old/new communities. Besides the possibility of recovering and repairing their homes, would-be returnees also base their decisions to return on the availability of work, their assessment of the security situation, their children's chances of getting a decent education,[24] the provision of basic public services and their access to pensions, health care and other social benefits.

Despite the multi-faceted political offensive on the part of the international community in support of minority return, it has not coupled its commitments to physical return with a similar commitment to ensuring its sustainability. While a lot of energy and resolve has been directed towards facilitating returns at a political and legal level, the country's persistent economic fragility invariably limits the success of such initiatives. Thus, the promotion of minority return on all fronts made sense from the perspective of recreating multi-ethnicity and righting the wrong of ethnic cleansing; from the perspective of economic development and growth, however, it would have made more sense to facilitate the free movement of people to areas where economic opportunities existed, regardless of domicile return.[25] The tension between the two perspectives has resulted in the socio-economic needs of minority returnees not being prioritized by key international economic actors.

Against this background, there are reasons to be concerned about the sustainability of the return process in terms of regenerating truly multi-ethnic communities.[26] Firstly, minority returnees often live in isolated rural enclaves, and a high percentage of returnees are elderly and retired people who have chosen to return in order to live out their lives in familiar surroundings. Many of the elderly have returned because they have strong emotional connections to their land, but return has proved to be much less attractive for younger people, more concerned about their economic futures.

Second, the situation of the IDP population and minority returnees remains fragile. Their living conditions are generally precarious.[27] For instance, the existence of separate welfare systems in each entity has created immense difficulties for returnees. Most continue to rely on assistance from aid agencies or family members living elsewhere in order to survive. National authorities have yet to fulfil their obligations under the DPA to ensure an environment conducive to sustainable return. As a facet of ethnic cleansing, members of the 'wrong' ethnic community were dismissed from firms and public institutions which came under the control of the nationalist parties. Although the necessary legal framework to get their jobs back is often in place, enforcement of the respective laws and agreements remains limited. The generally dire state of the economy and the paucity of new jobs means that returnees of all ethnic communities, including those belonging to the majority, have difficulty in obtaining jobs, and experience shows that 'minority' returnees face the added obstacle of institutionalized discrimination.

Where large-scale return has taken place, returnees have usually formed parallel institutions, led by returnee associations, serviced by token representatives in municipal government and sustained by a largely separate economy. Thus, return has not resulted in re-integration. In Foča in eastern RS, for example, where Bosniacs initiated a breakthrough return to villages violently cleansed in the war, economic malaise is a major obstacle to sustainable return to the town. Returnees have made inroads in establishing a presence in the municipal council, but a climate of unregenerate racism compels returnees to keep a very low profile. The case of Prijedor represents an RS municipality where significant Bosniac return has re-established a strong and highly visible Bosniac presence in the local economy, politics and society. Yet the continuing presence as well of unindicted war criminals, a divided education system and a largely un-integrated municipal administration have encouraged Bosniac returnees to establish a parallel existence, separated from their Serb neighbours (see further Roberto Belloni, this volume).

These examples demonstrate that the return of pre-war property is not equivalent to the return to the pre-war situation of 1991, particularly in the absence of equal opportunities for returnees and the genuine reintegration of returnee communities. In the case of Prijedor (and other success stories, such as Serb return to Drvar) it is instructive that large-scale return pre-dated the international community's push for implementation of the property laws, thus revealing that such implementation is but one of the many factors needed to ensure the rights guaranteed under Annex 7.

International efforts since have focused mainly on opening up space for return by ensuring that refugees and IDPs can reclaim and/or reconstruct their pre-war properties. As a result, 92 per cent of property claims lodged by pre-war owners were resolved by December 2003.[28] No international organization or government agency has precise figures on how many Bosnians, after reclaiming their houses and flats – or receiving reconstruction assistance – then decide to sell or exchange them and relocate elsewhere.[29] According to data collected by the International Crisis Group, about three-quarters of pre-war occupants do return to their reconstructed dwellings; but in a third of these cases, only a part of the family does so.[30] There is a tendency for only older family members to return permanently and for school-age children to remain in or be sent back to their majority areas. In 20 per cent of the verified cases, reconstructed houses and apartments remained empty, but less than 4 per cent had been let, sold or lent to an occupant other than the original beneficiary. These figures show that incentives for the return of younger refugee families remain weak, though also that such people seem to be keeping their options open by holding on to their reconstructed property.

As for repossessed houses and apartments, reports from the field illustrate varying patterns of return, sale and rental, depending on the area. After the OHR decreed an end to the two-year moratorium on resale in the Federation in July 2001, applications for repossession from people living abroad shot up. In some cases, potential returnees have repossessed their flats and rented them to displaced persons. This reflects an apparent desire among potential returnees to keep their options open and to secure some income while waiting for employment opportunities to arise or for the security environment to improve. In the meantime, permanent return is more often centred on villages, where subsistence agriculture can be practised. The percentage of sale of real estate is lower in rural areas, where people have at least the possibility to obtain some work and thus to survive.

Thus, the category of IDP is getting smaller – not only because displaced people are returning to their pre-war homes, but also because their property is being reinstated and they lose their IDP status. What is most worrying is that those returning are often the poorest and most socially vulnerable people who have no other options but to return. Yet, without major socio-economic changes the elderly and the vulnerable returning to their new-old environment will be without viable means of support, often in isolated and inward-looking enclaves without adequate social support networks, whether public or private.

The process of return has to be put into the context of the rural–urban and young–old dynamics of the country during and since the war. Internal displacement followed a rural to urban pattern. This was because, on the whole, the refugees who left BiH did so earlier in the war rather than later. These people tended to be urban, more cosmopolitan in outlook and better educated than the IDPs. At the same time, families driven out of the villages ended up in urban centres where they became integrated, thus 'the war effectively was a process of compulsory urbanization'.[31]

Since the war, age, education, economic and security calculations have meant that the process of return to rural areas has not meant the restoration of the pre-war age, ethnic and social balance. By and large, minority returns involve a process of re-ruralization, in which returnees have been encouraged to move from urban sites of displacement back to their pre-war homes in rural areas. This strong rural dimension to minority return is partly linked to the fact that BiH was one of the least urbanized territories prior to the war. At the same time, return to rural areas has been far less problematic politically, since many destroyed rural villages remain abandoned, and returns to these areas represent less of a threat to the majority community. However, this process does not appeal to many, especially the younger generation who have grown up with the experience of urban life, and importantly it runs counter to the broader economic reform and modernization agenda being promoted by the international community, which takes for granted that labour will be available where employment opportunities are, not vice versa. In general terms, current population movements are not individuals returning to their homes of origin, but rather people relocating in different directions in the search for employment opportunities or a secure living environment.

In the case of BiH, the international community has been simultaneously moving in two different directions: one backward-looking, in terms of trying to restore the pre-war status of multi-ethnicity, and the other forward-looking, in terms of trying to building a functioning market economy. But restoring multi-ethnicity is about more than simply the physical return to homes of origin.

Conclusion

Annex 7 of the DPA embodies the hopes and assumptions of its authors, if not of its signatories, that the return and reintegration of the different ethnic communities would serve both as the foundation of a stable state and as a counter to nationalist politics. The creation of ethnically-pure territories was at the heart of the conflict that tore BiH apart. Much of the post-Dayton period in the country has revolved around the struggle to achieve ethnic reintegration – and rebuild a genuinely multi-ethnic Bosnian polity – in the face of determined resistance by local elites. The international focus on return, especially on minority return, greatly politicized the question and has led to massive international interference which would otherwise not have been the case. As David Chandler has pointed out, 'return for the international community has become less a matter of choice, to be decided by individuals or negotiated between community representatives and more a matter of international policy-making'.[32]

With the push by the international community for return, especially minority return, to restore the status quo ante of multi-ethnicity across BiH, the reversal of ethnic cleansing has been the central issue of the country's post-conflict period. Starting in 1997, the UNHCR devoted almost its entire operational budget to supporting minority returns. Minority return, not the removal of the fundamental causes of displacement, became the goal of the peace process, leading to the reversal of the cause and effect relationship. In other words, rather than seeing physical reintegration of ethnic communities evolving at the end of the peace process, the international community viewed minority return as a tool through which to achieve multi-ethnicity. Refugees and IDPs, by returning to their previous homes were expected to erase the consequences of ethnic cleansing and contribute to the rebirth of a multi-ethnic state.[33]

Using returnees as a vanguard force in the fight for reintegration, without recognizing the transformation that the war, and the post-war environment, had wrought on Bosnia's economic and social framework (see Michael Pugh, this volume), not only raises questions about the effectiveness of such strategies in regenerating a multi-ethnic society but can also be seen as morally problematic. International policy appears to regard people's choices based on Bosnian society as it exists today as less legitimate than the Dayton commitment to domicile return; in this way international policy has exacerbated the vulnerability of those who were already among the most vulnerable of the country's citizens.[34]

Furthermore, placing return so high up the agenda made the issue automatically politicized, and therefore confrontational, instead of adopting a more consensus-based and less politicized approach. In this context, the challenge of today seems to be rather to support multi-ethnicity, tolerance and cohabitation as a constitutive and organizing principle for peacebuilding. The solution lies not only in promoting democracy and especially minority rights' protection but also, importantly, in reviving the state's capacity to overcome secessionist ethnic nationalism, through creating political institutions which have a broad popular legitimacy and are capable of commanding citizens' cross-ethnic allegiances. In BiH, neighbourliness (*komsiluk*) was secured so long as the state was trusted to guarantee stability and peace. Once the legitimacy of the state was brought into question, *komsiluk* became the object of fear and insecurities, despite the fact that there were no clear lines of territorial ethnic division and that integrative dynamics (common language, ethnic origin and life-style) had always existed.

Before the war, the different ethnic communities were not uniformly dispersed throughout the country; it was however very unusual for any one community to hold a hegemonic position. The geographic positions and ethnic compositions of the different localities were not without consequences for the war and the post-war period.[35] One of the characteristics of the Bosnian conflict was that it fundamentally disrupted not only ethnic but also social and economic relations across the country. These social and economic relations will never be re-established. Regardless of questions of ethnic 're-mixing' the pre-war 'normality' desired by the international administrators cannot be recreated as the future of the region. The international interveners in BiH will sooner or later have to face the fact that, rather than seeking to impose an unattainable past, the solution to Bosnia's war-time divisions can only be found by looking towards the future.

NOTES

1. I. Kempe and W. van Meurs, 'Europe beyond EU Enlargement', in W. Van Meurs (ed.), *Prospects and Risks beyond EU Enlargement – Southern Europe: Weak States and Strong International Support*, Opladen: Leske & Budrich, 2003, p.26.
2. The term 'refugees' refers to displaced persons who fled to other countries; 'internally displaced persons' (IDPs) are those who remained inside the state boundaries. The internally displaced population also includes returning refugees who cannot go back to their pre-war home. The term 'minority return' refers to the return of refugees and IDPs to areas in which their ethnic group is now in the minority; 'majority return' refers to returns by persons who belong to the majority ethnic group in the area.
3. N. Cigar, *Genocide in Bosnia: the Policy of 'Ethnic Cleansing'*, College Station, TX: Texas A&M University Press, 1995; X. Bougarel, *Bosnie: Anatomie d'un conflit*, Paris: Editions La Découverte, 1996.
4. M. Morokvasić, 'Ouverture des frontières à l'Est et nouveaux flux', *Les Migrations Internationales*, Mars-Avril 2002, pp.20–45.
5. International Crisis Group, *Going Nowhere Fast: Refugees and Internally Displaced Persons in Bosnia and Herzegovina*, Bosnia Report, No.23, 1 May 1997, at www.crisisweb.org/home/index.cfm?id=1572&l=1; D. Melcic (ed.), *Der Jugoslawien-Krieg: Handbuch zur Vorgeschichte, Verlauf und Konsequenzen*, Opladen-Wiesbaden: Westdeutscher Verlag, 1999.
6. Dayton General Framework Agreement, Annex 7, 'Agreement on Refugees and Displaced Persons', at www.ohr.int/dpa/default.asp?content_id=375.
7. G. O' Tuathail (G. Toal) and C. Dahlmann, 'The Effort to Reverse Ethnic Cleansing in Bosnia-Herzegovina: the Limits of Return', *Eurasian Geography and Economics*, Vol.45, No.6, 2004, pp.439–65.
8. For further information on the rights of refugees and IDPs see P. Prettitore, 'Refugee return in Bosnia and Herzegovina', presentation at Transferring Best Practice an international workshop on the comparative study of refugee return programmes, 9-12 June 2004, University of Exeter, UK, mimeo.
9. International Crisis Group, *Minority Return or Mass Relocation?*, Bosnia Report, No.33, 14 May 1998, p.2, at: www.icg.org/home/index.cfm?id=1507&l=5.
10. Ibid.
11. International Crisis Group (n.5 above), p.13.
12. International Crisis Group, *The Konjic Conundrum: Why Minorities Have Failed to Return to Model Open City*, Bosnia Report, No.35, 19 June 1988, at www.icg.org/home/index.cfm?id=1510&l=5.
13. D. Djipa, M. Muzur and P.F. Lytle, 'War-Torn Lives, in Bosnia-Herzegovina', in D. Narayan and P. Petesch. (eds), *Voices of the Poor: From Many Lands*, New York: World Bank, Oxford University Press, 2002, at www1.worldbank.org/prem/poverty/voices/reports/lands/lanbosnia.pdf.
14. 'Bosnia and Herzegovina 1998: Self-sustaining Structures', PIC Bonn Conclusions, §11.2, 10 December 1997, at www.ohr.int/pic/default.asp?content_id=5182#03.
15. The overall coordination of Return and Reconstruction was ensured, until 2003, through the Reconstruction and Return Task Force (RRTF) which comprised humanitarian and human rights agencies, development actors, such as the UNDP and the World Bank, and primary donors.
16. D. Heimerl, 'La politique de l'Allemagne à l'égard des réfugiés ex-yougoslaves', *Hommes et Migrations*, January–February 2002, pp.28–39.
17. International Crisis Group (n.5 above), p.11.
18. European Stability Initiative, *Interim Evaluation of Reconstruction and Return Task*, Sarajevo: ESI, 14 September 1999, at www.esiweb.org/pdf/esi_document_id_2.pdf.
19. Return was blocked by the myriad of war-time and post-war laws passed by the entities and the municipalities which legalized the theft of residences and property belonging to refugees and IDPs. The OHR eventually cancelled all entity property laws and imposed a uniform property law implementation process. In 1997 and 1998, the international community resolved to

support return by insisting that the right to repossess one's pre-war property should take precedence over any rights that local authorities had granted to the current occupant. In 1998, international arm-twisting compelled the entities, first the Federation, then the RS, to create legal frameworks for property repossession. These laws were strengthened and harmonized by the OHR in October 1999. See further, Prettitore (n.8 above), p.11.

20. International Crisis Group, *Too Little, Too Late: Implementation of the Sarajevo Declaration,* Bosnia Report, No.44, Sept. 1998, at www.icg.org/home/index.cfm?id=1514&l=1. See also the more negative assessment of the Sarajevo declaration in Prettitore (n.8 above), p.9.

21. 'Bosnia and Herzegovina', *2001 World Report,* Human Rights Watch, at www.hrw.org/wr2k1/europe/bosnia.html.

22. UNHCR, UN News Centre, 21 Sept. 2004. Note that the exact numbers of returnees are difficult to calculate. Information on refugee return is collected by UNHCR, OHR, RRTF and SFOR. Each agency utilizes a different methodology for gathering data.

23. La lettre d'information de l'Association de Sarajevo, 21 Sept. 2004, at http://beltegeuse.dyndns.org/association.sarajevo/.

24. Bosnian primary and secondary schools teach according to three separate, nationally specific curricula, in three allegedly distinct languages and often using textbooks replete with terminology and interpretations that are offensive to returnee children and their parents. The entity ministers of education signed an Interim Agreement on the accommodation of specific needs and rights of returnee children in March 2002.

25. T. Donais, 'Halfway Home': 'The Political Economy of Return in Post-Daylon Bosnia', York University Centre for International and Security Studies, Toronto, Canada, March 2002, p.11, at www.insanet.org/noarchive/donais.html.

26. The combination of a lack of economic space and ongoing political tension explains why, increasingly, it is exodus rather than return that characterizes demographic trends in contemporary Bosnia. Roberto Belloni reports that from 1996–98, some 250,000 Bosnians, many of them educated professionals, left Bosnia to join the more than 700,000 refugees who found 'sustainable solutions' abroad. The exodus seemed to gather momentum after the war rather than diminish. See R. Belloni, 'Blaming the Victims? The Challenge of Minority Return in Bosnia-Herzegovina', *Human Rights Working Paper,* No.13, University of Denver, March 2001, p.20, at www.du.edu/humanrights/workingpapers/papers/13-belloni-03-01.pdf.

27. Norwegian Refugee Council, 'Profile of Internal Displacement: Bosnia and Herzegovina', 28 Jan. 2004, at www.idpproject.org.

28. Ibid.

29. The Helsinki Committee on Human Rights in Bosnia and Herzegovina expressed concern that more than 75 per cent of the repossessed property is sold.

30. International Crisis Group, *The Continuing Challenge of Refugee Return in Bosnia and Herzegovina,* Bosnia Report, No.137, 13 Dec. 2002, p.11, at www.icg.org//library/documents/report_archive/A400847_13122002.pdf.

31. Tuathail and Dahlmann (n.7 above), p.449.

32. D. Chandler, *Bosnia: Faking Democracy after Dayton,* London-Sterling, Virginia, Pluto Press, 1999, p.107.

33. S. Albert, 'The Return of Refugees to Bosnia and Herzegovina: Peacebuilding with People', *International Peacekeeping,* Vol.4, No.3, 1997, p.2.

34. T. Donais, 'Halfway Home: The Political Economy of Return in Post-Dayton Bosnia', York University Center for International and Security Studies, Toronto, Canada, March 2002, p.13, at www.isanet.org/noarchive/donais.html.

35. J.A. Slack and R. Doyon, 'Population Dynamics and Susceptibility for Ethnic Conflict: the Case of Bosnia-Herzegovina', *Journal of Peace Research,* Vol.38, No.2, 2001, pp.139–61.

Empowering Women? An Assessment of International Gender Policies in Bosnia

VANESSA PUPAVAC

This essay considers international gender policies and the prospects they offer for the women of Bosnia (BiH) to move beyond post-conflict stabilization. Gender empowerment has become a standard tool of international peacebuilding in post-conflict societies and BiH is no exception in this respect. Maximizing the public role of women, whether as voters, journalists, political representatives or through women's organizations is viewed as useful to undermine the power of nationalist parties and to promote a more tolerant, non-violent, political culture. Voter education, gender quotas, media training and broadening the political role of women's organizations have been pursued in numerous initiatives.

The Dayton settlement itself did not address the issue of gender, but considerable international attention has been given to the issue since then. To pursue gender empowerment more systematically, a Gender Coordination Group was established, chaired by the OHR, with representatives from the OSCE, OHCHR (Office of the High Commission for Human Rights), the International Human Rights Law Group and other international organizations. Its remit includes implementing the Convention on the Elimination of Discrimination against Women (CEDAW) and integrating the gender dimension into 'national legislation, public policies, programmes and projects'.[1] A complimentary Gender Equity and Equality Project, supported by the Finnish government, operates through the Gender Centre of the Federation of Bosnia and Herzegovina (FBiH) and the Gender Centre of Republika Srpska (RS).[2] Both projects helped sponsor a Law on Gender Equality, passed in 2003,[3] codifying international gender thinking and building on ad hoc measures such as electoral gender quotas.

The Law on Gender Equality has been followed up by a two-year $400,000 project dedicated to its implementation supported by the UNDP as the lead international organization together with UNICEF, OHCHR, UNFPA and the ILO under the UN Gender Group. Importantly, they have been working with the Ministry for Human Rights and Refugees, the Entity Gender Centres and NGOs to establish a state-level gender agency. Initiatives also include gender awareness campaigns and the 'training of trainers (judges, teachers, NGO officials) and other capacity-building activities addressing gender equality and the elimination of gender-based violence.[4] Meanwhile international micro-credit programmes have often been directed towards women. The UNDP and other international organizations are keen to emphasize how their own programmes incorporate a gender dimension and how they strive towards a gender balance among their own employees.[5]

Below, I first consider international policies intended to politically empower women, analysing the impact of the quota system for appointment to government bodies and for political party candidate lists, and discuss the role of internationally-funded women's groups in political advocacy. I then consider in the following section international strategy aimed at enhancing the economic empowerment of women, focusing on the rise of micro-credit initiatives and the encouragement of small businesses.

Political Empowerment?

International gender policy has sought to redress discrimination against women in the political sphere. The war's impact on the number of female political representatives has been dramatic. Before the war, apparently, 24 per cent of the representatives in the Assembly of the Republic of Bosnia and Herzegovina and 17 per cent of the representatives in the municipal assemblies were women.[6] However, the number of women in parliament sharply plummeted in the first Bosnian elections held after the war. Women's strong presence in the NGO sector failed to translate into greater political representation. To cite just one figure, a solitary woman gained a seat out of the 42 seats in the Bosnian House of Representatives.[7] These election results have reinforced concern that economic crisis and war have undermined women's participation in the workplace too. Large-scale unemployment, it is feared, has encouraged thinking receptive to a more gendered division of labour along with the ethnicized divisions.

These reversals have encouraged international officials to adopt a more proactive approach. The Law on Gender Equality does not confine itself to outlawing gender-based discrimination, direct or indirect. Instead the law incorporates an affirmative approach requiring gender parity in the allocation of public posts. Crucially, Article 15 sets out the principle of equal gender representation in public life:

> State and local authority bodies, corporate management bodies, political parties and other non-profit organizations shall ensure and promote equal representation on the basis of gender in management and the

decision-making process... [T]he percentage of the sexes in government bodies *at all levels*, including the judiciary, legislature and executive, as well as all other public services, committees, boards, and bodies representing the state at the international level, *shall as a rule reflect the equal gender representation* (emphasis added).[8]

The requirement for equal gender representation has huge implications for public life in BiH. Post-conflict BiH is effectively expected to implement more radical fast-track measures than Britain, the High Representative Paddy Ashdown's own state, or the incremental track deployed in the Scandinavian countries.[9] Britain would have difficulty in demonstrating equal gender representation at *any level* let alone at *all levels* of government and the public services. British government bodies, public services, private sector institutions and corporations would fall foul of this article. Moreover, the principle of gender parity compliments constitutional provisions codifying ethnic representation in public life. Consequently gender parity will have to be implemented taking into account the extensive quota requirements which already exist for ethnic representation. Achieving gender parity and the required ethnic representation would only be possible with complex bureaucratic planning.

The Law on Gender Equality builds on various affirmative action initiatives seeking to challenge the political and cultural marginalization of women. A 'Women in Politics' programme was established by the OSCE, delegated responsibility for supervising elections under Dayton. As part of its programme, the OSCE changed the electoral rules and required 30 per cent of the candidates on candidate lists to be women. The measure did increase the number of women representatives in elected bodies. The percentage of women in the House of Representatives leapt up from a miserable 2 per cent to a much more respectable 26 per cent under a closed list system,[10] although the figure dropped back to 14 per cent when the closed list system was subsequently replaced with an open list system.[11]

Complementary initiatives seek to enhance the role of women parliamentarians. The remit of the Stability Pact Gender Task Force is to increase 'public awareness of women's political participation in elections and political processes in general; reform existing electoral systems and legislation...to promote women's political participation; [and] establish governmental institutions to promote gender equality.'[12] A 2001 conference held in Sarajevo on the theme of 'Partnership in Parliament – Strategic Steps towards Gender Equality', for female members of the Parliament, NGO members and others, called for 'continuous education' for parliamentarians as well as other measures to encourage women to enter politics.[13] Grassroots work has also been sponsored to enhance women's broader influence on the peacebuilding and reform process, such as the 'There Are More of Us, Let's Vote' campaign in 1998. The campaign was conducted under the auspices of the League of Women Voters, a coalition of women's NGOs backed by USAID and the OSCE. International organizations gave strong backing to the women's voter education project, although the turnout among women was relatively healthy, especially compared to that of young people. These projects are not simply concerned with ensuring that women vote, but also with influencing how women vote by empowering them not to follow their (nationalist voting) menfolk.

How effective is the quota system? The quota system has boosted the number of women standing in Bosnian elections, testifying that women can be politicians and providing role models for other women. Indeed, the idea of quota systems, whether gender- or ethnically-based, is not an alien concept to Bosnians as elsewhere in Eastern Europe. However, this familiarity with quota systems has made East European electorates more sceptical than international officials or women's NGOs about their impact. 'In the former communist countries...quotas are typically rejected out of hand because they are seen as being parallel to the systems of appointment/election that prevailed under communism', a Stockholm-based research project on gender quotas admits.[14] Bosnia's own pre-war quota system was widely criticized 'for being merely symbolic',[15] because many female politicians owed their position to their connections, and their politics tended to simply echo that of their male colleagues.[16] Similarly, in Britain, the calibre of recent female politicians whose candidatures were secured through quotas has been unfavourably compared to that of their predecessors. Rather than a distinct voice, it was observed that 'Blair's babes', as the 1997 intake were derogatorily named, were less likely to rebel and more likely to tow the government line than their male colleagues, even on matters touching on women's interests.[17] Strikingly, international reports have commented on the generally poor calibre of female politicians in present-day Bosnia.[18] Advocates concede some of these criticisms, but argue that quota systems provide professional experience and can therefore help develop their calibre.

However, the stunted nature of political life under international governance is not conducive to improving the calibre of politicians. To focus on the poor calibre of political representatives side-steps the degraded nature of the political rights which are promoted by advocates of quotas. Consider the research by the Stockholm-based Gender Quotas project – which advocates parliamentary gender quotas and increasing women's political participation in Iraq and Afghanistan – while pointedly disregarding the lack of political self-determination in the two states under external regulation.[19] What political powers do any politicians have when all major policies are made by external powers? The image of re-arranging the deckchairs on the Titanic springs to mind. The weak calibre of Bosnian politicians is unsurprising given the artificial character of Bosnian political life under international governance (see David Chandler, this volume). Women's advocates talk about ensuring the meaningful participation of women but without challenging the stunted and restricted nature of politics under international governance. What is the significance of more women becoming members of the Bosnian parliament when local politicians lack real political and legislative powers? Greater political representation, in this case, merely signifies a form of therapeutic inclusion since Bosnian politicians' role has been reduced to little more than role playing, rubber-stamping internationally determined legislation.

A 'so-called mandatory platform in which political parties have to take positions on the most important, vital issues for all people in BiH has been developed by the OSCE in its supervisory role'[20]. Over the last decade, not only has opposition to Dayton effectively been outlawed under international governance, but political candidates are expected to adhere to the wide-ranging policies determined by the international community. The often controversial reforms such as privatization or pension reforms go far beyond ethnic matters. Consequently, more women becoming politicians in Bosnia under international governance might be better understood as improved employment opportunities for some women rather than women's political empowerment. For all the image of women activists driving gender quotas, their introduction was bound up with the belief of international officials that female politicians would be more amenable than male politicians to international strategies and help legitimize international governance. Tellingly, these sorts of fast-track gender empowerment approaches are a feature of other weak post-conflict countries under heavy external intervention such as Afghanistan or Rwanda.

International officials seem to hold a rather impoverished and undemocratic view of political participation. The very process of realizing the Law on Gender Equality exemplifies how the population is marginalized from policy-making. International organizations were closely involved in drafting the gender equality law at every stage, so much so that even its style reflects how draft provisions spent much of their time being formulated in the English language rather than the language of the country. A snapshot of the process reveals how the Gender Coordination Group discussed a draft which was then 'distributed for review to the International Community and NGOs dealing with the issues contained in the draft' in summer 2001. Only subsequent to this review did the Ministry of Human Rights and Refugees begin organizing 'a public debate of the draft law'.[21] The public became involved following international determination – essentially to be instructed on its provisions. As such, the Law on Gender Equality, as with other such legislation, testifies to the powers of international officials over Bosnian public life rather than the empowerment of Bosnian women.

In this understanding of politics, different social groups are formally represented, but political contest revolves around bureaucratic wrangling over quotas rather than competing political visions. Progressive thinking risks being stifled in the bureaucratic mindset and backroom deals that BiH's gender or ethnic quotas encourage (as was the experience of former FRY).[22] Since representatives brought through a quota system owe their position to official sponsorship it should be no surprise that the women chosen are those regarded as the most loyal by their sponsors and also prove to be so. Their dependence on official sponsorship, rather than popular support, predictably encourages quota candidates to take their political cue from their sponsors, whether this derives from the main ethnically-based political parties or from the international community. Accountability to the constituency they ostensibly represent is also thereby weakened.

Quota measures risk ossifying representation, institutionalizing the position of quota representatives and insulating them from the need to galvanize popular support and address the core concerns of their constituencies. This criticism is particularly relevant to BiH, where a serious dichotomy exists between the gender parity required under the Law on Gender Equality and the social trends for women under international governance, discussed below. Quota systems can undoubtedly advance the position of women's representatives, but whether their advancement necessarily improves the circumstances of ordinary women is a moot point. The feminist political theorist Wendy Brown has warned that identity-based representation can create what she calls 'wounded attachments', a category of representatives with a vested interest in the perpetuation of difference since their own position is premised on their identity's victimized status.[23] The affirmative action approach of the Law on Gender Equality – requiring measures to ensure equal gender representation 'at all levels of government' – does not involve any commitment to broader social changes which would enable ordinary women to realize parity of opportunities or of incomes. Arguably the strongest achievement of women's representatives has been securing the retention of the gender quota system, that is, in protecting their own positions. They have been less successful in defending maternity provisions and other social rights relevant to ordinary women.

The quota system casts doubt on representation per se, even as it assumes an identity of interests between women. The feminist movement in the 1970s problematized the idea that the experiences of women, and therefore the interests of different groups of women, were the same. Consequently, if men cannot represent women's interests, as the gender quota system implies, and women's interests are not identical, how can it be assumed that urban middle class women can best represent the interests of working class or rural women? The Global Rights' *Shadow Report* observes of women politicians: 'They view the status of all women in BiH through the lens of their own elevated success or position, and for women politicians in BiH, that status is generally far removed from the position of the average woman in the country.'[24] Other social divisions may be more salient, as analysis of women in BiH acknowledges.[25] The limitations of this approach have meant that the potential role of women's organizations in the political empowerment of women has become a central focus.

At first glance, women's involvement in civil society seems much more vibrant and able to provide opportunities for women's grassroots activism. Advocates often present women's organizations as activists challenging a reluctant international community to support women's empowerment. More sober reports observe that women run many NGOs, although they have been reluctant to become involved in politics.[26] Women's organizations have generally been exempt from the critical scrutiny that the rest of the NGO sector has come under during the past decade (see Adam Fagan, this volume). But women's organizations share many of the problems of NGOs in general, although, among researchers, there is a great reluctance to identify these problems, as if to do so would disempower women.

Nevertheless, women's NGOs, like other local NGOs, are essentially orientated towards the international community and reliant on its continuing sponsorship for their survival, and they evidence a rather weak relation to the population. The observations that the NGO sector is dominated by a small minority of individuals from the urban elite equally applies to women's NGOs.[27] Criticisms of female politicians made by the Global Rights' *Shadow Report* are also relevant to women's NGOs.[28] NGOs have failed to galvanize popular support among women and have moreover no formal accountability to the population, unlike elected representatives. Without external sponsorship, many local women's NGOs would collapse.

Tensions observed among women's organizations[29] highlight their reliance on external funds and their need to compete for sponsorship from external donors. Competitiveness between NGOs has been exacerbated by the internationally-sponsored NGO sector becoming an important arena of international investment relative to the rest of the economy. This phenomenon has encouraged the emergence of NGO entrepreneurs, or 'anti-war profiteers' as they are nicknamed locally, whose livelihoods depend on the success of *their* organization attracting external sponsorship as opposed to another. The proliferation of NGOs is therefore better understood as representing the needs of the urban professional class, rather than representing any popular movement. Symptomatically, organizations are disinclined to merge or work together unless cooperating under externally-funded programmes. Even where individuals' involvement transcends these mundane motivations, the general problem remains that NGOs are primarily orientated towards gaining sponsorship from the international community rather than popular support. Indicatively, much of advocates' time is spent writing grant applications to international donors and implementing internationally-sponsored programmes.

Unsurprisingly, the gender policies pursued by women's advocates echo those of their international sponsors. Within the population there are strong views against privatization and new laws reducing social rights. Their negative impact on women is acknowledged, but there is little evidence that the women's organizations, sponsored by international donors, are opposing these structural adjustment policies which are detrimental to women. The agenda of local women's organizations reflects the international emphasis on cultural and personal change rather than material advancement. Tellingly, the different interests among women, in so far as the problem is acknowledged, are conceptualized essentially in terms of cultural prejudices (urban versus rural), to be addressed by cultural-awareness training programmes. Meanwhile, any economic improvements are envisaged as coming about through cultural and personal change. The following section considers these approaches to the economic empowerment of women.

Economic Empowerment

A 1997 ILO report observes that international strategies after the war re-orientated their programming for women 'away from therapy toward income generation, micro-enterprise and skills training'.[30] Bosnian women had already been trying to use international projects to support income-generating activities. I found this when I visited the Mostar offices of Stope Nade in September 1997. The remit of the internationally-sponsored project typified the international focus on counselling of female (rape) victims, reproductive health and community peacebuilding.[31] However, local women were adapting its office in eastern Mostar for their own income-generating activities. Instead of encountering counsellors providing women with therapy, I was greeted with a makeup demonstration by a local (Bosniac) 'Avon lady'. Previously, such activities would have been considered supplementary, but today many households rely on them as their main income given Bosnia's unemployment.[32] Likewise, international policy-makers increasingly rely on micro-enterprise as the core of their employment strategy, through organizations such Žene za Žene [Women for Women].

Before examining micro-enterprise, I will briefly highlight how micro-enterprise compliments international structural adjustment policies, eroding state employment and welfare provision.[33] This pattern is evident in Bosnia. Even before the war, women found themselves targeted for redundancy under restructuring programmes on the grounds that their salaries were secondary in the family. State sector employment had been important for women, providing not only financial security but also fostering greater social independence as well as associated social benefits such as maternity pay and access to state nurseries. Nevertheless, in the name of promoting 'a more flexible labour market'[34] and 'reforming provisions that now keep women out of the labour market',[35] women are losing protection they previously enjoyed such as 'very long maternity leave, prohibitions against their doing night work etc'.[36] Yet women's NGOs have criticized female politicians for focusing 'on maternity legislation and maternity rights as the most important women's issue' and falling into stereotypical women's issues, despite the pertinence of defending these in the post-war context.[37] The population is expected to lower its expectations and rely on private welfare provision. Human rights lawyers, for example, instruct that the right to health means basic health, not up-to-date specialist cancer hospitals – despite the fact that breast cancer is a major killer of Bosnian women. In sum, international economic governance is increasing the social vulnerability of women, and the social burden placed on them, by authorizing the further erosion of state support systems.

There is a need to rethink international economic governance because of its impact on women and Bosnian society as a whole. International neo-liberal economic policies, requiring the retreat of the state, have failed to regenerate the Bosnian economy to pre-war levels, and are exacerbating social inequalities (see Michael Pugh, this volume).[38] Internationally-sponsored privatization policies are fostering 'private affluence and public squalor', in the words of economist J.K. Galbraith. These policies are undermining the state's capacity to raise income through taxation and to regulate the informal economy, in turn undermining its capacity to enforce the rule of law and finance welfare provision. There has been the removal of 'punitive levels of employee-related taxes and welfare provision', that is, the erosion of employment rights in the private sector.[39] The privatization programme has thereby reinforced the shadow, ethni-cized, patrimonial economic networks, which evolved through the economic crisis and war economy.[40] World Bank research has found that the informal sector actually grew in 2001–03, rather than shrinking, employing 410,500 people, representing over a third of the employment in the country.[41] Women (and men), unable to rely on state employment or assistance, have had to resort to these shadow patrimonial economic networks as part of their survival strategies. Such patrimonial networks make women more subject to patriarchal relations. In sum, international economic governance implies women being more dependent on kinship ties, despite all its talk of gender policies. At best, gender equality legis-lation in the current circumstances ensures a fairer distribution of unemployment, social benefit cutbacks and poverty. Few women qualify, for example, for veteran benefits, such as exemptions from health service charges. Furthermore, inter-national policy favours addressing anomalies by taking away benefits rather than expanding eligibility.

International organizations have acknowledged that 'privatizing state firms will make things worse' for women, but nevertheless they treat privatization as unavoidable.[42] The ILO report refers to 'the new realities' that Bosnians are having to grasp,[43] the UNDP argues that privatization 'is necessary and inevita-ble',[44] and Global Rights: Partners for Justice accepts privatization 'as an essential aspect of the country's economic reform program' and, in fact, argues for more women representatives to be included in its implementation.[45] Alternative economic models, which could give the state a greater role, have not been considered by international policy-makers.[46] Little love may be lost between BiH's constituent ethnic groups, but one issue that the population is unified over is the role of the state as provider. As international reports observe, 'most people still expect "the state" to sort out their problems',[47] as job creator if not welfare provider.[48] Yet this affirmation of the state and suspicion of the private sector – a potentially powerful resource for state-building based on political and social consensus – tends to be dismissed by international officials as merely backward or outmoded prejudice. This is despite the fact that some rethinking on these questions is evident, even among Western policy-makers who previously advocated privatization and the rolling back of the state.[49] Alternative economic models, giving a stronger role for the state to create a safety net, would have better protected women's welfare and the social gains women had made since 1945. Interestingly, the former FRY managed to reach pre-war growth levels within five years of the end of the Second World War, whereas international officials do not expect BiH to reach pre-war growth levels until 2010.[50] Moreover, even this forecast may be optimistic given current worsening trends.[51] The 2003 UNDP Annual Report concluded that the current authorities are not offering 'any effective solution to this problem' and that 'the entire country can be considered a "welfare case"', even allowing for involvement in the informal economy and remittances from relations abroad.[52]

How does the international micro-enterprise approach address these serious economic problems which have hit women disproportionately, particularly female-headed households?[53] Micro-finance has not overlooked women. The

World Bank has stated that 50 per cent of its clients are women.[54] Indeed in the early years, international reports actually observed how men had difficulty accessing these schemes.[55] Advisers warned that since unemployment affected the majority of the population, micro-credit 'should not be pressed to meet donor demands for heavy concentration on social categories.'[56] Over $30 million has been invested in two World Bank projects to develop a micro-credit industry in Bosnia, and there have been numerous ad hoc initiatives in addition. The World Bank programme is implemented via government foundations based in the FBiH and in RS.[57] These two foundations have contracted with local micro-credit organizations to administer the loans. Micro-credit organizations receiving contracts have consolidated based on performance. At the end of June 2003, the World Bank reported that 201,421 loans had been distributed with around 51,000 active clients,[58] a third up from the previous year.[59] The spread of micro-finance is regionally uneven, but prevalent across both entities. The highest activism is recorded in Podrinje (in RS) and in Sarajevo-Rumenija, Tuzla and Western Herzegovina (in FBiH), involving over 2.5 per cent of the population in these four regions.[60] The average loan was recorded the previous year to be KM 3,122 (£1,050 approximately).[61] Loans for agriculture and small farming had risen to 39 per cent.[62] Women managed seven out of the 13 BiH micro-credit organizations listed as important by the World Bank.[63]

The analysis here is less concerned with questions of access to micro-credit than with its centrality to international strategies and how this approach embodies low expectations for the advancement of women. Micro-finance has become important as public sector work has declined while capital investment remains scarce. An ILO/UNHCR micro-finance study admits that micro-finance is about helping people survive: 'the only possible alternative people may turn to in order to earn enough for survival is self-employment through private entrepreneurship'.[64] However, the future of the small-scale private entrepreneurship envisaged for BiH is insecure given the population's weak purchasing power and competition from imports. Subsidies or tariffs, which might protect the local market, are eschewed under international economic governance.[65]

Essentially, micro-enterprise represents a shift from state responsibility for employment and a structural understanding of unemployment to an individualized understanding of unemployment, addressing the employability of individuals, their skills and motivation. Accordingly, the UN Common Country Study for BiH speaks of changing from an economy based on large state industries to one which 'places more responsibility on the shoulders of individual entrepreneurs and workers'.[66] Micro-credit caught the imagination of international policy-makers as empowering women, building upon the Grameen Bank initiative in Bangladesh. Yet, detailed research on these initiatives suggests that micro-credit has only led to modest gains for women. Indeed, micro-credit is frequently only made available to married women or widows, questioning the idea of micro-credit as emancipating women.[67] Interestingly, the rates of interest are not necessarily better than those of private lenders,[68] as is the case in Bosnia.[69] Micro-credit schemes, providing small capital investment, can only initiate small-scale household production, unless the loans are used to support successful existing family businesses. In Bosnia, it has been observed that 'the impact of micro-finance programs on enterprise development has been greater when people were relatively less vulnerable and had a stronger enterprise to start with'.[70] As a director of micro-finance has advised: 'micro-finance alone cannot reduce poverty, it can only supplement a comprehensive development programme'.[71] Yet micro-credit has become a stand-alone employment strategy despite the fact that it only appears to secure the position of women within their existing social roles.

Micro-enterprise, based on small-scale labour-intensive production or gendered service sector work, such as hairdressing,[72] simply does not address the employment expectations of Bosnian women of working age; instead it represents a step backwards. As a joint ILO/UNHCR report states: 'In BiH, the low-income entrepreneur may well be an electronic engineer with twenty years experience'.[73] Take the generation of women now entering their forties; many are newly poor with a relatively high education level.[74] This generation, even if they grew up in rural communities, aspired to work in the public sector – whether service provision, public administration or in public companies – or to set up their own businesses. Related to the latter, there was a certain gendered aspect to those able to start family-sponsored businesses: men would be in charge of cafes (predominantly for male clientele); women would run family shops. They did not desire or expect to remain in labour-intensive agriculture or other labour-intensive forms of household production. Such a way of life was viewed as backbreaking, anachronistic and only generating small returns – a fate they wished to escape. Despite these aspirations, the UN Common Country Study for Bosnia suggests that 'it is easy for planners and bankers alike to still aim too high and overlook "micro" enterprises that are often important income sources for women-headed households'.[75]

Micro-enterprise sounds more glamorous than petty trade, but the latter description is closer to the nature of the activities. The numerous hairdressing or taxi businesses make a scant living as they vie for customers and the purchasing power of the population that is 'more than weak, after meeting existential needs'.[76] Moreover, the locally produced goods are often uncompetitive compared to imports, as analysis readily admits.[77] The returns from small-scale agricultural production are also insecure – women (or their children) competing to sell homemade preserves along the main Sarajevo-Mostar road in the baking heat of summer have few buyers. Likewise, only a limited market exists for the production of handicrafts – the focus of many micro-credit advocates. Turnover is visibly slow even for well-established businesses in Bascaršija, the old Turkish commercial district in Sarajevo, where the main purchasers of traditional crafts are the international officials as 'tourism is practically non-existent'[78]. Some projects have sought to train women for work in non-traditional sectors, such as computing.[79] Regrettably the main international focus is on the employability of individuals, as if unemployment could be addressed merely by middle-aged women acquiring modern skills. In reality, skilled people also lack jobs and (particularly the young) only see a viable future abroad.[80]

Micro-enterprise may work as a coping strategy or a form of occupational therapy, but it does not provide secure employment or advance women's position. As international reports admit, involvement in micro-enterprise is no advancement for the many qualified women who have lost their jobs over the last decade. Interestingly, the World Bank has drastically reduced the figures for employment provided by micro-finance from over 180,000, claimed in 2002,[81] to 100,000 in 2003, despite its dramatic increase in loans.[82] Failure to generate secure employment perhaps explains why international reports often draw attention to micro-finance's impact on clients' confidence and 'individual and group motivation'.[83] This emphasis on attitudes rather than material circumstances indicates how international policy-makers would rather psychologize social problems.

In contrast to the present post-conflict situation, women experienced unprecedented social gains after the Second World War. Within a decade, large numbers of women, whose mothers had been illiterate and engaged in subsistence farming, went to school and gained employment in the public sector, widening their horizons and challenging the patriarchical extended family structures. Consider the establishment of the huge agricultural processing enterprise Agrokomerc in Kladusa, north-west Bosnia, at one time employing over 13,000 employees. Whatever criticisms can be levelled at the running of Agrokomerc, it did have a socially transforming impact on women's lives in Kladusa, a poor, isolated region holding very traditional attitudes towards women. Employment at the plant meant entry into the wage economy and experience of work outside the home, giving women new economic and social independence. In turn, the factory created new purchasing power and sparked off other businesses in the area to service the wants of Agrokomerc and its employees. Women from Kladusa still recall that the opening of Agrokomerc's factory gave them a new financial independence, enabling them to shake off their submissiveness and begin challenging their husbands' authority.

In contrast, the petty trading that characterizes much micro-enterprise represents a form of disguised unemployment. Unsurprisingly, micro-enterprise lacks the socially transforming impact that the massive expansion of public sector employment had after the Second World War. Instead, social transformation is tagged on, for example, by adding 'a gender awareness and assertiveness component' to skills-training and employment promotion programmes.[84] As a NGO delegate stated at an inter-regional conference, held in Srebrenica, on the Law on Gender Equality: 'it is difficult to speak about gender equality when it comes to employment... Here, neither men nor women are successful in finding jobs, for there are none.'[85] Nevertheless, her conclusions emphasized citizen 'education and motivation' and the 'awakening' of women,[86] reflecting the international policy assumption that the problem of social development can be addressed at the psychological level of individual attitudes.

Conclusion

In BiH, we are presented with the picture of enlightened internationals struggling to bring progressive gender ideas to an intransigent, backward, patriarchal and abusive culture. However, if progressive ideas on women are not flourishing in

Bosnia, it should be no surprise given that women and men are expected to lower their aspirations in so many aspects of their lives. International gender empowerment initiatives may legitimize international governance and empower a few female members of the urban elite, but the prospects of these policies advancing the position of ordinary Bosnian women are illusory.

Analysis of international policy-making in this sphere suggests that the emphasis on gender empowerment fits closely with the top-down approach of international policy development. International administrators seem much happier developing policies which are susceptible to bureaucratic target-setting – such as quotas and micro-credit – as opposed to policies capable of generating real changes in the political, social and economic opportunities of Bosnian women.

ACKNOWLEDGEMENTS

I am grateful to the British Academy for financial assistance towards a visit to Bosnia in July 2004. My thanks to David Chandler, Tahera Choudrey and Michael Pugh for encouraging my thinking on international gender policies. However responsibility for the views expressed in this article lies with me.

NOTES

1. OHR Sarajevo, 'Support to the Women of BiH on International Women's Day', Office of the High Representative, Press Release, 7 March 2001, at www.ohr.int/ohr-dept/presso/pressr/default. asp?content_id=4259.
2. Gender Centre, Government of the Federation of Bosnia and Herzegovina, at www.fgenderc.com.ba/.
3. Law on Gender Equality in Bosnia and Herzegovina, *Official Gazette of BiH*, No.16, 2003, at www.fgenderc.com.ba/txt/equality_law_in_bh.doc.
4. 'Implementation of Gender Equality Law', UNDP Press Release, 4 Sept. 2003. The project has been supported by $275,000 from the Government of Japan, $100,000 from UNDP and $25,000 from UNICEF.
5. 'The Special Adviser on Gender Issues visits the UN Mission in Bosnia and Herzegovina (UNMIBH)', *Network*, The UN Women's Newsletter, Vol.5. No.1, March 2001.
6. OSCE, *Women's Representation in Bosnia and Herzegovina: A Statistical Overview 1986, 1990, 1996, 1997*. Sarajevo, 1998, cited in M. Walsh, *Aftermath: The Role of Women's Organizations in Postconflict Bosnia and Herzegovina*, Washington DC: Center for Development Information and Evaluation/USAID, 2000, p.10. Quota measures had already been used in Bosnia prior to the war and facilitated the relatively impressive figures highlighted here.
7. International Human Rights Law Group, *Women's Rights in BiH*. Sarajevo: IHRLG, 1999, p.182. The Group has since renamed itself Global Rights: Partners for Justice.
8. Law on Gender Equality in Bosnia and Herzegovina (n.3 above).
9. D. Dahlerup and A.T. Nordlund, 'Gender Quotas: A Key to Equality? A Case Study of Iraq and Afghanistan', *European Political Science*, Vol.3, No.3, 2004, at www.essex.ac.uk/ECPR/publications/eps/onlineissues/summer2004/research/dahlerup_nordlund.htm.
10. Figures cited in Walsh (n.6 above), pp.10–11.
11. Global Rights: Partners for Justice, *Shadow Report on the Implementation of CEDAW and Women's Human Rights in Bosnia and Herzegovina*, Washington and Sarajevo: January 2004, p.55, at www.globalrights.org/resources/BH_shadowreport_cedaw.pdf.
12. 'Working table 1: Gender', Stability Pact for South Eastern Europe, at www.stabilitypact.org/gender/default.asp.
13. Human Rights Coordination Centre, Human Rights Quarterly Report, 1 April–30 June 2001, at www.ohr.int/.
14. Dahlerup and Nordlund (n.9 above), p.92.

15. Global Rights: Partners for Justice (n.11 above), p.77.
16. M. Walsh, *Post-Conflict Bosnia and Herzegovina: Integrating Women's Special Situation and Gender Perspective in Skills Training and Employment Promotion Programmes*, Geneva: ILO, 1997, p.25; Walsh (n.6 above), p.10.
17. P. Cowley and S. Childs, 'Too Spineless to Rebel? New Labour's Women MPs', *British Journal of Political Science*, Vol.33, 2003, pp.345–365.
18. Walsh (n.6 above), p.11; Global Rights: Partners for Justice (n.11 above), p.79.
19. Dahlersup and Nordlund (n.9 above).
20. OSCE, 'Women can Change Bosnia.' June 1999, at www.oscebih.org/events/events15-7-interview.htm.
21. Human Rights Coordination Centre (n.13 above).
22. D. Rusinow (ed.), *Yugoslavia: A Fractured Federalism*, Washington, DC: Wilson Center Press, 1988.
23. W. Brown, *States of Injury: Power and Freedom in Late Modernity*, Princeton: Princeton University Press, 1995.
24. Global Rights: Partners for Justice (n.11 above), p.79.
25. Walsh (n.6 above), p.2; Global Rights: Partners for Justice (n.11 above), p.64.
26. Walsh (n.6 above), p.8.
27. D. Chandler, 'Democratization in Bosnia: The Limits to Civil Society-Building Initiatives', *Democratization*, Vol.5, No.4, 1998.
28. Global Rights: Partners for Justice (n.11 above), p.79.
29. Walsh (n.6 above), p.2.
30. Walsh (n.16 above), p.31.
31. Marie Stopes International was the main international donor.
32. Walsh (n.16 above), p.10.
33. R. Abrahamsen, *Disciplining Democracy: Development Discourse and Good Governance in Africa*, London: Zed Books, 2000, p.58.
34. UNDP, *Early Warning System, Bosnia and Herzegovina, Quarterly Report*, July–September. Sarajevo: UNDP, 2003, p.52, at www.undp.ba/publications.asp.
35. Office of the Resident Coordinator for Development Operations, *The Transition to Development – Challenges and Priorities for UN Development Assistance to Bosnia-Herzegovina, Common Country Study*, Sarajevo: UN Bosnia and Herzegovina, 2000, p.43.
36. Ibid.
37. Dahlerup and Nordlund (n.9 above).
38. M. Pugh and N. Cooper with J. Goodhand, *War Economies in a Regional Context: Challenges of Transformation*. Boulder, CO: Lynne Rienner, 2004.
39. Office of the Resident Coordinator for Development Operations (n.35 above), p.54. See also Walsh (n.16 above), p.29.
40. Pugh and Cooper (n.38 above), pp.170-176.
41. UNDP, *Early Warning System, Annual Report 2003, a Year in Review*, Sarajevo: UNDP, 2003, p.22, at www.undp.ba/publications.asp.
42. Office of the Resident Coordinator for Development Operations (n.35 above), p.22.
43. Walsh (n.16 above), pp.11-12.
44. UNDP (n.34 above), p.52.
45. Global Rights: Partners for Justice (n.11 above), p.74.
46. M. Pugh, 'Liquid Transformation in the Political Economies of BiH and Kosovo', paper presented at the Seventh International Seminar, Institute for Strengthening Democracy in Bosnia, Konjic, Bosnia, July 2004.
47. Office of the Resident Coordinator for Development Operations (n.35 above), p.40.
48. UNDP (n.41 above), p.36.
49. Francis Fukuyama, 'The Art of Reconstruction', *Wall Street Journal*, 28 July 2004.
50. Pugh and Cooper (n.38 above), p.145.
51. UNDP (n.41 above), p.22.
52. Ibid p.33.
53. R. Kukanesen, *Families where Women are Heads of Households*, UNDP, May 2003.
54. World Bank Local Initiatives Project, Sarajevo, 2002, at http://siteresources.worldbank.org/INTBOSNIAHERZ/Resources/LIP.pdf.
55. Walsh (n.16 above), p.10.
56. N. Goronja, *The Evolution of Micro-finance in a Successful Post-Conflict Transition: The Case Study for Bosnia-Herzegovina*, Geneva: ILO/UNHCR, 1999, p.16. See also Office of the Resident Coordinator for Development Operations (n.35 above), p.54.

57. World Bank Bosnia & Herzegovina – Micro-finance in Bosnia and Herzegovina, 2004, at www.worldbank.org/.
58. World Bank Local Initiatives Project II, Sarajevo, 2003, at http://siteresources.worldbank.org/INTBOSNIAHERZ/Resources/LIP2.pdf.
59. World Bank (n.54 above).
60. World Bank (n.57 above).
61. World Bank (n.54 above).
62. World Bank (n.58 above).
63. World Bank (n.54 above).
64. Goronja (n.56 above), p.8.
65. Pugh and Cooper (n.38 above), pp.163–9.
66. Office of the Resident Coordinator for Development Operations (n.35 above).
67. A.M. Goetz and R.S. Gupta, *Who takes the Credit? Gender, Power and Control over Loan Use in Rural Credit Programmes in Bangladesh*, IDS Working Paper, No.8. Institute of Development Studies, University of Sussex, 1994; S. White, *Evaluating the impact of NGOs in rural poverty alleviation. Bangladesh Country Study*. Working Paper, No.50, Overseas Development Institute, London, 1991.
68. Tahera Choudrey, University of Nottingham, private communication with the author.
69. Goronja (n.56 above), p.4.
70. M. Matul and C. Tsilikounas, 'Role of Microfinance in the Household Reconstruction Process in Bosnia and Herzegovina', *MFC Spotlight Note*, No.6, Warsaw: Micro-Finance Centre, 2004, p.8, at www.ids.ac.uk/impact/Publications/PartnerPublications/MFC_SN6.pdf.
71. Interview, 'Bring micro-financing under regulatory body', *Daily Star*, Dhaka, 28 June 2003.
72. Walsh (n.16 above), p.32
73. Goronja (n.56 above), p.9.
74. Matul and Tsilikounas (n.70 above), p.3.
75. Office of the Resident Coordinator for Development Operations (n.35 above), p.52.
76. UNDP (n.41 above), p.32; Goronja (n.56 above), p.17.
77. Goronja (n.56 above), p.18. In 2004, I noticed how IKEA rugs featured among the handicraft items women were selling. Evidently it made more commercial sense to buy ready-made goods to sell than to engage in labour-intensive production.
78. UNDP (n.34 above), p.59.
79. Walsh (n.16 above), p.36.
80. Ibid., p.31; UNDP, *Are You Part of the Problem or Part of the Solution? Youth in Bosnia and Herzegovina, 2003*. Available at: http://undp.ba/publikations.asp.
81. World Bank (n.54 above).
82. World Bank (n.58 above).
83. Walsh (n.16 above), p.31.
84. Ibid., p.37.
85. Quoted in D. Pelemis, 'Gender Equality in Bosnia and Herzegovina', OSCE Press Release, 9 July 2004.
86. Ibid.

Civil Society in Bosnia Ten Years after Dayton

ADAM FAGAN

It seems as though all aspects of Bosnia's internationally-led post-conflict transition hinge on civil society development.[1] There is an implicit assumption that a vibrant sector of local advocacy networks can entrench democratic values, heal the wounds of ethnic conflict, and facilitate economic growth, bringing an end to the international administration of Bosnia (BiH).[2] In other words, a developed civil society will be the hallmark of successful state-building, the point at which the Bosnian state is able to be left to rule without the international community. Thus, to suggest that civil society development is anything less than central to the international community's state building agenda would be an understatement.

Practically every international NGO, foreign donor organization and multilateral agency involved in the country makes explicit reference to civil society development as a key objective of their involvement. But it is not just the international community in BiH that has used the language of civil society promotion; local NGOs providing services within the community, running small education programmes or providing practical assistance to displaced persons, the elderly, or those with medical conditions also express their objectives in terms of civil society.[3] The term has thus become eponymous for almost every aspect of Bosnia's transition; the lingua franca of interaction between international and local actors, politicians, agencies, citizens and commentators.

From the perspective of 2005, this essay will analyse the changing nature of international approaches to civil society development and assess the role of international donors, their patterns of interaction and the support given to the capacity-building of local NGOs. The conclusion drawn is that whilst aspects of what has emerged under the rubric of civil society are to be applauded, to view NGO development as instrumental in the envisaged transition to a democratic and multi-ethnic autonomous state exaggerates their capacity to deliver fundamental change. Whilst NGO activity crosses nationalist and ethnic boundaries, challenges the agendas of local elites, and does seem to be mobilizing citizens to make use of democratic processes, the capacity of civil society to realize radical transformation is contingent upon more fundamental institutional and political change.

The next section considers the approach of the international community to civil society development in the initial post-Dayton period, and the various criticisms that have been levelled at such intervention, in particular, of the high levels of NGO dependence on external funding, their isolation from Bosnian society and from governing institutions, and the instability of the NGO sector in a highly competitive project-led environment. The following sections consider the changing nature of international policy over the last three to four years, particularly focusing on international funders' attempts to engage NGOs more in the policy-making process and on the shift in international emphasis away from externally-directed projects and towards NGO sustainability. The essay concludes that, although policy may now seem to be moving in the right direction, many of the initial problems of external dependency remain – resulting in NGOs being less able to play a civil society advocacy role in BiH than elsewhere in the region.

Initial Approaches to Civil Society-Building

The strategy of civil society-building, core to the international community's peacebuilding efforts in BiH, has been centrally-focused on the development of NGOs. What is envisaged is a sector of advocacy organizations; schools for democracy in the Tocquevillian sense, that will, through their advocacy role, bring about a new culture of interaction and political engagement based on compromise, tolerance and participation. As well as kick-starting the economy and facilitating the policy process, these NGOs will represent an alternative to the nationalist-ridden political elites, and imbue a new generation with notions of tolerance, compromise and moderation. The development of NGOs will also serve to balance the top-down influence of the international community by stimulating local political activity. It is deemed that all this can be realized through the transfer of know-how and assistance from Western donors and international NGOs.

The vision of civil society development in BiH is thus typical of the conceptual understanding at the core of the mainstream democratization/transition literature.[4] It is based on the key role played by NGOs which have been developed and supported by the international community. There is an implicit assumption that any existing civil society legacy, from the communist and pre-war periods, could have only a limited and perhaps restrictive impact on the necessary reform of political, social and economic relations. Rather than attempt to resurrect social networks of the past, the international civil society development programmes have attempted to begin anew with strata of professional, policy-oriented advocacy NGOs.

However, under the rubric of civil society development, international donors have predominantly supported various service-provision initiatives, ranging from help for internally displaced persons, to education organizations, business services organizations and health care initiatives. Indeed, for many Bosnians, it is Western-funded local NGOs or an international donor agency located in the country that provide, for example, credit and new technical skills, psychosocial support for women and children,[5] childcare,[6] medical training and access to breast cancer screening. For others, Western-funded NGOs are a source of relatively secure and well-remunerated employment. In other words, the conceptual understanding of civil society employed by donors is fluid and extends to include notions of a third sector, a realm of voluntary non-profit organizations operating between the market and the state in order to compensate for the short-comings of both.[7]

To an extent, the existing analysis of civil society development in BiH has tended to echo the issues and constraints seen as limiting the political capacity of donor-created civil society in post-communist Europe, the former Soviet Republics of Central Asia and parts of the developing world.[8] Based on research undertaken at the end of the 1990s, a host of British and American scholars charted the extent to which the donor-dependent sector of NGOs in BiH was characterized by low levels of citizen involvement, and an apparent separation from society at large.[9] The picture painted was of a small sector of NGO professionals, a handful of people, drawn mostly from the urban middle-classes, clustered predominantly, though not exclusively, in the towns and cities of the Federation (FBiH).[10] Typically, these people were involved in a multiplicity of different donor-driven initiatives, their sense of accountability and political focus being the international donors, NGOs and agencies that supply the funds and devise the projects. Though the role of international donors in terms of resource provision was acknowledged, the condescending nature of know-how transfer, of assumptions about Bosnian citizens lacking the capacity to engage with democratic procedures and institutions, and the political implications of donor intervention were echoed in practically all the studies.

In addition to the usual concerns – regarding the true benefactors of donor aid, the colonial nature of Western intervention in NGO development, and the immeasurability of added value – the critique of the civil society development project in BiH extended significantly beyond concerns about sustainability, dependency and societal linkage. It was argued that the new tier of NGO professionals had been encouraged by Western donors to see their function and role as essentially technical and apolitical, distinct from the nationalist-dominated political sphere. Jens Sörensen claimed that this separation led to the lack of an overall democratization/civil society development strategy, and had resulted in the inability of the NGO community to challenge dominant political discourse or to mobilize significant political support.[11] The contradiction that civil society was expected to achieve heady political objectives but through using apolitical means. The reality of the international community's confused efforts, it was claimed, was a divided and politically enfeebled civil society, which lacked the capacity to deliver the sort of political change envisaged by donors.[12]

Whilst so much was expected of the new NGOs, in terms of achieving democracy and healing wounds, the main thrust of civil society development aid focused on grooming NGOs as service providers. The fact that 'civic groups and NGOs were becoming contractors for the provision of services commissioned by foreign donors' was seen by critics as a constraint on the political change dimension of civil society, and as a hindrance to the emergence of civil society as a vehicle for the articulation of local political agendas.[13] It was claimed that Western-funded NGOs, trained in how to write project proposals and apply for donor funding, were being drawn into substituting for the state in areas such as social policy, fiscal reform and social and economic provision, at the expense of a more politicized local advocacy role. Although less controversial studies have explained the emphasis on service provision in terms of a continuum with the communist period,[14] others felt that devolving services to NGOs within the existing political and economic framework of BiH served only to maintain 'the fragmentation and multiplication of political authority'.[15] The overriding depiction was of NGOs operating within the constrictions of the post-Dayton infrastructure – plugging gaps, duplicating provision and generally trying to compensate for the absence of state-level authority and a nascent market economy.

But the critique of civil society development in BIH was actually more nuanced than the claim that NGOs were propping-up the status quo instead of acting as agents of change. It has been suggested that Western-funded and trained NGOs were, in fact, exerting a negative effect on the country's long-term sustainability and socio-economic development in the sense that the sector siphoned off the intellectual elite and those who would otherwise be engaged in the public sector and the local labour market. That the professionalism and growth of the NGO sector occurred at the expense of the public sector, civil service and state administration, not to mention the expansion of the market, was a fairly damning critique of the international community's intervention when so much politically depended upon the economic regeneration of BiH.

Of even greater concern was the related claim that – by assuming functions such as social provision, regulation, redistribution and education – NGOs allowed nationalist elites to shun any responsibility for the misappropriation of funds by local authorities, or for their failure to permit displaced persons to return to their pre-war locations. NGOs were thus accused of providing a smokescreen for the feudalist, corrupt and ethnicized politics of the nationalist elites and for actually preventing the empowerment of multi-ethnic state authorities.[16] It was sadly ironic that internationally-funded NGOs, championed as agents of democratic change, were accused of undermining the contractual relationship between citizen and state that is so fundamental to democratic governance.

NGOs and Good Governance

With regard to the role and function of organizations, their political engagement, and their interaction with donors, local elites and grassroots communities, empirical research conducted during 2004–05 broadly reveals a somewhat more positive picture than that recorded in the earlier literature. Whilst the long-term capacity of civil society to deliver substantive change remains somewhat uncertain, there have undoubtedly been significant developments in the past few years that point towards the emergence of a new tripartite relationship between NGOs, citizens and the state.

The earlier literature identified a series of key inter-related problems: the lack of rootedness of NGOs, who were seemingly operating without civil society; a 'proposal' culture amongst NGOs who switched project areas in response to the latest available funding; the lack of connection between NGOs and other sectors, particularly government; and – the greatest threat to civil society development and the sustainability of NGOs – the decline in donor revenue, a process that had started in 1998 and threatened to shrink the NGO sector before it had reached maturity.

It is important to acknowledge, when making any assessment of the contemporary capacity of civil society or making assumptions about the role of NGOs in general, that there is still a great variation in circumstances across the country. Progress is far greater in multi-ethnic urban areas within FBiH. In cities such as Tuzla, where there is civic engagement and a commitment by government officials to deliver change, NGOs are gaining access and influence. However, in rural mono-ethnic villages in Republika Srpska (RS) or parts of western Herzegovina, where NGO activity is virtually non-existent and nationalist-led local authorities make no attempt to develop civil society, the status of NGOs is very different.[17] Commenting on such disparity in March 2004, Milan Mirić, the Network Coordinator of the International Council for Voluntary Agencies (ICVA), a Bosnian-run organization that supports and helps develop the NGO sector, claimed that 'in some areas of the country – such as eastern BiH – it is still dangerous for NGO activists to travel. Hard-line Serbian politicians in this region still deliberately disrupt the efforts of NGOs and see them as enemies.'[18] Regional variation was observed in all the earlier studies of civil society development in BiH, and it remains as much of a problem in 2005. As foreign donors gradually withdraw their support, and those that remain suffer a certain degree of fatigue, the prospect of aid and assistance reaching the more remote and neglected areas of the country seems increasingly unlikely. This is a particular problem for parts of RS, where donor aid is still needed.

A similar note of caution must be issued with regard to the number of NGOs registered, which in 2003 was 7,874.[19] This figure is deceptive as the majority are not operative and are simply a registered entity. Only a handful of the NGOs registered are active, of which the majority are service-provider organizations with little or no political aspiration. ICVA estimates that there are about 200 active NGOs operating in the country, of which no more than 60 could be described as strong – denoting good management structures and developed strategies.[20] Despite some positive developments outlined below, the overall picture is still of a weak civil society, almost entirely dependent on foreign funding, with small pockets of networking activity and attempts being made by a few key individuals from within the sector to strengthen capacity and sustainability. The bulk of NGO activity involves providing services in the community that would not otherwise be provided.

Despite such caveats, the most important development over the past few years, and in marked contrast to the situation in 2000, is the willingness of certain government authorities (municipal, canton and entity levels) to work with NGOs. Though politicians may be co-operating with NGOs under pressure from the international community, and though there is indeed significant variation between individual municipalities and cantons, this is undoubtedly a new and positive impetus. Earlier research recorded that NGOs operated entirely within the orbit of the international community, worked on projects proposed by donors, and paid little attention to the local administration.[21] This was seen as a rational response on behalf of NGOs, who identified the international community – rather than municipalities and state authorities – as the source of real power and influence. Today there is evidence of cooperation between government and NGOs.

In the initial post-war period NGOs were treated with suspicion by government officials – the term 'non-governmental' (*nevladina*) was interpreted as opposition to government, and the issues that NGOs worked on were perceived as contentious and threatening. The situation has altered; today there are several examples of new linkages having been forged between networks of NGOs and government. For example, the Tuzla Reference Group, a coalition network of over 50 local Tuzla-based NGOs, has established good relations with the government and local mayor, and has entered into joint projects with regard to displaced persons and education.[22] The BiH Economic Women's Initiatives has gone a stage further and forged relations between local women's organizations, government and business.[23]

The momentum for NGOs to forge relations with government and the responsiveness of certain state authorities to such cooperation is driven by various factors. Most significantly, the international donors – multilateral agencies, charities, foundations, international NGOs and national government organizations – on whom the bulk of NGOs rely, either directly or indirectly for funding, have made a concerted effort to connect NGOs with government as part of their emphasis on developing the long-term sustainability of the NGO sector. Donors are driven in large part by a concern that NGOs need to discover alternative sources of revenue. The approach has been twin-track, with donors exerting pressure simultaneously on NGOs and on state authorities (at municipal, canton, entity and state levels) to establish such partnerships. The provision of funding, training and assistance has been made dependent on such linkage. For example, at the core of the World Bank's Poverty Reduction Strategy for BiH is linkage between civil society organizations, parliamentarians and trade unions. In devising the strategy in 2002, the World Bank insisted that civil society organizations be involved in the process of deliberation, constituting a significant turning point in the policy-making role of Bosnian NGOs. Not only has the Bank made the distribution of assistance and its small grants contingent upon the continued partnership between government and civil society organizations, but the BiH government has been compelled to channel credits, received from the Bank for poverty reduction programmes, through NGOs. Without firm evidence of intra-sectoral cooperation, neither NGOs nor government will receive World Bank revenue.[24]

The World Bank is not the only international organization to demand such cooperation as the sine qua non for external support. The Canadian International Development Agency and Catholic Relief Services similarly insist that all the initiatives they fund involve NGOs working with state officials and government. In effect, donors have successfully pushed the two sides together and forced cooperation around specific projects, training and poverty reduction. The EU has also made recent efforts to promote NGO–government cooperation. One consequence of this approach has been the strengthening of the service-provision function that NGOs can offer government at the local level. NGOs have positioned themselves to offer the skills training to state authorities that the international donors (particularly the EU) demand. It is likely that NGOs will be able to access this form of income from international donors for some time, particularly if EU membership for BiH becomes a realistic prospect.

A recent mapping exercise was undertaken, by the EU delegation in BiH, into the areas of policy in which cooperation with NGOs was most appropriate and where it was not necessary, and which organizations to involve. The underlying aim was to standardize such interaction and to coordinate donor assistance to ensure that NGOs were given a greater role in the policy-making process. The EU essentially coerces reluctant municipalities to open up to civil society organizations as the hallmark of good governance – if they refuse they are heavily criticized and denied access to structural funds and other assistance. The most responsive municipalities are, not surprisingly, in Tuzla and Sarajevo, areas where NGO activity is most developed and established.

There is evidence to suggest that such initiatives have become embedded and have established a new relationship between state authorities and NGOs, though much does of course depend on the particular canton. For example, Sarajevo Canton made KM 1 million (approximately £300,000) available to NGOs in 2004. Although currently the bulk of the money goes to sports clubs and old established apolitical organizations, the hope is that this will change as NGOs become more adept at advocating for the available funds.[25] Yet even in the case of Sarajevo, where the authority is clearly inclined to support NGOs, no announcement is made of projects to be funded, and details regarding the process of application are not clearly displayed.[26]

However, as a source of sustainable revenue, public funds distributed by the more enlightened cantons are no match for international donor money. Though the amount of international donor revenue available for NGOs has diminished considerably over the past five years, the level of dependency has remained more or less static.[27] The state of the economy and high poverty levels make it impossible for NGOs to raise revenue from citizens. There is little prospect of this changing in the near future, and NGOs are generally reluctant to consider fund-raising as a source of income.[28] Corporate sponsorship is heralded by many NGOs as an option for the future, but this will depend on a new tax regime and a significant increase in foreign investment in the country. Some environmental organizations and NGOs concerned with cultural and leisure activities do receive donations from business, but levels of funding tend to be low.[29]

Currently, NGOs have little option other than to continue accessing foreign donor funds and public revenue from local authorities. The implications of both these options for the long-term development of civil society are worrying. If NGOs become too dependent on municipal funds the fear is that they will become a subsidiary or extension of the state. As Ruth Mandel has observed, in her research on NGOs in Central Asia, organizations that receive substantial proportions of their revenue from state sources end up performing more of a civil service role – providing research and policy advice to the government on the development and implementation of its policies. They thus become GONGOs – government organized NGOs – that are run and controlled by government, for government.[30] As cautioned in the earlier literature,[31] this is a particular concern in the case of BiH, where the combination of the legacy of NGOs delivering humanitarian aid during the war, and the ineffectiveness of the post-Dayton state to deliver basic social provision, alleviate poverty and social deprivation and implement social policy, make the prospect of NGOs acting as para-state organizations a likely scenario. The danger is that such an NGO sector would not just substitute for the state, but would further weaken its remit by gradually siphoning off experts and officials with the offer of higher salaries and more favourable working conditions.

From Projects to Sustainability?

A shift in focus away from short-term projects has been an important development over the last three-four years, with international donors placing far greater emphasis on sustainability and skills training.[32] This has been assisted by the complexities of EU funding mechanisms and the focus on skills training at the local level. The EU is now the largest donor in BiH, both for government and NGOs. It typically offers grants in the region of €50,000–€100,000 to organizations for specific projects. The EU Delegation in BiH does not initiate specific projects as such, but identifies broad areas it wishes to support, and then invites NGOs to submit applications for projects that fall in line with these designated national objectives. But the emphasis of EU funding varies from year to year, for example, from a focus on sustainability and network development to strengthening democratic institutions. Because the focus of EU funding changes quite often, the provision of funds for specific projects is only ever likely to be short-term, despite the emphasis placed on sustainability. However, it could be argued that the EU's funding application process itself tends to be a powerful mechanism for perpetuating NGO sustainability.

The application process for such funds is extremely complicated. It involves the applicant organization having a basic knowledge of project psycho-management tools. NGOs are required to submit a log frame, a logic matrix identifying how the overall objectives of the proposed project would further EU national objectives for BiH. The specific objectives of the project must then be identified with reference to the sustainable development of the organization and to the methodology for measuring outcomes and identifying indicators of achievement. Applicants are requested to identify quantitative and qualitative base-line assessments against which the EU will measure success on completion of the project. Submissions can end up being 150-page documents and the product of many hours of work.

Paolo Scialla, the team coordinator for the Democratic Stabilization Programme of the Delegation of the European Commission to BiH, concedes that this is an extremely difficult process. He acknowledges that 'such complex management tools are not easy for people who have been using them for years'. It is recognized that the reason that funds repeatedly go to a few larger NGOs, with whom the EU has worked over the past three-four years, rather than newer local organizations, is to do with the complexity of the process and the insistence that NGOs obtain match-funding.[33] Invariably this rules out smaller NGOs and benefits those that have already established contacts with USAID, the OSCE or some other large international donor. In other words, an NGO has to be pretty well established and connected to gain access to EU funds.

Not surprisingly perhaps, the EU found it hard to allocate funds for the current network-building round. The quality of the applications was considered poor, and out of a potential €7 million, only €1.5 million could be allocated. The local delegation has concluded that the process is too complex for most local NGOs and that there is a lack of capacity to develop the kind of projects that the EU wishes to support. However, the solution to this is seen in terms of providing more training for NGOs to develop the specific technical skills required to complete grant applications. At the outset the delegation was motivated by the evident need to support and help develop local NGO networks, to encourage grassroots capacity and orientate smaller NGOs more towards complementing the work of others, and to develop intra-sectoral partnership. However, the process of accessing that potential support is seemingly prohibitive for those who require it most. It seems to be a Catch-22 situation in which organizations need to have the developed capacity and know-how before they can access the EU funds to develop it.

Though the process of applying for EU grants is particularly complex, the issue of NGOs having to acquire very specific skills and expertise to obtain funding is an endemic problem and one that leads NGOs to deploy resources towards skills development rather than advocacy campaigns.[34] Local NGOs applying for grants to the USAID, OSCE and the World Bank must demonstrate developed internal management practices and structures and be proficient in organizational management concepts. Several of the large NGO networks have made it through the hoop and, having acquired the necessary skills, are able to access these funds. They then distribute some of the resources and know-how to smaller local NGOs within the community, which is, of course, positive. The critical indicator of success will be whether the ownership of this knowledge and expertise, which is currently in the hands of a few – an elite of civil society organization professionals – will in time be diffused to more enmeshed local organizations, outside of Sarajevo, Tuzla and Mostar.

The case of the Quaker Peace and Social Witness (QPSW) mission in BiH provides a good illustration of this change in emphasis to focus on skills training to ensure sustainability in the sector. QPSW initially worked on delivering humanitarian aid and later began offering small grants to NGOs working on a variety of issues. However, since 2000, QPSW have acted as consultants for NGOs, providing specific skills and training through short training seminars, with the objective of developing the sustainability of NGOs.[35] Similarly, the OSCE, which has long been involved in democracy development in BiH, has shifted away from the project-based approach of the late 1990s – where the local office identified specific projects that they wanted NGOs to work on – to a more organization-based approach. For instance, a recent project entitled 'Successor Generation Initiative', involved inviting young people from across the country to submit proposals under the general rubric of 'making a difference'. It was then up to the applicants to come up with the project, rather than the OSCE.[36] The organization no longer talks in terms of grants, but refers to funding 'initiatives' and 'building capacity'. Reflecting on the change, Zinaida Dedić, the Deputy Spokesperson of the OSCE in BiH, claimed that:

> In the past journalists from abroad would come and give a two-day session, lectures on modern media, all paid for by the OSCE. That was it; done after two days. Now we think long term, ask what every initiative will achieve, what will be the long-term results. Self-sustainability is our key aim – we'll help you out in the beginning.[37]

There is a sense that the lessons of the earlier period – when donors were entirely project-focused and sought to achieve their objectives as cost-efficiently as possible and with little regard to local agendas – have been learnt.

The bulk of funding today is directed towards sustainability programmes and for the building of links with communities and local authorities.[38] The local NGO networks – such as TALDi, the Tuzla NGO development agency, the Centre for Civic Initiatives, and the Civil Society Promotion Centre – which work with smaller community organizations to develop local capacity, attract the bulk of donor money. The initiative TALDi, based in Tuzla but operating across the country, contends that there is significant capacity within communities that local NGOs need to learn how to access. Rather than being obsessed by the acquisition of resources from foreign donors, NGOs need training and assistance with their internal organization and long-term strategic planning.[39] The implicit suggestion is that the experience of the last ten years, whereby NGOs have been locked into a continuous pursuit of short-term funding, has failed to strengthen the sector and, in fact, developed the wrong skills amongst NGOs.

The coalition of NGOs established, in 2001, by the Civil Society Promotion Centre, which includes over 140 organizations, has developed a code of practice for NGOs, a series of benchmarks for interaction between NGOs and government, and a document outlining standards for the quality of services between government and NGOs. The Coalition has also established a series of Reference Groups across the entire country with the aim of coordinating grassroots NGO activity, spreading good practice and linking community groups to the larger network. The aim is to raise the standard of NGO activity, develop and foster professionalism, and to help small operations to gain access to know-how. The leading figure in the Coalition, Fadil Sero, contends that progress has been made in terms of improving the quality and quantity of interaction between government and NGOs. A key objective has been to encourage local NGOs to think long-term, to consider their motives and objectives, and to think beyond short-term projects.[40] However, Sero acknowledges that amongst the coalition members, their potential political advocacy role is still undeveloped and that the bulk of NGOs involved remain focused on service provision.

Despite the recent sensitivity of donors to sustainability and the perils of 'projectization', the dependency of NGO development on donor funding has resulted in the emergence of an NGO sector which, in its lack of autonomy and independence, is, paradoxically, more akin to the voluntary associations of the former FRY (on women's NGOs, see Vanessa Pupavac, this volume). While service provision may evolve into political advocacy, it has to be acknowledged that this sector has little in common with civil society networks evolving in Central and Eastern Europe or those existing in Western Europe; this is in large part the product of extensive external donor involvement.

Whether it is feasible for NGOs to acquire the necessary skills to develop their capacity whilst they remain locked into donor-dependency is debatable. There is a sense that developing sustainability and capacity has simply become the latest short-term project that donors, through the local network organizations, are keen to promote. However, those employed within the network organizations referred to above point to the fact that NGOs have gained a new respect amongst citizens and government, and are now recognized as service providers and sources of expertise and empowerment for sections of the community. This is a marked contrast with the situation five years ago when they were treated with suspicion.[41]

Conclusion

Studies compiled in the late 1990s painted a somewhat gloomy picture of a tier of NGOs which masqueraded as civil society but fulfilled few of its democratic functions. NGOs were seen as legitimizing divisions and substituting for the state, with organizations providing employment for people who were motivated more by personal gain than the desire to heal wounds and generate civic engagement. The fledgling NGOs that seemed to institutionalize the ideals of Western civil society were, in fact, totally dependent on foreign donors and were largely project-driven.

In a number of respects the situation today is different. Donors have shifted the emphasis of their support for NGOs towards sustainability, development and capacity-building. There exists a core of NGOs that are more focused on government and are more tuned to their own long-term development. Local capacity is being mobilized and drawn into the activities of NGOs, and there is more of a sense that organizations are aware of their role and function than that suggested in the earlier literature. The bulk of NGO activity involves local people, working for local organizations. This is in marked contrast to the earlier period when international donors funded international NGOs which employed foreign nationals.

However, most NGO activity in BiH today involves service provision, with organizations plugging gaps and acting either in conjunction with or in place of the state. The rationale voiced by many within the NGO sector is that political advocacy will eventually develop through service provision, and that NGOs need first to enmesh themselves with government and communities before they can take on a more political role. But it is hard to envisage how, or at what point, NGOs will shift from partnership to advocacy. The terms of their engagement with government dictate that they provide information, and assist and support rather than oppose.[42]

What must also be acknowledged is that, despite the emphasis placed by donors on sustainability and capacity-building, assistance is still delivered through short-term projects. When the OSCE talk about helping NGOs, what they seem to mean is developing their capacity to apply for funding and to devise OSCE-fundable projects. Moreover, as the example of the EU so clearly illustrates, donor requirements can reinforce an existing elite of NGOs. The worthiness of an NGO's project and the criteria for providing grants is still based on how well the proposal is drafted and whether the objectives are clearly expressed. Far less, if any, consideration is given to the needs of the individual organization or the importance of the particular project for the specific community. The processes of awarding grants remain bureaucratic and managerial.[43] To an extent, the emphasis on sustainability and capacity-building is a smokescreen as the main driving force for donors is value for money, visible impact and tangible evidence of their assistance. Whilst this is perhaps understandable, it is arguably not the most conducive context to build the long-term sustainability of NGOs.

Professional, elite-focused organizations able and willing to contribute to the policy process and assist government are important for BiH and undoubtedly constitute the bedrock of civil society. However, whether they can also realize societal linkage, contest power and mobilize marginalized sections of the community will be the true indicator of their success as civil society institutions. The legacy of 15 years of donor funding for NGO development in Central and Eastern Europe suggests that the shift towards elite-focus and the dependency on donor-aid distances the professional NGOs from their constituents and from societal campaigns and issues.[44]

That NGOs are being drawn into some form of partnership with the state could also lend credence to the view that NGOs are legitimizing rather than transforming the status quo. Yet the ability of a small corps of NGOs to engage government, to access state resources, to participate in policy debates and to articulate political agendas that are different from those of the local political elites suggests power is shifting, however slightly and slowly. The fear, expressed by many within the sector, is that what is being created in the name of civil society has very little in common with that which exists in Western Europe, or even in other parts of post-communist Europe. This is largely indisputable and is an inevitable consequence of the unique external context in which NGOs are developing.

But to dismiss NGOs as fulfilling no political function other than legitimizing the status quo and the nationalist grip on power ignores recent significant changes that do perhaps herald the prospect of a more positive future for NGOs as moderators of state power, facilitators of social protection, and institutions for mobilizing local capacity.

NOTES

1. R. Belloni, 'Building Civil Society in Bosnia-Herzegovina', Human Rights Working Papers, No.12, Jan. 2000, p.2, at www.du.edu/humanrights/workingpapers/papers/02-belloni-01-00.pdf.
2. D. Chandler, *Bosnia: Faking Democracy after Dayton*, 2nd edn., London: Pluto Press, 2000, p.143; Y. du Pont, 'Democratisation through Supporting Civil Society in Bosnia and Herzegovina', *Helsinki Monitor*, No.4, 2000; S. Freizer and M. Kaldor, 'Civil Society in Bosnia and Herzegovina', unpublished paper, 2002; B. Deacon and P. Stubbs, 'International Actors and Social Policy Development in Bosnia-Herzegovina: Globalism and the New Feudalism', *Journal of European Social Policy*, Vol.8, No.2, 1998, pp.99–115.
3. ICVA, *Guide to Civil Society in BiH: Directory of Humanitarian and Development Agencies in Bosnia and Herzegovina*, Vol.1, Sarajevo: ICVA, 2002.
4. For an excellent discussion of the ethnocentric nature of civil society development, see C. Hann, 'Introduction: Political Society and Civil Anthropology', in C. Hann and E. Dunn (eds), *Civil Society: Challenging Western Models*, London: Routledge, 1996, pp.1–3.
5. For example, Žene za Žene International, a local NGO.
6. For example, Pomozino djeci, Visegrad.
7. Such a notion of civil society tends to be used more by sociologists. See L.M. Salamon and H.K. Anheier, *Defining the Nonprofit Sector: A Cross-national Analysis*, Manchester: Manchester University Press, 1997.
8. R. Mandel, 'Seeding Civil Society', in C.M. Hann, *Postsocialisms: Ideals, Ideologies and Practices in Eurasia*, London: Routledge, 2002; J. Wedel, *Collision and Collusion: The Strange Case of Western Aid to Eastern Europe, 1989-1998*, New York: St. Martin's Press, 2001; B.A. Cellarius and C. Staddon, 'Environmental Nongovernmental Organizations, Civil Society and Democratization in Bulgaria', *East European Politics and Societies*, Vol.16, No.1, 2002, pp.182–222; S. Sampson, 'The Social Life of Projects: Importing Civil Society to Albania', in C. Hann and E. Dunn (n.4 above), K.F.F. Quigley, 'Lofty Goals, Modest Results: Assisting Civil Society in Eastern Europe', in M. Ottaway and T. Carothers (eds), *Funding Virtue: Civil Society Aid and Democracy Promotion*, Washington, D.C: Carnegie Endowment for International Peace, 2000, pp.191–216.
9. Chandler (n.2 above), pp.151–3.
10. Freizer and Kaldor, (n.2), p.34.
11. J.S. Sörensen, 'Pluralism or Fragmentation', *War Report*, May 1997, p.35.
12. Belloni (n.1), p.4.
13. Ibid.
14. Freizer and Kaldor (n.2).
15. Deacon and Stubbs (n.2).
16. Belloni (n.1), p.6.
17. An example of such a rural setting is the village of Tegare in RS, where a handful of Bosniac families have returned to an economically devastated village. No public funds were made available to help displaced persons or indeed to alleviate the poverty of the Serb majority. The international community also has no visible presence here.
18. Interview with Milan Mirić, Network Coordinator, ICVA, Sarajevo, 24 March 2004.
19. USAID, 'The 2004 NGO Sustainability Index for Central and Eastern Europe and Eurasia', p.42.
20. Interview with Milan Mirić (n.18 above).
21. S. Sali-Terzić, 'Civil Society', in Ž. Papić et al. (eds), *International Support Policies to South-East European countries: Lessons not Leaned in Bosnia-Hezegovina*, Sarajevo: Muller, 2002, pp.175–94.
22. Interview with Tuzla Reference Group, Tuzla, 9 November 2004.
23. Interview with Milan Mirić (n.18 above).
24. Interview with Goran Tinjić, Operations Officer, World Bank Country Office Bosnia and Herzegovina, Sarajevo, 8 Nov. 2004.

25. Interview with Milan Mirić (n.18 above).
26. Ibid.
27. As there is very little published data available regarding NGO funding, this is a guesstimate, but one that is echoed by almost all those involved in the NGO sector.
28. Interview with Tuzla Forum, Tuzla, 9 Nov. 2004.
29. Interview with Milan Mirić (n.18 above).
30. Mandel (n.8 above), p.286.
31. Deacon and Stubbs (n.2 above).
32. Interviews with: Goran Tinjić, (n.24 above); Paolo Scialla, Team Coordinator, Democratic Stabilization Programme, Delegation of the European Commission to BiH, Sarajevo, 24 March 2004; Armina Dedić, Small Grant Scheme Programme Officer, DFID, Sarajevo, 23 March 2004; Selma Sijercić, Project Management Specialist, USAID, Sarajevo, 10 Nov. 2004; Almir Tanović, Programme Officer, CIDA, Sarajevo, 11 Nov. 2004; Nikola Yordanov, Civil Society Coordinator, OSCE, Sarajevo, 8 Nov. 2004.
33. Interview with Paolo Scialla (n.32 above).
34. Interview with Lejla Sonum, Independent Bureau for Humanitarian Issues, Sarajevo, 22 March 2004.
35. Interview with Goran Bubalo and Sladjana Rakonjac, Quaker Peace and Social Witness mission, Sarajevo, 22 March 2004.
36. Interview with Zinaida Delić, Deputy Spokesperson, and Caroline Cliff, Information Officer, OSCE, Sarajevo, 22 March 2004.
37. Ibid.
38. CRS, DFID, USAID all make their grants conditional on either linkage with the community, or the development of long-term sustainability of the organization.
39. Interview with Indira Prljaca, Director, TALDi, Tuzla, 9 November 2004.
40. Interview with Fadil Sero, Sarajevo, 11 November 2004.
41. This was endorsed by recent OSCE public opinion surveys which recorded a much more positive opinion of NGOs.
42. Several of the NGO leaders interviewed reported that the expectation of local political elites was that, in return for co-operation, NGOs must give up their opposing position.
43. For instance, the EU allows NGOs 48 hours to submit any additional information it requires to process an application. Sometimes this will include an improved translation into English (the language of EU grants), or some extra data. If the NGO has not supplied the information in that time frame the application is simply discarded, even if the missing data is rather inconsequential.
44. This claim is based on an extensive empirical analysis of Czech NGOs. See A. Fagan, 'Time to Take Stock? Civil Society Development in the Czech Republic', *Democratization* (forthcoming, 2005).

Local Institutional Engineering: A Tale of Two Cities, Mostar and Brčko

FLORIAN BIEBER

The northern Bosnian city of Brčko, built in Austro-Hungarian style on the Sava River, and Mostar, the capital of the Herzegovina in the south, just an hour's drive from the Adriatic and straddling the Neretva river, are as different in appearance as cities in Bosnia (BiH) get. Yet they share a decade of international institutional engineering designed to bring together communities which had been separated by war.

Governance in BiH is a complicated matter. The asymmetry of the state, the high degrees of decentralization and of international intervention, has made it an unwieldy country to govern. In this context, local governance has been much neglected in the face of concerns over international coordination with state- and entity-level institutions. In fact, local governance has been the key to post-war BiH: the way municipalities were run determined the return of refugees and greatly impacted on the economic and social development of the locality.

Local government in the Republika Srpska (RS) is regulated at the entity level, whereas in the Muslim (Bosniac) and Croat-dominated Federation (FBiH), a general framework law left it to the cantons to define the specific competences (and funding) of the municipal level. As a consequence, there are 12 different types of local government – ten in the FBiH, one in the RS and in Brčko.[1] Complex institutional systems in BiH are not limited to higher levels of government. In parts of BiH, municipal arrangements are equally complex, due to international attempts to accommodate and balance the competing interests of the different communities residing there. As a result of the war, only a few municipalities remained ethnically diverse, mostly in FBiH. Even Sarajevo, prior to the war thoroughly multi-ethnic, became a predominantly mono-ethnic, Bosniac city. With about half of all refugees and internally displaced persons (IDPs) having returned by the summer of 2004, some areas of BiH –homogenous at the end of the war – have regained some of their diversity. Even so, most municipalities are dominated by one ethnic community, threatening to undermine the formal legal status of Bosniacs, Croats and Serbs as equal 'constituent people'. Brčko and Mostar were two cities which were the post-war exception, rather than the rule. Mostar is shared and contested between Croats and Bosniacs – few of the Serbs from before the war are left – and Brčko is shared between Bosniacs and Serbs.

This essay is not only about two contested cities in BiH. These two case studies allow for an evaluation of two types of power-sharing in post-conflict settings: on the one hand, rigid consociationalism with territorial decentralization and, on the other, flexible power-sharing.[2] In addition, Brčko and Mostar can shed light on institution-building in post-conflict settings – with international policy, in the former case, emphasizing institution-building and integration before democratic elections and, in the latter, focusing on the holding of elections prior to the establishment of viable institutions.[3] Much of the literature on power-sharing and post-conflict institution-building focuses on national or regional institutions. The cases of Brčko and Mostar demonstrate the variety and significance of institutional design and multi-national governance at the local level.

The War in Mostar and Brčko

The war left both Mostar and Brčko divided, in Mostar the dividing line ran through the city centre; in Brčko the city remained under Serb control, the rural regions were part of the Bosniac–Croat FBiH. In both towns, the demographic balance had dramatically shifted in the course of the war. Serbs emerged as the largest community in Brčko after the war, whereas in 1991, Serbs were third in size after Muslims and Croats. In Mostar, on the other hand, the number of Serbs dropped drastically to less than five per cent and Croats made up the largest group, outnumbering Bosniacs who had been more numerous before the war.[4] Irrespective of the shifts between groups, both cities had seen a sharp drop in the number of inhabitants, with many refugees living abroad or elsewhere in BiH.

In the aftermath of the war, the communal division was severe and few dared to cross the borders which ran through the municipalities. In Mostar, crossing to the other side of the city was even formally restrained, with only a limited number of people allowed to cross in the immediate post-war period. Brčko did not experience the same degree of segregation, largely due to the fact that the city itself was not divided. In the outskirts of the city, the Arizona Market was established – a cross-communal trading place in no-man's land where ethnic belonging and citizenship mattered little and everything was for sale. In both cases, the end of the war did not mean an end to the existing territorial divisions between the communities. Rather, post-war life began in both municipalities by cementing the lines of division. The contested nature of both towns made them a target of the post-war nationalist leaderships keen to consolidate their grip symbolically and demographically. In Mostar and Brčko, Croat and Serb authorities explicitly attempted to resettle as many refugees from their own community as possible, in order to secure their post-war claims. The symbolic markers fulfilled a similar role. In Brčko, the Serb administration symbolically 'secured' the town by erecting a monument to Draža Mihailović, the leader of the Serb nationalist Četnik movement during the Second World War,[5] while Mostar became notorious for the gigantic cross on Mount Hum above the city and the disproportionately large cathedral tower in the Croat west of the city. If Brčko provided the link which made the RS *one* territory, Mostar was the only city and the 'capital' of the Croat secessionist project. It was against this backdrop that the Office of the High Representative (OHR) and, in the case of Mostar also the European Union (EU), sought to reintegrate these thoroughly divided cities.

Institutional Design and International Administration

Due to their contested status, tensions continued longer in Brčko and Mostar than elsewhere in the country and the lines of division remained tangible. Thus, Mostar and Brčko have been focal points of international intervention in BiH. International efforts have taken very different forms in both cities, with very different results. In Mostar, quick elections and the institutionalization of the status quo dominated, whereas in Brčko an international protectorate took precedence over elections and new institutions were more inclusive and flexible.

Governing Mostar

After the end of Bosniac–Croat fighting, Mostar was placed under EU administration, lasting from July 1994 to January 1997. The aim of the international administration was to reconstruct the wartime damage and reintegrate the city, whose facilities, including the university, had been entirely divided between the Croat and Bosniac-controlled parts of town. As part of the Washington Agreement (which established FBiH), Mostar was established as a joint Bosniac–Croat city and the capital of the mixed Croat-Bosniac Herzegovina–Neretva canton. Reflecting its nature as a cease-fire agreement the new municipal boundaries were drawn on the basis of the distribution of forces, not on economic, social or historical criteria. The city itself was divided into six municipalities, three Bosniac and three Croat, with a small central zone to be administered by the joint city government. The EU reduced the size of the central zone following riots and attacks against Hans Koschnik, the first EU administrator, by supporters of the Croat Democratic Union (HDZ).[6] This concession in the face of violent resistance undermined international efforts in Mostar for years to come.

The Interim Statute, imposed in 1996, established Mostar as a highly decentralized city with far-reaching power-sharing mechanisms which sought to counteract the territorial control of the communities, while at the same time recognizing, and thereby institutionalizing, the ethnic divisions. The system of governance was excessively complex in its attempt to prevent domination by either Croat or Bosniac parties. In the six municipalities, the local councils were set up to represent all three population groups according to the 1991 census. In addition, Muslims, Croats and 'Others' were represented in the municipal government and administration, replicating the power-sharing structures at the city, cantonal, entity and state level. Originally, the HDZ delayed the establishment of the local municipal councils and sought to prevent their statutes from including any power-sharing mechanisms, fearing that this would allow the Bosniac Party of Democratic Action (SDA) to challenge the absolute dominance of the HDZ in West Mostar.[7]

The allocation of seats in the municipal councils ensured that no one community would have an outright majority. In the predominantly Croat municipalities, for example, Croats were restricted to only between 10 and 12 seats (out of 25) with the rest reserved for other groups. This complex system was not free from abuse. The leading Bosniac and Croat parties (the SDA and HDZ respectively) sought to get round the ethnic quota system by placing Serb (or other) candidates on their party electoral lists and thereby managed to 'capture' the seats reserved for 'Others'. In other cases, there were not enough candidates from non-dominant communities, resulting in vacant seats.[8] Thus, the municipalities continued to operate as mono-ethnic, and segmented administrations, despite the international intention of using the complex electoral framework to ensure cross-ethnic consociational practices.

The competences of the city government were minimal[9] and the decision-making system cumbersome, with a mayor and a deputy mayor (each from a different community, that is, one Bosniac, one Croat),[10] who regularly rotated. In addition, the post of mayor was linked to the canton by requiring the governor of the canton and the mayor of Mostar to be from different communities.[11] The election of the mayor required a cross-community consensus, with all candidates requiring support from one third of Croat and Bosniac deputies.[12] In practice, this cross-community support did not result in the election of mayors who could command authority from both Croats and Bosniacs.

The mayor and deputy have been largely governing 'their' respective part of town through parallel institutions rather than governing the city jointly. The city council has been equally divided. During the first electoral cycle (1996/ 1997), the council contained a total of 37 seats, 16 of which were reserved for Bosniacs and Croats and five for others. Later, the membership of the city council was reduced to 30 with an equal share for Bosniacs and Croats and 'Others' (10 each), on the basis of the pre-war 1991 census. The council was elected through a city-wide list (12) and three deputies from each of the six municipalities, making elections rather cumbersome.[13] Power-sharing mechanisms also operated at this level with the president and the vice-president representing different ethnic constituencies.[14] In addition, all 'people' (Croats and Bosniacs) could invoke a veto if their 'fundamental interests' were affected. Unlike the current 2004 statute, there was no definition of what constituted a vital interest and the threshold for invoking a veto was relatively low (majority of representatives of one community), opening opportunities for blocking decision-making.[15]

In consequence, the city council failed to exercise properly even the limited responsibilities accorded to it by the interim statute and met on relatively few occasions.[16] Similarly, the central zone – comprising the historic town centre – never functioned, and the other municipalities encroached upon it. The institutional set-up of post-war Mostar was additionally plagued by the existence of fragmented formal institutions and parallel institutions which further weakened the already fractious municipal bodies. As a consequence, the six municipalities were, in fact, operating largely as if they comprised two separate municipalities: one Bosniac and one Croat. The central city administration was largely ineffective due to the complete parallelism of most institutions and double budgeting. According to the findings of the Commission on Mostar – appointed by the OHR in 2003 – this duplication of administration came at a cost: maintaining the bureaucracy required KM 288 (approximately €150) annually or five per cent of the average annual income of an inhabitant of Mostar.[17]

Ironically, the international presence reinforced the division between Bosniac and Croat parts of town. While the OHR declared attempts to unify the Croat municipalities illegal, unfortunately the interim statute and the substantial aid disbursement (some €150 million during the EU administration period alone) consolidated the segmented political structure of post-war Mostar. In addition, the limited foreign investment, for example, in the hydroelectric power plant and the aluminium factory, largely benefited the Croat parallel institutions in the city.[18] Finally, the frequent elections – citizens of Mostar chose their city council four times between 1996 and 2004 – legitimized the institutions and the office-holders, both representing the segmented structure of the city. Rather than challenging the ethnic division of the city, the rigid power-sharing system – instituted by the international administrators – both accepted and perpetuated the post-war status quo.

Over the years, the international community was able to ensure that – despite the failure of the institutional structures – a number of agreements were made between the Bosniac and Croat representatives, for example, overcoming obstacles to the freedom of movement and preventing continuing ethnic cleansing from West Mostar. However, in the face of the dominant Bosniac and Croat parties' continued resistance to institutional reform, the OHR established the Commission for Mostar. The Commission – composed of domestic and international experts and political representatives from political parties – proposed the creation of a single municipality. Community interests were to be protected through preserving the six municipalities – albeit only in the form of electoral units – to prevent outvoting, and, in addition, 'vital interests' were to be protected through a system of super-majority voting and veto rights, as is the case at the entity and cantonal levels.

When the local political parties refused to adopt the proposals, Paddy Ashdown, the High Representative, imposed the recommendations in early 2004, thus ending the formal ethno-political division of the city. The main opposition to the plans was led by the Bosniac SDA. The Croat HDZ had, in the post-war period, been the main opponents of the unification proposals; however, it was now aware that the Croat community formed an ethnic majority across the city as a whole.[19] This meant it was the SDA that raised vocal concerns that the ethnic minority might find the veto rights and other protective mechanisms inadequate for promoting their particular interests.[20]

The general response to the international imposition was mostly one of passive acceptance (see Sumantra Bose, this volume), while most political parties welcomed or at least accepted the final statute. Croat and Serb parties criticized the separate electoral units: Croat opposition was based on a preference for city-wide elections, leading to their numerical domination of the city council; Serb parties feared that the fragmentation of the small Serb community into six electoral units would deprive them of representation (as it in fact did in the October 2004 elections).[21] Prior to the unification, a number of unrecognized referenda in some of the six municipalities revealed the sharp divisions, with Croat municipalities supporting a unified city and Bosniac municipalities sharply opposed.[22] These referenda results had no impact on international policy but strongly highlighted the lack of consensus over the future of Mostar.[23]

The new Mostar statute tones down the rigid power-sharing practised until 2004, indicating a learning process on behalf of the international community. There has been a move away from formalized rigid systems which can be dysfunctional, merely consolidating ethnic segregation. The 2004 city statute abolished the six municipalities, which had existed since 1996, and returned the city to its pre-war status as one municipality.[24] The city council is no longer composed of a pre-set number of representatives from each community, but on the basis of fixed parameters of a minimum number – four for the three constituent people and one for 'Others' – and a maximum number (15) of the 35 council members. Thus, electoral representation is geared at preventing both exclusion and domination.[25] While power-sharing might be weaker in regard to representation, consociational elements can be identified throughout the statute. The president and the vice-presidents of the council and the president and the mayor, for example, have to hail from different constituent peoples. The statute abolishes the position of the deputy mayor, but instead sets up the post of chief adviser, who manages the mayor's secretariat and has to be from a different constituent people than the mayor.[26]

National interests in Mostar are protected through both super-majorities and veto rights. All core decisions, such as amendments to the statute, the budget, symbolic issues (naming and city symbols) and the election (and dismissal) of the mayor require a two-thirds majority, that is, support from more than one community.[27] In addition, vital interests, as defined in the FBiH constitution (after the 2002 constitutional amendments),[28] can be invoked to veto council decisions.[29] A decision can be vetoed by a simple majority, if supported by at least two community caucuses, or a two-thirds majority, if only one community invokes a veto. In case the veto succeeds, the issue is referred to the Federation Constitutional Court; however, this has raised concerns over the court's already overbearing caseload. Unfortunately, there is no provision in the statute that would suspend the decision, pending the court's ruling, which may have the result that some vetoed decisions cannot be effectively nullified.[30]

The 2004 institutional set-up departed in a number of ways from the interim statute.[31] First, and most importantly, it abolished the six municipalities and thus put an end to the formal parallel governance structures which existed. In addition, it reduced the rigidity of the power-sharing system at the city level by no longer firmly setting the number of representatives per ethnic nationality and abandoning the position of the deputy mayor. Finally, the status of Serbs was formally upgraded to be equal to Croats and Bosniacs, even though numerically the community is only marginally represented. Other than that, the city remained firmly governed by power-sharing, requiring grand coalitions between the different communities, guaranteeing the representation of the communities and protecting vital interests through veto rights.

Governing Brčko

Brčko has adopted a different model of local governance. As discussed earlier, the status of the city was left to be resolved by an arbitration tribunal.[32] In preliminary decisions in 1997 and 1998, the municipality was placed under international supervision. In the final arbitration decision in 1999, the entire pre-war municipality was made an autonomous district, governed by its own laws and only subordinate to the state level, on the grounds that neither of the entities had fulfilled international demands with regard to refugee returns and good governance.[33] The 'autonomous' district became a full protectorate, whereby an international administrator appointed the mayor and all members of the assembly until 2004. Unlike the rest of BiH, which has been an informal semi-protectorate since 1997, the intervention of the international supervisor was direct and not in parallel to local institutions. The supervisor's powers allowed for a much more effective international administration than that available to the EU and the OHR in Mostar. The international administration faced similar opposition to its rulings, especially in the immediate post-war period, as in Mostar, but its opponents could not claim any electoral legitimacy.

Institutional engineering in Brčko was consequently more heavy-handed and direct than in Mostar, until the reforms imposed in January 2004. The international administration of Brčko had the *integration* of the district as its core task. Most decisions of the supervisors have been aimed at dismantling the entity-structures which were established prior to the arbitration decision. The new administration of Brčko, replacing the mono-ethnic systems, has been structured less along ethnic lines than in the rest of BiH. In particular, the system of governance lacks some of the formal power-sharing features possessed by the cantons and entities. For example, there are no veto rights for constituent nations, but instead most key decisions (election of the mayor, budget, laws, and appointment of police chief and their deputies) require a three-fifths majority, which prevents the marginalization of either of the two large communities (Bosniacs and Serbs). This type of decision-making could be described as an integrative system which requires cross-community consensus rather than a narrow majority subject to vetoes. The indirect election of the mayor was an exception (together with Mostar) from the rest of BiH, in an attempt to prevent the election of a mayor on the basis of the support of one community alone.

Prior to the 2004 elections, the 13 Serb, 9 Bosniac and 7 Croat members of the assembly were selected by the internationally-appointed supervisor on the basis of their 'quality of the application, professional background and potential constituencies',[34] and included representatives of the main political parties of both entities.[35] The international supervisor also sought to strike an informal balance between communities by allocating the three highest offices – the mayor, deputy mayor and the president of the assembly – to representatives from the three constituent nations. Veto rights – which do not explicitly exist in Brčko – have been frequently criticized for blocking decision-making in other parts of BiH. Thus, Brčko has been an experiment in decision-making not based on institutionalizing ethnic divisions, in a deliberate attempt to prevent special political privileges for the different communities, which would render governance more difficult.[36] Nevertheless, international intervention in decision-making has been commonplace due to a lack of consensus between the three constituent nations as represented in the local assembly. In this case the super-majority has often been no easier to attain than the task of avoiding circumventing vetoes (or their threats) elsewhere in BiH.

While in both Brčko and Mostar, the institutions were internationally imposed, their substance differed greatly. Mirroring the larger power-sharing systems in BiH, Mostar was governed (or rather not) by territorial decentralization along ethnic lines and weak power-sharing at the centre. The devolution of powers to the unit of greatest ethnic homogeneity increased the effectiveness of decision-making at this level but permanently weakened power-sharing. The emergence of parallel institutions in Mostar was thus a consequence of the rigid power-sharing structure which provided no incentives for cooperation at the city level. The power-struggle between the HDZ and the SDA (their cooperation not withstanding) meant that governance in Mostar was subject to other levels of power-sharing at the canton and entity levels.

Governance structures in Brčko, on the other hand, not only removed policy-making from the political party competition for power at the entity level, but also abolished any territorial decentralization along ethnic lines. Governance in Brčko, focusing only at the district level, thus provided greater incentives for compromise than in Mostar. Decision-making without veto rights further reduced the blockages of the ethnically-divided competitive party system. As it has been under international tutelage until 2004, the real test began only after the October 2004 local elections. Nevertheless, Brčko has already become a model of sorts. The statute imposed on Mostar by the OHR in 2004 follows a similar approach to that taken in Brčko and gives up on the gradualist approach towards integration. While having stronger consociational elements, it abolishes the territorial dimension of power-sharing and shores up the central institutions.

Measures of Success: Political Moderation and Refugee Return

The different trajectories of institutional design, at least until 2004, have resulted in divergent developments in both cities with regard to the development of the politics of moderation and, in particular, the return of refugees. Such discrepancies attest to the importance of institutional design, especially at the local level where the impact on the return of individuals from a no-longer dominant community is most significant.

Electoral Dynamics and Moderation

Electoral dynamics have been fundamentally different in Brčko and Mostar. The first post-war elections in BiH took place in Mostar in June 1996, followed by three more local elections (in 1997, 2000, and 2004). Mostaris have had more opportunities to cast their vote than those living anywhere else in BiH. In Brčko elections took place only in 1997 and 2004.

Since 1996, elections in Mostar have been about which community controls the city. In the first post-war years, the slight dominance of the Bosniac community translated into SDA political dominance and demands from the party for an abolition of the separate municipalities and the unification of the city. As the demographics began to tilt towards the Croat population, support for unifying Mostar grew among the HDZ and dissipated within the SDA. In 1996, the votes were nearly evenly split between the two parties, squeezing out the only alternative, the United List, comprising a number of moderate candidates and parties. Despite the close race between the two national parties, the SDA was able to gain 21 seats on the city council – the 16 reserved for Bosniacs and the five set aside for 'Others', as its Serb and other non-Bosniac candidates received slightly more votes than those allied to the HDZ. The attempt at designing an institutional system which prevented the electoral domination of either community thus failed spectacularly.[37] This should have come as no surprise, considering that quota systems had a long history of use (and abuse) in former Yugoslavia (see Vanessa Pupavac, this volume). In 1990, for example, the SDA gained the upper hand in the Bosnian presidency by winning the seat reserved for 'Others'.

The new city council was only established in early 1997 – following protests by the HDZ over the SDA's dominance, which were placated only after the party received the position of mayor. Following the BiH-wide local elections in 1997, the balance of power remained similar and the mayor and his deputy merely switched positions. Elections a mere three years later, in 2000, gave some greater influence to the moderate Social Democratic Party (SDP) with nearly 13 per cent, but the SDA and HDZ remained unchallenged in the six municipalities. The elections in 2004, under the new statute, evidenced the reduction in influence of the two main nationalist parties since the end of the war. The SDA only received half the votes it got in 1996 (24.9 per cent) and the HDZ vote fell by about a tenth since the first elections (36.6 per cent). However, taking into account the votes for other nationalist parties, the dominance of the national Croat and the Bosniac voting blocks remained unchallenged. In addition, the weakness of the Serb parties is striking – even though some 6,000 Serb refugees have returned to the city since 2000, no Serb party managed to gain seats in the city council.[38] There has been little movement towards political moderation in Mostar since 1996 and the permanent polarization over who controls the city has fuelled the electoral chances of nationalist parties on both sides.

In Brčko, the elections were not fought over control of the city. Here, the core issue in the post-war period was not the unification of the city but rather the return of refugees. A full return of all refugees would have shifted the political balance back towards the Bosniac population. However, even the refugee question has declined in importance as Brčko largely ceased to have any strategic political relevance, once it became an autonomous district. This loss of the strategic link between the two halves of the RS was not the result of a demographic shift, or of changes reflected at the ballot box, but of the international arbitration decision. Subsequently, under international administration, the main political conflicts – between the Serb parties and international administrators – have been played out through bargaining behind closed doors rather than in any public competition for votes.

Brčko has seen some moderation in political preferences between 1997 and 2004, but this has mainly been in line with broader shifts across the whole of BiH. In 1997, the nationalist parties collectively gained a total of 71.3 per cent of the vote.[39] By 2004, this share had dropped to 43.52 per cent. The different social democratic parties increased their share in the meantime from just below 22 per cent to just above 30 per cent. As mentioned, the Brčko party situation closely reflects that of the two entities. Among Serbs, the Serb Democratic Party remains the most popular party, the HDZ has the most support among the Croats and among Bosniac voters the SDA is in second place. The main electoral shift has been away from the dominance of parties based in the RS; this has been caused by relatively successful levels of refugee return,[40] resulting in a majority in the city council for parties from FBiH.[41]

The post-election coalition brought together moderate Serb, Bosniac and Croat parties after the nationalist parties failed to gain support in the assembly for their coalition. This picture suggests that while FBiH parties may be gaining the upper hand in Brčko, nationalist parties continue to be strong, and it would be misleading to attribute any weakening of the national triumvirate in Brčko to any specificities of the district alone. However, cooperation between programmatically similar parties across the ethnic divide is rare in BiH – as even social democratic parties are shaded by their respective national perspective and there have been few opportunities for coalitions, except at the state level. The electoral dynamics of Brčko suggest that the city could possibly emerge as a starting point for cross-ethnic and cross-entity coalitions on the basis of programmatic similarities.

The results, however, do undermine the assumption that heavy-handed international intervention, as has taken place in the district since 1998, would automatically benefit more nationalist forces. Both Mostar and Brčko have seen political moderation between 1996/7 and 2004, with similar declines in nationalist party support. The comparison of political preferences thus suggests that the Brčko protectorate and the more integrative power-sharing system did not per se result in greater moderation, but neither did it lead to a political radicalization. It could be argued that there was little differential impact between the two cities when it comes to the politics of moderation. While territorial fiefdoms provided a disincentive of cross-ethnic cooperation in Mostar, international intervention in Brčko had some of the same effects.

Refugee Returns and Integrative Strategies

Bearing in mind the fact that the election results do not point to a fundamental difference between the two cities, regarding ethnic division and public sentiment, Brčko's success at the level of integrative strategies and the number of refugees returned since the war, is all the more remarkable. Both towns had been severely affected by the war. In Brčko, two thirds of the pre-war inhabitants became internally displaced or refugees, and some 39,000 Bosniacs fled the town, as did half of Brčko's Croats. In addition, some 28,000 Serb refugees displaced from elsewhere settled in the town, dramatically changing the city's demography.[42] Mostar saw similar large refugee flows which resulted in West Mostar becoming nearly exclusively Croat with most Serbs living in nearby regions in the RS and Bosniacs living in East Mostar.

In the first post-war years, virtually no non-Serb refugees or displaced persons returned to live in Serb-controlled Brčko. Since the first substantial minority returns started taking place in 1998, numbers in Brčko have exceeded those in any other area of BiH. The first arbitration decision in 1997 created a Return Commission, including the main international organizations as well as three mayors from each of the mono-ethnic regions of Brčko; however, by early 1998 only 710 families had returned. The conditions for return changed drastically with the creation of a multi-ethnic police force in late 1997 and the dissolution of pre-existing administrative structures and the establishment of the autonomous district in 1999. Between 2000 and mid-2004, more than 21,000 refugees and IDPs (15,000 Bosniacs, 3,800 Croats, 2,500 Serbs) returned.[43] During this period, Brčko received significantly more returnees than other regions of BiH, although latterly return rates across BiH have began to catch up.

In Mostar, the rates of returns have remained well below the BiH-wide average in the first years after the signing of Dayton. In fact, Mostar was one of the few places where families continued to be expelled after the end of the war. Obstruction, especially in Croat municipalities, kept returns low. However, between 2000 and 2001, numbers of minority returns increased 13-fold from just below 400 to nearly 5,000. In particular, Bosniacs began returning to Western Mostar and Serbs moved back to both halves of the town. By mid-2004, nearly 15,000 minority refugees had returned to Mostar in a four-and-a-half year period; but this figure was still lower, in both absolute and relative terms, than Brčko. Mostar is no longer a place where little movement across the imaginary and real borderlines takes place. Until the unified status of 2004, the reasons for returns lay in the stricter enforcement of property law and the increased international supervision of the return process since 2000.

In Brčko, the underlying social and economic climate has become more conducive to the return of citizens who are in a minority. Since 2001, schools have been unified and are teaching according to one school curriculum. While highly contested, including major protests by Serb students in 2000, and with exemptions for 'national subjects' (such as history and culture), the different nationally homogenous schools have been abandoned and gradually all classes have become integrated.

Mostar on the other hand, has had probably the most divided educational system in BiH, including the divisive establishment of two universities, one Croat and one Bosniac, and segregated schools with no reference to the 'other' in curricula and teaching. This degree of separation only began to be tackled seriously in late 2002 with the abolition of the special regime in the Herzegovina–Neretva canton, which delegated competences such as education to the municipalities, and these changes have been reinforced with the unification of Mostar in 2004. Echoing the delay in refugee reform, and indeed in integrative institutions, the education system lagged behind BiH-wide reforms, whereas Brčko pioneered them.

Conclusion

Overall, the differential impact of international intervention in the governance of these two cities was greatest when Brčko became an independent district, while Mostar still struggled with its administrative divisions. Since the international administration has taken a tougher approach to centralizing authority in Mostar, the gap between the two cities has decreased, reflecting to a degree the increasing convergence of their institutional frameworks as well as larger BiH-wide trends. The differences between the cities nevertheless remain stark. Brčko has exceeded the rest of BiH in terms of average salaries and economic opportunities,[44] whereas Mostar has lagged behind with high unemployment and less than average salaries.

In as much as both cities have been the target of extensive international aid, assistance and intervention since the end of the war, it appears that the resources invested have yielded more tangible results in Brčko. The relative success of the district has been conditioned by three factors. First, the fully-fledged protectorate was beefed up by considerable international resources and tax advantages over the rest of BiH, which enabled the international administration to fully integrate the city and pay higher salaries for civil servants.[45] This factor contributed to the success of integration, but not necessarily to its sustainability. Second, by creating an autonomous district, directly administered by an international appointee, Brčko was divorced from power-struggles both within and between the entities, whereas the firm division of Mostar was reinforced by the struggle for control over power and resources in the canton and in FBiH at large. This is not to suggest that the political system in Brčko is divorced from the entities; entity parties dominate, and social and cultural life remains divided by ethnicity. Third, while institutional design at the local level cannot be entirely divorced from the larger political context, decision-making has been more effective and no parallel power-structures emerged which were based along ethnic lines. Consequently, Brčko has been and probably will be a model for institutional design in other regions and at different levels of governance in BiH. Mostar, on the other hand, portrayed the weaknesses of the immediate post-war peace throughout BiH: the combination of weak power-sharing with decentralization along ethnic lines was taken to its logical conclusion in Mostar. The result was the failure either to create a functional city or to reduce fears of ethnic domination.

NOTES

The research for this article was supported by the Luxembourg Ministry of Education in the framework of the Bourse Recherché & Développement.

1. New entity laws were being drafted in late 2004, which sought to simplify this unruly legal framework.
2. See A. Lijphart, 'Constitutional Design for Divided Societies', *Journal of Democracy*, Vol.15, No.2, (2004), pp.96–109.
3. See B. Reilly, 'Post-Conflict Elections: Constraints and Danger', in E. Newman and A. Schnabel (eds), *Recovering from Civil Conflict*, London: Frank Cass, 2002, pp.118–39.
4. W. Sommers, 'Brcko District: Experiment to Experience', paper delivered at the conference, 'Delivering Public Services in Central and East European Countries', Krakow, 25–27 April 2002; Federal Office of Statistics, 'Estimation of Population of Federation of Bosnia-Herzegovina', 30 June 2004.
5. The statue was removed in October 2003. *Glas Srpske*, 16 Dec. 2003.
6. See S. Bose, *Bosnia after Dayton: Nationalist Partition and International Intervention*, London: Hurst, 2002, pp.109–10.
7. International Crisis Group, *Reunifying Mostar: Opportunities for Progress*, Balkans Report, No.90, 19 April 2000, p.16, at www.icg.org/home/index.cfm?id=1521&l=6.
8. Bose (n.6 above), pp.121–2.
9. They included public transport, the airport, urban planning and infrastructure, *Interim Statute of the City of Mostar*, 7 Feb. 1996, Art.7.
10. Ibid., Art.44.
11. *OHR Bulletin*, No.13, 6 Aug. 1996.
12. Interim Statute (n.8 above), Art.41.
13. Bose (n.6 above), pp.119–20.
14. *Interim Statute* (n.8 above), Art.26.
15. Ibid., Art.31.
16. International Mediator for the Federation of Bosnia and Herzegovina and Republika Srpska, 'Trip Report', No.4, 21–27 Aug. 1999.
17. Commission for Reforming the City of Mostar, *Recommendations of the Commission, Report of the Chairman*, 15 Dec. 2003, at www.ohr.int/archive/report-mostar/pdf/Reforming%20Mostar-Report%20(EN).pdf. It should be noted that the number of employees in the city administration in Mostar and Brčko was not that different. According to the Commission Report for Mostar, some 550 employees staffed the municipalities, plus 124 at the city-level. As of 2001, Brčko had approximately 720 employees – excluding police (322), health (594) and education (703) – possibly suggesting that in Mostar the ineffectiveness of the administration has been a greater problem than size. Global-Kontakt, Vodič za građana kroz Brčko Distrikt Bosne i Hercegovine, 2001.
18. International Crisis Group (n.7 above), pp.3, 6.
19. Ibid., p.6. The ICG suggests that the change of heart of the HDZ was the direct result of the electoral commission publishing the list of eligible voters in 2002. On the basis of this data, the Croat dominance of the Mostar municipality became obvious.
20. An overview over the different proposals can be found in Commission for Reforming the City of Mostar (n.17 above), pp.59–69.
21. 'Reaktionen aus Sarajevo und Banja Luka auf das Mostar-Dekret des internationalen Bosnien-Beauftragten', *Deutsche Welle Radio*, 29 Jan. 2004.
22. FENA, Federal News Agency, 10 and 26 Jan. 2004.
23. M. Martens, 'Versöhnung durch Dekret', *Frankfurter Allgemeine Zeitung*, 23 July 2004.
24. Only a small slice of land from the pre-war municipality remained with the RS. The six municipalities continued to exist only in the form of electoral constituencies and administrative areas. See further, *Statute of the City of Mostar*, 28 Jan. 2004, Art.7, at www.ohr.int/decisions/mo-hncantdec/default.asp?content_id=31707.
25. Ibid., Art.17.
26. Ibid., Art.51.
27. Ibid., Art.33; Art.44.
28. See F. Bieber, 'With More Complexity towards Better Governance? The 2002 Constitutional Amendments and the Proliferation of Power-Sharing in Bosnia and Herzegovina', C. Solioz and T. K. Vogel (eds), *Dayton and Beyond: Perspectives on the Future of Bosnia and Herzegovina*. Baden-Baden: Nomos, 2004.

29. *Statute of the City of Mostar* (n.24 above), Art.35.
30. See International Crisis Group, *Building Bridges in Mostar*, Europe Report, No.150, 20 Nov. 2003, p.10, at www.icg.org/home/index.cfm?id=2374&l=1.
31. The statute largely follows the recommendations of the Commission for Reforming the City of Mostar (n.17 above), and the International Crisis Group (n.30 above), p.6.
32. The tribunal comprised an international member and one nominated by each entity.
33. Brčko Arbitral Tribunal for Dispute Over the Inter-Entity Boundary in Brčko Area, 'Final Award', 5 March 1999.
34. OHR, 'Brcko Supervisor Appoints New Councilors in the Brcko Interim Assembly', Brcko Press Release, 25 Sept. 2001.
35. N. Herceg and Z. Tomić, *Izbori i izborna kampanja u Bosni i Hercegovini 2000 godine*, Mostar: Sveučilište u Mostaru, 2001, p.70.
36. International Crisis Group, *Bosnia's Brčko: Getting In, Getting On and Getting Out*, Balkans Report, No.144, 2 June 2003, pp.12–13, at www.icg.org/home/index.cfm?id=1475&l=5.
37. P. Shoup, 'The Elections in Bosnia and Herzegovina: The End of an Illusion', *Problems of Post-Communism*, Jan./Feb. 1997, p.8.
38. D. Savić, 'Mostar bi prvi put u istoriji umjesto gradonačelnika mogao dobiti - gradonačelnicu?', *Slobodna Bosna*, 21 Oct. 2004, pp.17–18.
39. In 1997, elections only took place in the Serb-held region, with the Bosniac and Croat refugees located on the Federation-controlled parts of the municipality being allowed to vote in RS.
40. C. Dahlman and G. O. Tuathail, 'Territorial Conflict and Displaced Populations: The International Supervision of Brčko, Bosnia', paper presented at the Conference on Territorial Conflict Management, University of Illinois, Urbana-Champaign, 1–3 Oct. 2004, at www.acdis.uiuc.edu/Research/TerrConMng/TCMPapers/Dahlman.pdf.
41. M. Pargan, 'Hrvatske stranke ne žele Dapu za gradonačlnika,' *Slobodna Bosna*, 21 Oct. 2004, pp.18–19.
42. See International Crisis Group, *Brčko: What Bosnia Could Be*, Balkans Report, 10 Feb. 1998, at http://intl-crisis-group.org/home/index.cfm?id=1506&l=1.
43. UNHCR, *Returns summary to Bosnia and Herzegovina from 01/01/1996 to 30/06/2004*, 2004.
44. B. Lomović, 'Distrikt Brčko: Država u državi', *Politika*, 8 Sept. 2003.
45. Due to tax advantages and its own customs service, the district has disproportional resources at its disposal. The Public Administration in Brčko is the most costly in the country due to high salaries. See European Stability Initiative, *Post-Industrial Society and the Authoritarian Temptation: Governance and Democracy in Bosnia*, Berlin and Sarajevo, 2004, p.18, at www.esiweb.org/pdf/esi_document_id_63.pdf.

Peacebuilding at the Local Level: Refugee Return to Prijedor

ROBERTO BELLONI

This essay analyses the local-level dynamics of peacebuilding. Of the widely differentiated Bosnian localities, it focuses on a (relatively) successful case – the post-Dayton intervention in Prijedor, a municipality in northwest Bosnia (BiH) which had been under Serb control since the beginning of the 1992–95 war, and was formally granted to Republika Srpska (RS) under the Dayton peace settlement of November 1995.

Peacebuilding in Prijedor is significant for at least two reasons. First, much scholarly literature has focused on highlighting how international intervention has often not worked as intended, and why there remain stumbling blocks to securing self-sustaining peace. Instead of highlighting what has not worked, Prijedor offers an opportunity to draw positive lessons by identifying what has worked and why. Second, while macro-level issues such as the building of central political institutions enjoy the lion's share of scholarly and policy analysis, intervention is most relevant at the level of the municipality, where citizens struggle to re-build their communities and lives (see also Florian Bieber, this volume). As Carrie Manning argues, 'establishing legitimate state institutions at the central level is just the tip of the iceberg.'[1] It is at the local level where a peace settlement has the most immediate and far-reaching consequences for ordinary citizens, and where the long-term support for peace must develop.

Prijedor is also a daunting case for international peacebuilding. By the time the peace agreement was signed, the presence of the non-Serb population had been erased from the municipality.[2] Because of the legacy of fear and hate left by wartime crimes, most international officials believed that Prijedor – dominated by hard-line nationalists – should be isolated and dealt with at a later stage. Yet, unexpectedly, within a few years the municipality witnessed significant improvements. Most notably, thousands of Muslim displaced persons (DPs) returned home against all odds, and the wartime Bosnian Serb leadership was marginalized by the emergence of moderate and pragmatic politicians. Prominent international community representatives concluded that 'when the majority of places look like Prijedor, we can leave the process of return to the Bosnians'.[3]

As this essay will show, the idea of 'leaving the process of return to the Bosnians' unjustifiably implies that local organizations and groups had a largely passive role in the process. This is inaccurate, to say the least. Contrary to the perception of international agencies, successful return home was in large part due to the autonomous organizing of local DPs. International activism did facilitate the process of return at crucial junctions. However, such activism became necessary in order to redress previous policies which had exacerbated inter-ethnic tensions. Only a more proactive international approach could break a dangerous deadlock and prevent the risk of further de-stabilization.

This essay begins with a brief background on Prijedor and reviews the final vicissitudes of the war which left the town under Serb control. Second, it shows how post-settlement international policy risked undermining the peace process. Third, it highlights the crucial role in diffusing ethnic division played by returning DPs, who returned home after the war even against the advice of international agencies. Finally, it considers the political impact of DPs' return, and draws lessons for improving approaches to international peace-building at the local level.

Prijedor: From Peace to War and Back Again

A Typical Bosnian Town

Before the outbreak of war in April 1992, Prijedor was a typical multi-ethnic Bosnian town. Like many others, its population of 112,543 citizens was a microcosm of the rest of the state. According to the 1991 census, the two largest ethnic groups were Muslims (49,351) and Serbs (47,582), living alongside Croats (6,316), Yugoslavs (6,459) and a smaller number of other ethnic groups (2,836). These different groups shared a struggle of resistance against Nazi forces during the Second World War. This common history of struggle was erased almost overnight, when, in the summer of 1991, Prijedor became the main supply town for the Yugoslav Federal Army fighting in Croatia. A 'crisis committee' was created to organize a Serb-only alternative administration of the town.[4]

The chair of the committee was Simo Drljaca, head of the local police and agent of the federal secret service. Under his leadership, on 30 April 1992, the committee began implementing the plan to take over the municipality. SDS member Milomir Stakić replaced the duly elected Muslim mayor. On 23 May, the village of Hambarine was subjected to several hours of artillery bombardment; when the bombardment stopped, the village was stormed by Serb paramilitary units and razed. The next day, the town of Kožarac came under attack; between 2,500 and 3,000 people were killed during the siege. Some 25,000 Muslims and Croats were expelled; men and boys older than 15 were interned in detention camps and Kožarac's 16 mosques were desecrated.

In the following three-and-a-half years, ethnic cleansing led to the opening of at least three detention camps, in Omarska, Keraterm and Trnopolje.[5] Their dramatic existence soon reached an audience outside BiH, yet, despite world outrage, no international military intervention materialized until late summer 1995. In the meantime, Prijedor's crisis committee turned the municipality into a Serb nationalist stronghold.

The Dayton Peace Accord and the Prijedor Region

In September 1995, NATO bombing, combined with the shifting military balance among the parties, formed a situation approximating the proposed basis for peace. The Bosnian Serbs controlled roughly 50 per cent of the territory, while the Croat/Muslim alliance dominated the other 50 per cent. The parties agreed on a ceasefire, but the war carried on in the Prijedor region. A final wave of mass expulsion of non-Serbs occurred in September and October,[6] and in response, American chief negotiator Richard Holbrooke urged the Muslim/Croat troops to continue their western advance and 'take Sanski Most, Prijedor, and Bosanski Novi – all important towns that had become worldwide symbols of ethnic cleansing'.[7] The Serb Army was in disarray and the Muslim Army, led by General Atif Dudaković, took Sanski Most, about 30 kilometres east of Prijedor, but unexpectedly decided to stop. Dudaković's soldiers were exhausted and resented the idea of fighting for a town likely to be retuned to the Serbs as part of the peace settlement.[8]

The Dayton peace accord (DPA) established a territorial division based on the 'leveling of the cleansing field',[9] that is, land conquered through ethnic cleansing and forced population removal. The two entities that constituted the Bosnian state, the Bosniac[10]/Croat Federation (FBiH) and the Republika Srpska (RS), divided by an Inter-Entity Boundary Line (IEBL), were granted control over a variety of standard instruments of sovereignty – from the judiciary, to the police, to taxation rights – with a 'thin roof' of central institutions to carry out those state activities not assigned to the entities. At the same time, the DPA affirmed the right of those displaced by the war (more than half of Bosnia's population) to return to their homes in conditions of dignity and safety. This goal was to be facilitated by the deployment of a 60,000-strong NATO force.

Among the contentious issues at Dayton was the fate of Sanki Most. According to Carl Bildt, who served as first post-war High Representative, one of the goals of the RS was to get Sanski Most back under its control. Serbs feared that leaving the town in Bosniac hands would provide a bridge-head for an assault on Prijedor.[11] In one respect, these fears proved to be well founded; against expectations to the contrary, Sanski Most indeed became a bridge for thousands of Bosniac DPs to return to the areas from which they had been expelled.

After the Peace Settlement

An Unlikely Case

Scholars of peacebuilding argue that there are two key variables to explain progress (or lack of) in building peace after a communal war: the country's local capacity and the level of international assistance. If there are few domestic political, economic and social resources available, only the assertive presence of international humanitarian organizations and bilateral donors can sustain the post-settlement transition. Thus, higher levels of international intervention compensate for lower levels of local capacity.[12] Michael Doyle and Nicholas Sambanis add to this equation levels of war related-hostilities. In their view, peacebuilding is a triangle composed of net local capacities, international capacities, and level of war-related hostilities. The higher international and local capacity, and the lower the war-related hostilities, the more likely peacebuilding will be successful.[13]

A brief analysis of the 'peacebuilding triangle' reveals how Prijedor, at the end of the war, was an unlikely case for successful peacebuilding. First, Prijedor had few 'local capacities'. The municipality was dominated by the same political/economic leadership responsible for the war, and opposed to the presence of NATO troops and the return of non-Serb DPs. Since the signing of the DPA, Simo Drljaca and his group provided a formidable obstacle to the implementation of Dayton.[14] In the spring of 1996, Drljaca systematically organized violent responses to any attempt by non-Serbs to return to Prijedor to visit their homes.[15] Intimidation continued at the September elections, when Bosniacs crossing the IEBL 'were in fact prohibited from entering their home towns at all.'[16] Two days after the elections, Drljaca was involved in a shooting incident with NATO troops and was removed from his position as chief of police. However, he continued to exert considerable influence from behind the scenes, in conjunction with the other former members of the crisis committee. The police force was staffed with many individuals involved in the implementation of wartime crimes;[17] their threatening presence was an additional disincentive for Bosniac DPs to return home.

Second, in addition to the presence of a tense local situation, international assistance (what Doyle and Sambanis call 'international capacities') was at a low point.[18] The US Congress Lautemberg Amendment, which prohibits the US government from providing assistance to communities suspected of harbouring war criminals, placed Prijedor under an aid embargo. For this reason no US-funded programmes could be implemented. Perversely, despite its sound intentions, the Amendment deprived Bosniac DPs from the resources they needed to return to Prijedor, and thus perpetuated the war-time status quo.

In the early post-Dayton phase, the British Overseas Development Agency (ODA) was one of the few donor agencies active in Prijedor, providing economic and financial assistance. Unfortunately, international monies often had the effect of enriching the local political/economic criminal elite, instead of 'improving the human condition' (as required by ODA's mission statement). As Human Right Watch argued in its review of early international activities in Prijedor: 'well-intentioned assistance programs are serving to financially reward those persons who participated in war crimes, and who actively seek to obstruct the Dayton Agreement, particularly those provisions relating to human rights and return of refugees and displaced persons'.[19] In response, the ODA argued that allegations against Drljaca and the other members of the crisis committee were based on 'rumours' and continued funding projects in the municipality.[20]

Prijedor's relative isolation continued even after 'minority return'[21] became the international agencies' priority in BiH (see Daniela Heimerl, this volume). Despite the presence of thousands of Bosniac DPs willing to move from Sanski Most back to Prijedor, international agencies excluded this town from internationally-organized return schemes. In 1998, for example, in an effort to promote the return home of Bosnian DPs, the UN High Commissioner for Refugees (UNHCR) adopted the 'Open Cities' programme, whereby municipalities willing to accept the return of ethnic minorities would receive additional reconstruction funds. Fifteen towns were declared 'open cities', but Prijedor was never awarded this status because of the obstruction of local politicians and the presence of indicted war criminals.

Third, not only did 'local and international capacities' much complicate the peacebuilding task, but also the high level of war-related hostilities further problematized the situation. The wartime presence of detention camps in the region understandably worried potential returnees. Those who were interned, beaten, tortured and sexually abused were likely to reason that they would be better off re-building their lives elsewhere, rather than returning to live in areas under the control of the individuals who perpetrated crimes against them.

In sum, hard-line politics, international isolation, and the recent history of violence all made Prijedor a very unlikely case for successful peacebuilding. Yet, a decade later, international agencies could highlight the achievements made in the town. They cited the return home of thousands of Bosniac DPs and the election of a moderate administration as the main indicators of success. How was Prijedor transformed into an example of successful international policy? As the rest of this essay illustrates, the role of international agencies in the peacebuilding process was not always positive. Not only did international isolation risk leaving the town with its immediate post-war political leadership and ethnic composition, but the post-settlement policy of repatriating Bosnian refugees from European states exasperated inter-ethnic tensions and risked endangering the peace process and further reinforcing ethnic divisions, as the next section will show.

Forced Repatriation and the Risk of a New War

After the signing of the DPA, some European states offered permanent residence to about 100,000 Bosnians who were accepted during the war. But most states were concerned about the welfare costs of maintaining a sizeable refugee population, and desired to avoid turning 'temporary protection' (accorded to Bosnian refugees during the war) into a tool for permanent immigration.

By early 1996, Germany (which had hosted more than 500,000 Bosnian refugees) began placing considerable pressure on the UNHCR to devise a repatriation plan. The plan foresaw the lifting of the temporary protection clause and the return of refugees on the basis of the fulfilment of specific benchmarks, including the implementation of the military provisions of the DPA, the proclamation of an amnesty for crimes other than serious violations of international humanitarian law, and the establishment and effective functioning of mechanisms for human rights protection.[22] Between 1996 and 1998, about 150,000 refugees were repatriated. Many human rights organizations protested against this policy, believing that at least the third benchmark, the presence of 'mechanisms for human rights protection', had not been fulfilled.[23]

The repatriation of Bosnian refugees further contributed to the ethnic homogenization of the country (see Daniela Heimerl, this volume). In an effort to increase their electoral support, nationalist politicians in Bosnian municipalities encouraged individuals from their own ethnic group to join their towns and resisted the return of individuals of other ethnic backgrounds. As a result, it is estimated that at least 100,000 people, for the most part Bosniacs originally from the territory of the RS, went to join their own ethnic group. Most of them deeply resented being prevented from exercising their right to return. Their living conditions made them vulnerable to nationalist manipulation and, faced with a future of misery and rootlessness, they constituted a real threat to the peace process. Amnesty International perceptively warned that: 'as long as territories within BiH remain ethnically exclusive the region will remain unstable, since victims of the war who were forcibly expelled from their homes, are likely to dwell upon that injustice'.[24]

Many thousands of those repatriated individuals settled in Sanski Most. The city mayor welcomed the returnees in order to consolidate his own political power as well as the military victory – taking the town from the Bosnian Serbs at the end of the war. By mid-1997, about 40,000 displaced Bosniacs had moved into Sanski Most, raising the total population to the pre-war level of 61,000. Hosted in poor living conditions, these DPs constituted a menacing presence just across the IEBL, many of them only a few miles away from their town of origin– Prijedor. A journalist described them, at the time, in these terms: 'These people are disenfranchised, unemployed and miserable. Many of them want to return home, support themselves, and not spend the next couple of generations as a new Bosnian underclass.'[25]

International authorities did little to facilitate their return home. The High Representative believed that minority return, at that time, would be politically de-stabilizing. At the same time, international agencies were reluctant to permanently relocate Bosniac DPs because of the concern that this would legitimate wartime ethnic cleansing. As a result, the proclamation of the right of return home, combined with the lack of enforcement and the international resistance to relocation, produced the worst possible outcome: it undermined the DPA's goal of reversing ethnic cleansing, while leaving many Bosnians in an indeterminate and potentially unsustainable state of internal displacement.

Change of Policy and the Return Home

Faced with a critical mass of individuals possibly ready to retake by force what was denied to them, international agencies refocused on the problem of internal displacement and the need to facilitate minority return. They took two initiatives. First, in May 1997 the Peace Implementation Council (a collective body tasked to provide supervision and direction to international agencies operating on the ground) met at Sintra, Portugal, and endorsed a more vigorous approach in the implementation of the DPA. Second, international agencies declared 1998 as the 'Year of Return', underlining the fact that return was a dangerously ignored provision of the DPA. The UNHCR hoped that more than 50,000 people would go back to their pre-war communities by the end of that year. Because of the US-embargo, Prijedor could not be included in the newly devised 'open cities' programme. Yet, despite international isolation and Bosnian Serb resistance, returns occurred in considerable number to the Prijedor region, while they remained sluggish in most other Bosnian localities.

Failed Early Efforts and NATO Activism

Early efforts to return to Prijedor proved dangerous. In the spring of 1996, Drljaca announced that not one person would be allowed to return. Mayor and SDS hard-liner Milomir Stakić explained that: 'A visit by seven or eight buses, four hundred people, a third of whom are extremists whose names alone irritate the citizens…would lead to an incident.'[26] As predicted (or perhaps planned), in May 1996 a busload of Bosniac women trying to return to Prijedor was stoned.[27] In October, the UNHCR gave Prijedor police the list of Bosniac DPs who were planning to visit their houses in Hambarine. The following day, arsonists destroyed 96 houses, all of them owned by the DPs whose names where on the list. As a UNHCR official concluded: 'Given the organization required for such systematic destruction, it was inconceivable that the Prijedor authorities had not been involved or known in advance.'[28]

   In mid-1997, following the PIC meeting at Sintra, a more assertive international military presence paved the way for important changes. Operation *Tango* was NATO's first post-Dayton coercive intervention. On 11 July 1997, British troops attempted to capture Milan Kovacević and Simo Drljaca, both named by the International Criminal Tribunal for the former Yugoslavia (ICTY) in a sealed indictment. Kovacević was arrested and immediately transferred to The Hague. Drljaca engaged in a shootout with British troops and was killed. NATO's actions were applauded by several human rights organizations, including Human Rights Watch, which had previously released a damning report on war criminals in the Prijedor region.[29]

   The July 1997 arrest of an indicted war criminal and the killing of another, in addition to the removal of police officers involved in wartime atrocities, had a profound impact. Following NATO's overdue activism, mayor Milomir Stakić (fearing that the ICTY had issued a secret indictment for his own arrest) went 'on permanent vacation'.[30] Instead of the feared backlash against international peacekeepers, important political changes at the municipal level paved the way for a breakthrough. SDS member Borislav Marić became the new mayor. Marić endorsed the idea of accepting Bosniac returns, albeit gradually. In the summer of 1999 he called for restraint when a Bosniac returnee to Kožarac shot two Serbs at a coffee bar. His moderate stance enjoyed broad support among the Bosnian Serb political elite. Several politicians even switched allegiance from the SDS to the more moderate leadership of Biljana Plavsić (and later that of Milorad Dodik).[31] From this time onward, hardliners were no longer capable of generating broad support for a campaign of intimidation against potential Bosniac returnees.[32]

The Return Process

These changes gave many Bosniac DPs a sufficient sense of security to seriously consider returning home. They began to return on a 'spontaneous' basis, that is, one made possible by the determination of the DPs themselves, rather than the international agencies' planning and direction.[33] Starting in the spring of 1998, the Prijedor area became the first site for significant Bosniac return to the RS – at a time when internationally sponsored return schemes (such as the 'Open Cities' programme) failed to produce concrete results.

On 18 May 1998, the Prijedor municipality selected Kožarac as the first area where return could begin. The choice was facilitated by an agreement between Bosnian Serb DPs in Prijedor and Bosniac DPs in Sanski Most, who decided to lobby their respective authorities on the basis of return based on reciprocity.[34] DP associations, often acting against the advice of international agencies, made initial assessment visits, provided information to potential donors, and reassured potential returnees about the safety of return. One of the best examples of this grassroots, bottom-up organizing was the women's group *Srcem do Mira* [Through Heart to Peace], which since 1993 held annual conferences bringing together the parties involved in the return process. In 1998, when return was tentatively beginning, the UNHCR did not even put in an appearance at the conference, an unmistakable sign of the lack of interest among international agencies for local initiatives.[35] Instead, the main Bosniac nationalist party, the Party for Democratic Action (SDA), provided construction material in the effort to capitalize politically from the homecoming.

In July 1998, 200 Bosniac DPs conducted an assessment visit to Kožarac, and many returnees slept in improvised tents to put pressure on international agencies to support their return plans. By the summer of 1999, some 90 families had returned to Kožarac and the number rose to 200 the following year. In August 2000, the town became the site of the first mosque to be rebuilt in the RS without incident. Eventually, more than 10,000 Bosniacs (about half of the pre-war population) returned to the town.[36] A few returns occurred to Prijedor itself; Muharem Murselović was the first Bosniac to return to the town centre, where he re-opened a coffee shop in the busy pedestrian area.[37] The return of Murselović, who is recognized by Bosniac DPs as one of the most prominent leaders of their community, contributed to improving the morale and determination of those still in Sanski Most.

International agencies responded to these developments in two ways. First, they blamed the returnees for going back home. According to a UNHCR official, Bosniac DPs and their leaders 'pressed ahead with an agenda of return without consideration of the safety of potential returnees'.[38] The sporadic violence that resulted from return was thus blamed on the returnees, and those who encouraged them to return 'too rapidly', instead of the perpetrators. As Murselović pointed out, this argument was exactly the same one endorsed by Bosnian Serb nationalists to justify the outbreak of violence against returnees.[39] The argument was also compatible with NATO's policy, which preferred to discourage return instead of providing security for the returnees.

Second, eventually the lessons learned in Prijedor convinced international agencies to make important changes to their BiH-wide return strategy. In late 1998, there was a change in the approach of the Reconstruction and Return Task Force (RRTF). This coordinating body – which included all major agencies involved in the return process – identified strategic axes of likely return movements based on the interest of the DPs themselves, thus reversing the failing top-down peace-building approach. The RRTF's main innovation was the decision that international activities should follow the flow of DPs, instead of requiring DPs to follow the flow of international activities. This change was the crucial policy innovation that would finally break BiH's population logjam.

Making Return (almost) Irreversible

The key to making the return process a sustainable and potentially irreversible reality was securing individual property rights. During the war, all three communities tried to solidify their territorial gains by promulgating property laws aimed at accommodating the large numbers of DPs belonging to their respective ethnic groups. At the end of the war, the property regime made minority return practically impossible.[40]

Property repossession became part of international policy only in 1998, when the promulgation of new property laws, first in the Federation and subsequently in the RS, created some legal certainty. In 1999, the High Representative intervened to harmonize these laws in the two entities. He imposed a package of property-related decrees to create a legal framework to ease return and reinforce 'the duty of the authorities at all levels ... to actively implement their [citizens'] rights to their homes and property'.[41] At last, a clear procedure was in place to make it more difficult for local housing officers to ignore requests of repossession and the need to evict illegal occupants. The presence of this framework, which applied in principle to all, regardless of ethnicity or status, was an important step towards establishing the rule of law based not on ethnic affiliation but on universal principles of equity.

The creation of the Property Law Implementation Plan (PLIP) in 2000 gave additional necessary support to the return process. The PLIP replaced the positive conditionality incentives of the 'Open Cities' approach with the principle that the same pressures, demands and expectations must be applied to all officials and municipalities.[42] By linking return to minority issues and group rights, positive conditionality had exacerbated resistance and opposition among the general population. Because the priority given by donors to minority returnees explicitly discriminated against the local majority (who often were as much in need as the returnees), positive conditionality quickly became counter-productive, solidifying war-time ethnic cleavages.

The PLIP required the eviction of families living in someone else's apartment. Implementation initially focused on the cases of 'multiple occupants', defined as individuals able to otherwise meet their housing needs (by dint of income or access to housing elsewhere). These cases were much less controversial than those where temporary occupants could not meet their own housing needs and were therefore entitled to alternative accommodation. Compounding this problem was the housing authorities' discretion over the order of processing eviction cases, inviting both bribery and pressure not to act against politically protected families. As a UNHCR report noted, 'political interference, corruption, and often pure arbitrariness have dictated which claims are processed and when'.[43]

Once again, the experience of Prijedor provided a test case for the rest of the country. In the fall of 2001, Prijedor introduced the principle of 'chronological order', whereby eviction orders would be processed according to the registration of claims.[44] There was no negative public reaction to the evictions. The first four families evicted without alternative accommodation moved in with friends and relatives. As the evictions were enforced, an increasing number of illegal occupants voluntarily turned over the properties they had occupied during the war.[45] On the grounds of this successful test, on 4 December 2001, amendments were imposed on the property laws making chronological processing an explicit legal obligation binding on all housing authorities throughout BiH. Despite some initial resistance and delays, the process of enforcing the property laws soon gained momentum.

By winter 2004, the Prijedor office of the Ministry for Refugees and Displaced persons had resolved 1,628 claims for socially-owned apartments and 6,023 claims for private property and had returned these properties to their pre-war owners or occupants.[46] At the end of April 2004, the PLIP reported that 7,439 cases had been resolved by the municipal authorities in the favour of the claimant, with only 212 refused on the basis of contested property claims. As a whole, Prijedor has an implementation ratio (the number of closed cases divided by the total number of claims) of 97.18 per cent, five points above the national average.[47]

The Political Impact of Return

The return of Bosniac DPs had a moderating impact on Prijedor's political life. In the autumn 1997 local elections, the SDS won a relative majority of votes, obtaining 14 seats out of 65. But the Bosniacs voting *in absentia* elected 24 councillors – 37 per cent of the seats. All political parties participating in the Municipal Assembly signed a power-sharing agreement, stipulating that the post of Speaker should be held by a Bosniac – a decision honoured with the appointment of Murselović. In January 1998, Prijedor was among the first municipalities to be certified by international agencies as having fully implemented the municipal election results. The political representation of Bosniacs in the Municipal Assembly contributed to convincing Bosniac DPs in Sanski Most that return to Prijedor was now a feasible option.

Following the 2000 elections, the percentage of Bosniac seats decreased to 28 per cent (9 out of the 32 seats, reflecting a decrease in the number of Bosniacs voting with absentee ballots). Their vote, however, still helped tip the power balance at the local level, and led to the ousting of the SDS from power, by enabling a coalition of moderate Serb and Bosniac parties to garner a slim majority of seats in the municipal assembly. Nada Sevo, a Serb politician and member of the Party of Independent Social Democrats (one of the three relatively moderate parties that arose from the 1997 split of the SDS),[48] was elected mayor. Sevo obtained 16 votes against the 15 votes of the candidate supported by the SDS, the ultra-nationalist Serb Radical Party (SRS) and the Bosniac nationalist SDA. The local SDS–SDA coalition shows that differences in BiH are political, and not simply ethnic, and involve hard-line nationalist parties vis-à-vis moderate political alternatives.[49]

The ousting of the SDS and the election of Nada Sevo suggests that the political participation of returnees can help marginalize hard-liners and have an overall positive impact towards accommodation and compromise. The active presence of ethnic minorities at the local level increased the need for a pragmatic approach; politicians were compelled to step up and provide solutions to diverse local demands. In 2002, the first elementary school in a Bosniac majority area was opened by a decision of the RS Ministry of Education. Local authorities also took over sensitive return-related responsibilities. Municipal funds – KM (convertible marks) 250,000 in 2001 and KM 350,000 in 2002 – were allocated to implement projects in return areas. As a UNHCR report explains, this new pragmatic stance came 'as a result of both the pressure from the international community and the adoption of more moderate political platforms in order to gain the support of a larger returnee community'.[50] On 16 May 2002, the United States acknowledged the many positive changes achieved and lifted the sanctions on Prijedor, previously imposed by the Lautemberg Amendment.

To be sure, Prijedor did not turn into an oasis of inter-ethnic harmony. Many Bosniac returnees took possession of their houses only to sell them and leave again. Occasional incidents worry Bosniac and Croat minorities alike. With a police force still dominated by Bosnian Serb officers, violence and harassment against returnees is not always prosecuted with the necessary vigour. The lack of employment opportunities is a chronic problem for all Prijedor citizens, and in particular for Bosniac returnees. Furthermore, following the general elections of October 2002, when the three main nationalist parties won control of all the main state-wide political offices, the situation in Prijedor deteriorated. The SDS was able to engineer a political stalemate – out of 34 sessions held by the Municipal Assembly, the Mayor's recall was attempted 32 times.[51] Higher levels of government in the RS supported these local attempts to undermine the Mayor. In late 2003, for example, the RS government unexpectedly 'promoted' Prijedor to the category of a 'developed municipality', thereby slashing revenue returns to the municipal budget by 20 per cent.[52] This occurred in the context of a steep decline in the economy in the municipality and inevitably, the resulting negative impact on the municipality's social service provision, was blamed on the mayor.

The Lessons for Peacebuilding

The dynamics of minority return in the Prijedor region provide insights into how peacebuilding works at the local level. Of the three components of the 'peace-building triangle' – local capacities, international intervention and level of war-related hostilities – the third has proved to be the least consequential. Even though this region witnessed numerous atrocities during the war, Bosniac DPs returned in large numbers to Prijedor and have proceeded to participate fully in the political, social and economic life of the municipality. Despite the presence of many unresolved problems still affecting returnees, return has been indispensable to improving inter-ethnic relations, avoiding the much-feared possibility of DPs turning into a destabilizing force, and even to marginalizing hard-line Bosnian Serb nationalists. The experience of this town suggests at least two lessons for international and local contributions to peace-building.

First, it is worthwhile re-stating the truism that the quality of international intervention is more important than its quantity. International agencies initially provided little of either quantity or quality. They placed Prijedor under international embargo, leaving it in the hands of the Bosnian Serb hardliners. They exacerbated ethnic tensions by repatriating Bosnian refugees from Europe and thus increasing the problem of international displacement and the risk of renewed conflict. And they blamed returnees for their quest to return home. The non-sustainability of this policy convinced international agencies that an alternative approach had to be implemented.

One single action by international forces had far-reaching consequences. The 1997 arrest of one indicted war criminal and the killing of another demonstrated the positive impact of a more active international military presence – this did not lead to a dangerous environment for international peacebuilders and was, in fact, an important factor in securing the implementation of the peace agreement. According to the International Crisis Group: 'The lesson is clear: the removal of suspects indicted for war crimes, who are symbols of impunity and are among the most obstructionist, has a ripple effect that can fundamentally alter the disposition of an area towards DPA implementation.'[53] In the following years, a total of 19 wartime leaders from the Prijedor region were arrested and sent to The Hague. By contrast, few people from eastern BiH have been indicted and arrested, and minority return to that area has been much lower. The capture of Radovan Karadžić, who is thought to be hiding in eastern RS, would, on this basis, probably have a major positive impact on minority return to this region.

Second, at its core the peacebuilding *problematique* is essentially a domestic issue. International agencies can (and should) arrest indicted war criminals – and support local actors struggling to rebuild their communities – but the ultimate success or failure depends on the choices, determination and resilience of Bosnians themselves, as the process of DPs return to Prijedor exemplifies.

In Prijedor, refugee groups themselves pushed the agenda of return in the face of international community resistance and in returning made a vital contribution to the transformation of the town and the marginalization of the main nationalist parties (Serb and Bosniac alike), eventually pushing them into opposition. Ultimately, the main lesson of Prijedor is that peacebuilding is a political process that needs the support and participation of people on the ground to turn international policy declarations into achievable ends. It is only when the people become the subjects – rather than objects – of policy-making that the peacebuilding process becomes sustainable in the long-term.

ACKNOWLEDGEMENTS

I would like to express my thanks to David Chandler and Arnaud Vaulerin for comments on a previous draft.

NOTES

1. C. Manning, 'Local Level Challenges to Post-Conflict Peacebuilding', *International Peacekeeping*, Vol.10, No.3, (2003), p.36.
2. Human Rights Watch/Helsinki Report, *The Unindicted: Reaping the Rewards of Ethnic Cleansing*, New York: HRW, Jan. 1997, Vol.9, No.1, Section 1, n.16 (citing Pulitzer Prize winner Roy Gutman), at www.hrw.org/reports/1997/bosnia/.
3. International Crisis Group, *The Continuing Challenge of Minority Return in Bosnia and Herzegovina*, Balkans Report No.137, 13 Dec. 2002, p.25, at www.icg.org/home/index.cfm?id=1473&l=1.
4. Human Rights Watch (n.2 above), Section 1.
5. I. Wesselingh and A. Valeurin, *Bosnie, La Mémoire à vif: Prijedor, laboratoire de la purification ethnique*, Paris: Buchet/Chastel, 2003, pp.63–80.
6. Human Rights Watch (n.2 above), Section 1.
7. R. Holbrooke, *To End a War*, New York: Random House, 1999, pp.160, 166, 172, 193.
8. General Dudakovic confirmed this circumstance to researcher Fotini Christa who interviewed him in July 2004. Author's personal communication with Fotini Christa, Aug. 2004.
9. S. Bose, *Bosnia After Dayton: International Intervention and Nationalist Partition*, Oxford: Oxford University Press, 2002, p.60.
10. During the war 'Bosniac' replaced 'Muslim' as an ethnic term, in part to avoid confusion with the religious term Muslim – an adherent of Islam.
11. C. Bildt, *Peace Journey: The Struggle for Peace in Bosnia*, London: Weidenfeld & Nicolson, 1998, p.140.
12. See, for example, R. Paris, *At War's End: Building Peace after Civil Conflict*, Cambridge: Cambridge University Press, 2004.
13. M.W. Doyle and N. Sambanis, 'International Peacebuilding: A Theoretical and Quantitative Analysis', *American Political Science Review*, Vol.94, No.4, 2000, pp.779–801.
14. E. Neuffer, *The Keys to My Neighbor's House: Seeking Justice in Bosnia and Rwanda*, New York: Picador, 2002, p.187.
15. Human Rights Watch (n.2 above), Section 5, §7: 'Obstruction of Freedom of Movement by Prijedor Authorities'.
16. Ibid., Section 5, especially §8: 'Elections'.
17. In October 1996, an American journalist identified four indicted war criminals in the police force, see Neuffer (n.14 above), p.186.
18. Doyle and Sambanis (n.13 above).
19. Human Rights Watch (n.2 above), section 7.
20. M. Marcus, 'Reconstruction in Bosnia: International Aid and Non-Compliance with Dayton Agreements', *Helsinki Monitor*, Vol.8, No.2, 1997.
21. The expression 'minority return' refers to return to an area where one's own national group is not demographically predominant. However, it should be pointed out that Bosniacs, Bosnian Croats and Bosnian Serbs are not legally 'minorities' but 'constituent peoples' of the state of BiH.

22. S. Bagshaw, 'Benchmarks or Deutchmarks? Determining the Criteria for the Repatriation of Refugees to Bosnia and Herzegovina', *International Journal of Refugee Law*, Vol.9, No.4, 1997, pp.566–92.
23. See, for example, the open letter Physicians for Human Rights wrote to the interior ministers of Germany's sixteen federal states; 4 June 1999. Copy on file with the author.
24. Amnesty International, *Bosnia-Herzegovina: All the Way Home: Safe 'Minority Returns' as a Just Remedy and for a Secure Future*, 1 Feb. 1998, at http://web.amnesty.org/library/Index/ENGEUR630021998?open&of = ENG-BIH. See also Z. Zlokapa, 'A Human Bomb', *99: Review of Free Thought*, No.7–8, April–June 1997, pp.7–10.
25. P. Lippman, *The Advocacy Project: OTR Bosnia*, Vol.7, No.2, 12 May 1999, at http://advocacynet.autoupdate.com.
26. PBS Interview, 'Sadako Ogata – UN High Commissioner for Refugees', 20 May 1996. Transcript at www.pbs.org/newshour/bb/bosnia/ogata_5-20.html.
27. K.R. Roane, 'Muslim Visitors Called Mortal Dangers by Serbs', *New York Times*, 28 May 1996.
28. A. Ito, 'Return to Prijedor: Politics and UNHCR', *Forced Migration Review*, Vol.10, 2001, p.36.
29. Wesselingh and Vaulerin (n.5 above), p.114.
30. This is what the municipality's staff communicated to international officials asking to meet him. Interview with Massimo Moratti, OSCE Human Rights Officer, Sarajevo, July 2003. Stakić was arrested in early 2001 in Belgrade and sent to The Hague to stand trial. In September 2003, he was convicted of crimes against humanity, crimes against the laws and customs of war, and murder. He was sentenced to life imprisonment.
31. N. Caspersen, 'Intra-ethnic Challenges to Nationalist Parties: SDS and Serb Opposition Before, During, and After the War,' paper presented to the 7th international seminar 'Democracy and Human Rights in Multiethnic Societies,' Konjic, Bosnia, 12–17 July, 2004.
32. Interview with Massimo Moratti, OSCE Human Rights Officer, July 2003.
33. As the International Crisis Group (n.3 above) point out, the term 'spontaneous return' does not reflect the considerable amount of organized work by DP associations that preceded return. There is little or nothing 'spontaneous' about the work of DP associations, whether lobbying local and international authorities, participating in municipal elections, or repairing destroyed houses.
34. While this agreement facilitated the return process, it was questionable in human rights terms. The agreement created an unjustifiable market for human rights, suggesting that one person's right can be defended in exchange for someone else's.
35. Interview with Emsuda Mujagić, president of Screm do Mira, Kožarac, July 2004.
36. The process of return was recorded, step by step, by the Advocacy Project (n.20 above).
37. C. Schaffer-Duffy, 'A Tenuous, Dramatic Homecoming', *National Catholic Reporter*, 18 June 1999.
38. Ito (n.28 above), p.35.
39. Interview with Muharem Murselović, Prijedor, July 2004.
40. T.W. Waters, 'The Naked Land: The Dayton Accord, Property Disputes, and Bosnia's Real Constitution', *Harvard International Law Journal*, Vol.40, No.2, 1999, pp.517–93.
41. Office of the High Representative, *A Comprehensive Strategy for a Just and Efficient Return Process in Bosnia-Herzegovina*, Sarajevo, 27 Oct. 1999.
42. Wolfgang Petritsch, *Bosna I Hercegovina od Daytona do Evrope*, Sarajevo: Svjetlost, 2002, pp.144–50.
43. UNHCR, *Prijedor: Municipality Background Report*, Banja Luka: UNHCR, 2002, p.4.
44. Ibid., p.12.
45. Interview with Jose Luis Martinez Llopis, OSCE Head of Office, Prijedor, July 2002.
46. Interview with Jeff Ford, OSCE Human Rights Officers, Prijedor, July 2004.
47. Property Law Implementation Plan, *Statistics: Implementation of the Property Laws in Bosnia & Herzegovina*, Sarajevo: PLIP, 30 April 2004.
48. See Caspersen (n.31 above).
49. UNDP, *Rights-Based Municipal Assessment and Planning Project: Municipality of Prijedor*, Sarajevo, 2004, p.28.
50. UNHCR (n.43 above), p.12.
51. UNDP (n.49 above), p.20.
52. Ibid., p.24.
53. International Crisis Group, *The Konjic Conundrum: Why Minorities Have Failed to Return to Model Open City*, Balkans Report, No.35, 19 July 1998, p.39, accessed at www.icg.org/home/index.cfm?id=1510&l=5.

Transformation in the Political Economy
of Bosnia since Dayton

MICHAEL PUGH

This essay focuses on the political economy of Bosnia and Herzegovina (BiH) in the post-Dayton period. It is concerned first with the crisis of 'public squalor and private affluence' (in the phrase popularized by J.K. Galbraith),[1] occasioned by the diminishing public realm through the privatization of public enterprises. Second, it is concerned with the extent to which shadow economies are criminalized, while externally-imposed and socially stressful policies are legitimized. The presentation of both aspects here are influenced by Zygmunt Bauman's critical theory of capitalist modernization in *Liquid Modernity* (2000).[2] BiH can be characterized as 'un-modern'. While the shapes of class, territory and social order have evidently changed since 1992, identity groups remain highly configured. Individuals have not been freed from collective constraints, social norms or society itself.[3] Indeed, collective restraints and social norms have been re-defined in national terms as protection of, and justice for, the social group, contributing to the diminution of the state's role in determining a just society. Peacebuilding in BiH appears to conform to characteristics of Bauman's thesis in at least one significant respect, the diminution and changing functions of public space. This has been achieved not only by domestic anti-statism, but also by external direction, contradicting Bauman's contention that global power elites are disinterested in administration and civilizing missions, which they supposedly avoid as 'costly and ineffective'.[4]

The analysis here also has affinity with theories of capitalist modernity and its relation to warfare as developed by researchers associated with the Research Centre for War, Armament and Development, University of Hamburg, and the

'Micropolitics of Armed Groups' at the Humboldt University, Berlin.[5] Their research is grounded in analysis of historical social, political and economic processes, including the interactions between social orders and the economic structures within war-prone societies. Relevant to BiH are the findings that violence in areas of former socialist governance is generally a consequence of systemic failures and highly differentiated and attenuated modernization – and is accompanied by a reassertion of neo-patrimonial political economies.[6] The significance for this study is that post-conflict peacebuilding under external guidance that addresses only economic symptoms of social unrest, such as corruption and crime, overlooks the functionalism of clientistic networks for economic survival and social cohesion.[7]

Squeezing Public Space

Public space can be defined as an arena for civil society, configured and set aside by the state, in which citizens organize themselves collectively for the common good.[8] This presupposes a distinction between state and civil society – though the latter was often state subsidized and furnished with social ownership and legal guarantees of free association. A broader definition allows that, through social provision, common ownership and direction of economic enterprises, states themselves – notably states with socialist-oriented governments – can also claim to be providing public goods and protecting public space. Whether defined as the civil society space between state and individual, or as a socio-economic function to provide public goods (as distinct from private accumulation), public space in many societies has been increasingly squeezed by monetarism, privatization and limitation of the state's economic role. Even the apparatus of state security is increasingly privatized.[9] Although presented as a 'golden rule' of economic development, this agenda is hotly debated by Massimo Florio, Joseph Stiglitz and others. They argue that the agenda has less to do with economic rationalism than political ideology and the reflection and maintenance of a particular structure of global power.[10]

In liquid modernity, economic power is no longer exerted from a territorial base or from the commanding heights of a national economy, and this has an impact on political participation. As Robert Cox notes, politics is about depoliticizing people, by removing the economic determinants of everyday conditions from political control. Politics becomes irrelevant: 'The sense of civic efficacy is removed; and many people, the most disadvantaged, are left in the futility of alienation.'[11] In BiH the meaningful function of formal politics, to protect group interests from other groups, produced high levels of participation and voter turn-out in early election contests. But depoliticization and low turn-out (see Richard Caplan, this volume) lates occurred, not simply because economic reforms are removing a key interest in participation, but because the population has not been re-politicized in the sense of controlling formal 'state' politics – as a consequence of external governance.

It may transpire that external actors *are* rapidly losing their appetite for civilizing subordinate populations – as a consequence of experience in southeast

Europe and other unruly contexts. A much 'lighter touch' by peacebuilders was evident in Afghanistan than in BiH and Kosovo, and Iraq's invaders can be said to have attempted to exert control through centralized indirect rule. Moreover, the urge to engineer is often doomed to disappointment because the security situation is too risky, the market small or the business context alien. Nevertheless, in BiH society has been vulnerable to raids on the public sphere from intervenors equipped with a neoliberal agenda of political economy as part of a civilizing mission to introduce a 'liberal peace' to war-torn societies (see Dominik Zaum, this volume).[12]

The legacy of conflict seems to provide a blank canvas on which external actors can introduce a doxa (in Bourdieu's sense of beliefs and practices elevated into such a status that they cannot be called into question). State budgets have typically been plundered by local actors during civil war, and the regulation of finance and economic exchange is weak or non-existent. New incentives have been created to enrich the individual and impoverish the collective. Collective assets, social property, public utilities, government factories, infrastructures and lootable resources are targets which emerge depleted or destroyed. Ruling elites are disoriented, captured or catapulted into office to continue their wartime exploitation. Yet such an apparently barren canvass seems to have an extraordinary attraction for war entrepreneurs, international administrators and foreign carpetbaggers.[13]

Paradoxically, then, the determination of external agencies (notably the OHR, USAID, the IMF and World Bank) to engineer BiH into peace and the good life has produced a sludge rather than liquid modernity. The people of BiH stand accused of resisting the modern condition, clinging to primordial identities, political clientism and forms of economic exchange that brought them into contention with globalization and structural adjustment, as well as with each other.[14] The transformation of the political economy of public space has been a purposeful strategy of territorial administration and social management by missionaries from outside. The strategy has not been completely effective, far from it in terms of privatizing socially-owned property and public enterprises. But such transformation that has occurred for reducing public space and public goods has been in partnership with, or connived at, by war entrepreneurs and local power brokers in a coincidence of interest.

Coincidence of Interest in Privatizing Public Assets

In each of the Croat and Bosniak areas of the Federation and the Serb-controlled Republika Srpska, the organizations that took BiH into war adapted to peace through appropriation of local resources. The embedded networks, such as the Herceg militias controlled by soldiers and nationalists in Zagreb and Mostar, survived the Dayton accords until Franjo Tudjman left office. The ruling nationalist parties also extended a post-war amnesty for deserters to include 'economic crimes' committed from the start of 1991 to the end of 1995, including the misuse of humanitarian aid. This immunized those politicians and wartime commanders who were otherwise vulnerable to investigation.[15] It enabled thousands of others to safeguard their wartime gains and to consolidate their economic control. Tele-communications (including broadcasting) and energy (electricity and gas) were divided along ethno-party lines to provide major sources of revenue for the nationalist parties and their parallel structures.[16] Command and influence in the peacetime political economy could then be exerted on the public space through clientalism, rentier fraud, corporatism and capture of privatization processes.

A glaring example of crony capitalism concerns the giant Mostar aluminium plant. In 1996 the Democratic Croat Union (Hrvatska Demokratske Zajednica – HDZ) took over management of Aluminij Mostar with a board led by Mijo Brajković. Although the plant suffered little war damage the management had it valued at US$84 million, compared to its prewar value of US$620 million. Its exports in the first year of revival exceeded its valuation by US$1 million. Brajković 'privatized' it through a co-capitalization process, the majority of shares going to the Croat workers and management. A team of international auditors found that illegalities had occurred, but 'for political and practical reasons' recommended that the ownership structure should remain undisturbed. The Bosniak-dominated Federation government subsequently sought to re-privatize it.[17]

Although resistant to legalized privatization and the spirit of transparency promoted by the Office of the High Representative (OHR), from 1998 onwards elites sought to gain control of privatization so that they could take advantage of donor funds that were conditional on withdrawing the state from the economy.[18] Mechanisms to distribute public assets, through voucher schemes for example, were complex and vulnerable to corruption.[19] The banking sector was particularly ripe for plucking, partly because the international financial institutions and donors first privatized the sector (through cash investments, not vouchers) and then exerted pressure to reduce the burgeoning number of private banks. Jadranko Prlić, former Prime Minister of wartime Herceg-Bosna and Mostar tycoon, had an empire estimated at US$1.3 billion and acquired a holding in Hrvatska Postanka Banka at a remarkably low price.[20] Privredna Banka Sarajevo, a respected pre-war financial institution, was privatized via an offshore company in the Cayman Islands in 2004. Its true owners were a mystery, and neither the FBiH Privatization Agency nor the FBiH Banking Agency could (or would) throw light on the matter.[21]

A lack of industrial investment going back decades, the wartime loss of markets and a dislocated labour pool meant that many former public enterprises were already bankrupt. Complemetary privatization strategies of the inter-national agencies and the nationalist appropriators in BiH underpinned bank-ruptcy. International donors withheld support for public enterprises, and new nationalist managements engaged in asset stripping and undervaluing enterprises for sale. In RS, the Kristal Bank was sold for one euro to forestall liquidation by the Mladen Ivanić government without any attempt to estimate its value.[22] And the indebted Banja Luka dairy was under threat of closure in a privatization process that would have left the city without milk.[23]

By 2004 the Federation government seemed caught between accelerating bankruptcies to write off losses and decelerating the resale of enterprises to

protect the 'new elite', which, as Edhem Biber, president of the BiH Independent
Syndicates' Union, suggested, had 'gained plenty of property, created by workers',
for little outlay through share offers and the pre-war Marković privatization.[24] In
January 2005 the Federation Prime Minister, Ahmet Hadzipasić, announced that
privatization of key companies (Energopetrol, Energoinvest, Agrokomerc, KTK
Visoko, Hidrogradnja, and the Mostar Tobacco Factory, for example) would
be delayed, claiming that it was first necessary to improve the conditions for privatization.[25] Hadzipasić maintained that the time was not right, there needed to
be 'restructuring of mines and modernisation of thermal-energy capacities ...
investments in the telecommunication sector, solving of property-related
issues. ... I think the state is not mature enough to go into the privatisation in
these sectors in the next two to three years.'[26] Paradoxically, the delay to some
privatizations brought workers out on strike, for example at the Kamengrad
coal mine near Sanski Most and the Tesanj UNICOFILTER company, because
they had not received pay for months.[27] By contrast a privatized Tuzla iron-
casting plant ceased production because of its debts, leaving 180 workers who
claiming back-pay and pension fund contributions, and resulting in the canton
had to revoke the privatization contract.[28]

Indeed the progress of legislation to facilitate bankruptcy proceedings and to
curb the money laundering, bribery and sleaze of privatization was marked by
inadequate provision for the workers who were adversely affected by the
process. The Federation government estimated that 10,000 workers would lose
their jobs as a consequence of acclerated privatization and restructuring, but
amendment of the bankruptcy law supposedly required trade union participation
in planning social care for redundant workers of enterprises with a minimum of
51 per cent of state capital. Biber objected that the necessary funds for social protection were lacking, and when parliament amended the law in March 2004,
miners staged a mass protest at the parliament building and Biber pledged to
sue the government.[29]

It was from rather different perspectives, then, that a consensus about the
shambles had emerged by 2004 between proponents of privatization, politicians
who had failed to line their pockets, workers whose jobs were threatened and
non-nationalist elements in civil society. Donald Hays, the American Principal
Deputy OHR in charge of economic transformation, and an unabashed zealot
for privatization, announced that another name for it in BiH was 'theft', for
which he blamed government authorities.[30] The RS Prime Minister, Dragan
Mikerević, bemoaned the slowness in implementing privatization, for which he
blamed the international community.[31] Biber, asserted that: 'the principles of
theft, corruption and immoral[ity]' had characterized the process.[32] The Sarajevo
civil society group, Circle 99, concluded that privatization was a 'dogma' that had
destroyed BiH companies, the economist Dragoljub Stojanov arguing that: 'the
only thing privatization made possible was robbery.'[33]

The coincidence of anti-statist interests between an OHR obsessed with
squeezing public economic space as a key to developing the liberal peace, and
nationalist management elites anxious to hold on to the public space they had
captured for private gain, diverged only in the methods by which the general

population would be marginalized and workers excluded community leaders engaging in varieties of blatant discrimination. It was more mired, than liquid, modernity.

Poverty and Growth

Capturing and selling public assets for private profit had been determined by the external agencies as a key to economic growth, with the specific intention of attracting foreign direct investment (FDI). But economic recovery was occurring too slowly to reach the 1991 level before 2010, and had failed to reduce poverty. Ten years after Dayton GDP per capita in BiH was only 50 per cent of the average for southeast Europe and still less than 50 per cent of its pre-war level (the official pre-war level being understated because it was accounting practice to exclude the service sector). The real average annual growth rate fell markedly: from 10 per cent in 1999, reaching a low of 3.5 per cent in 2003, before recovering to an estimated 5 per cent in 2004–05 (see Table 1). Hopes for export-led growth were stalled by a trade deficit equivalent to 36 per cent of GDP in 2003. The fiscal deficit improved, but deficit financing was ruled out for

TABLE 1:
BiH ECONOMIC AND FINANCIAL INDICATORS

Indicators	1990	1999	2000	2001	2002	2003	2004*	2005*
GDP ($US m.)	10,633**	4,540	4,252	4,795	5,610	–	–	–
GDP per cap., current prices ($US)								
BiH	2,429**	1,135	1,093	1,222	–	–	–	–
FBiH	–	1,458	1,373	1,453	–	–	–	–
RS	–	821	806	873	–	–	–	–
Real GDP growth % (i.e. allowing for inflation but not shadow activity)								
BiH	–	9.9	5.5	4.4	5.5	3.5	5.0	5.5
FBiH	–	9.5	7.0	7.0	–	–	–	–
RS	–	11.3	2.6	1.9	–	–	–	–
Industrial output								
FBiH	–	11.0	8.8	12.2	9.2	4.8	14.0	7.0
RS	–	2.0	5.3	-12.9	-2.5	5.8	8.0	6.0
Consumer prices yearly average % change								
FBiH	–	-1.0	1.4	2.1	1.0	0.6	0.2	1.8
RS	–	14.0	14.0	7.0	1.7	1.9	2.2	2.2
Budget Balance (% of GDP)	–	–	-7.0	-3.3	-2.2	0.4	-0.1	0.0
Recorded unemployment (% labour force)								
BiH	–	–	–	–	40.9	42.0	–	–
FBiH	–	–	38.9	39.9	42.7	44.0	–	–
RS	–	–	40.2	38.5	36.5	37.0	–	–

Notes:
*Forecast.
**Service sector was excluded in Yugoslav GDP accounts.
Sources: Dragoljub Stojanov, 'Poverty Reduction Strategy Paper', forum for Albania, BiH and FR Yugoslavia, Policy Notes, November 2002; European Commission, *European Economy: The Western Balkans in Transition*, Occasional Paper no.1, DGA Economic and Financial Affairs, Brussels, January 2003; Bank Austria Creditanstalt, *CEE Report*, 4, 2004.

BiH, both ideologically and because there is limited ability to attract FDI and to borrow from abroad.

Receipts from privatization have been temporary, irregular and low (partly because asset stripping reduces the market value). In 2002, privatization in BiH yielded receipts amounting to only 1.3 per cent of GDP, and in 2003 the Federation Privatization Agency recorded a deficit of 2.3 KM, partly because it failed to attract buyers for companies and partly because procedures were not completed in a satisfactory way.[34] Only 50 contracts were made with foreign buyers, and although net inflow doubled between 2001 and 2002, the total stock of FDI had reached only 16 per cent of GDP, half the level in Croatia (see Table 2).[35] Most of it came from other parts of former Yugoslavia, Austria, Germany and Kuwait. The country's *Strategy for Economic Development* (the poverty reduction paper) of May 2004 aimed to attract US$2 billion in FDI and $1.5 in donor grants by the end of 2007.[36]

Even if this could be achieved, studies of reliance on and privatization to stimulate economic growth suggest that productivity does not increase and benefits are heavily skewed towards entrepreneurs who take control of public enterprises.[37] FDI appears to make little impact on growth, varying according to the level of repatriated profits, but it increases the risk of instability in production and consumption because of the volatility of external investment. Moreover, economic deregulation and withdrawal of the state from the economy to tempt FDI contradicts the requirement for strong institutions of public authority to establish a social contract between society and the new state.

The dynamics of political economy that concern foreign investors, administrators and international financial institutions are: financial stringency to pay back loans, market penetration, cheap labour and cheap exports. Monetarism brought inflation down to below 1 per cent by 2002, but in a depleted land this was virtually a contribution to stagnation. The high cost of borrowing (over 10 per cent for business and individuals in 2002) has also smothered opportunities for growth. In addition, the effort accorded to attracting private sector investment has been inversely proportional to the attention paid to measures that

TABLE 2:
SOUTH-EAST EUROPE INFLOWS OF FOREIGN DIRECT INVESTMENT (€ MILLION)

	BiH	Croatia	Slovenia	Serbia & Mont.	Macedonia
2005*	320				
2004*	310				
2003	340				
2002	275	750**	390**	300**	75**
2001	133	470	385	200	350
2000	158	827	110	25	169
1999	90	1,445	144	112	27
Population	3.8m	4.5m	2m	11.4m	2m
FDI (€ per cap. in 2002)	230	1,900	2,600	200	500

Notes: *Forecast. **Approximate.
Source: Bank Austria Creditanstalt, *CEE Report*, 4, 2004 (at www.ba-ca.com).

might reduce the adverse social impacts of neoliberal policies. Poverty and unemployment, industrial and trade policy have been either neglected or treated as a kind of unavoidable collateral damage in the mission to make BiH profitable for investors. Poverty levels, income generation, employment opportunities, the cost of borrowing, social protection and the functionality of shadow economies do not figure highly, if at all. The World Bank and OHR could only wonder at the mystery of the demand for KM and invisible capital inflows apparently greater than annual FDI.[38] This 'excess liquidity' in the economy clearly reflected a high dependence on cash transactions to facilitate services and exchange that would evade auditing. In this respect, the shadow economy as well as the high proportion of government spending (20–30 per cent on welfare), although distorting in its budgetary impact, has been a cushion against even worse distress.

Dilemmas of Survival

Measurement of poverty and living standards is notoriously difficult, especially in BiH where data are unreliable. A living standards survey conducted in 2001 indicated that 16 per cent of the population in the Federation and 25 per cent in RS were living below the poverty line. A further 30 per cent were only just above the line and vulnerable to falling below it, and displaced persons in collective centres (who are among the poorest) were excluded from the survey.[39] The UNDP's 'early warning survey' for the spring of 2002 suggested that poverty was widespread, serious, and rising. Some 40–49 per cent in the Federation and 67–68 per cent in RS had insufficient income to cover a basic basket of consumer goods.[40] One might reasonably surmise that the shadow labour market was acting as a survival mechanism to enable people to exist at, or just above, the general poverty level.

In response to various developmental crises, the IFIs signalled general reforms to mitigate the harmful impacts of economic liberalization. In May 2000, the World Bank's Country Assistance Strategy for BiH included strengthening the social safety net. The Bank approved a US$14.6 million credit, repayable over 35 years, for educational development and welfare policies for the most vulnerable.[41] However, this represented only about a third of the sum committed to merely managing the privatization process.

Modification, rather than a fundamental questioning of structural adjustment, characterized the adoption of a poverty reduction strategy paper (PRSP) in 2004. Supposedly driven by local conditions and requirements, and directed by local political 'stakeholders', PRSPs are typically drafted with rigid budgetary and other macroeconomic rules by the 'distant but omnipresent' World Bank.[42] There is little room for negotiation by local political elites. As such, the BiH Development/Poverty Reduction Strategy portrayed poverty reduction and employment as ancillary to the absolute necessity of enticing business and investment.[43] The only new aspects of the strategy were designed to reinforce the neoliberal agenda: convergence towards EU integration through the Agreement on Stabilization and Association; integration into the global world economic space by attracting foreign investments; and membership of the WTO. Although there was reference to providing 'appropriate' welfare, health and educational systems, the PRSP contained no indication of the extent to which these sectors would be subject to market principles. Poverty was thoroughly profiled in the main section of the report, but curiously for a poverty reduction strategy, the vision statement mentioned poverty only briefly and contained virtually no employment or industrial policy.

A third of respondents surveyed by the UNDP in the spring of 2002 cited unemployment as their chief concern.[44] But employment creation has not exercised the external agencies unduly. In spite of the OHR's introduction of a 'Jobs and Justice' programme in 2002, the working assumption was that there was excessive labour capacity and that social protection would follow market principles. This rationale peddled blatant dishonesty about the choices available. According to the Economic Reform Agenda agreed by the BiH authorities and instituted by the IMF, the World Bank and the EU: 'Governments cannot create jobs. But they can create the conditions in which private enterprise can thrive and generate growth and with increased employment.'[45] Obviously, governments can and do create jobs, otherwise reforming officials would be out of work themselves.

The official unemployment rate in 2003 was about 42 per cent of the labour force and had been rising by about 1 per cent a year since 1999. However, this figure is misleading because evading the registration and taxation of labour became a major industry in itself. The IFIs assume a much lower rate on the grounds that over half the unemployed work in the shadow economy and that the true rate was 16–20 per cent.[46] Nevertheless, unemployment was still a significant drag on purchasing power and growth, and those officially employed did not necessarily get paid. The majority of the poor were employed people in families with children.[47]

The effort accorded to social protection by the external actors in BiH has also been consistently counteracted by the priorities of neoliberal policy. In this context, shadow markets act as a survival mechanism, enabling people to exist at, or just above, the general poverty level.[48] And this is the main paradox of economic survival in southeast Europe. Policies that add to social stress and reliance on crime are legitimized, while economic survival through shadow economic activity is criminalized. Indeed southeast Europe's political economies seem to have been archived as 'criminal',[49] and regional traffickers and corrupt political leaders have been held responsible by peacebuilding agencies for resistance to economic modernization and integration with the world economy.[50]

There are, evidently, varied representations and forms of shadow economy. As a legal concept, the term 'criminal' signifies behaviour contrary to legislative controls and beyond the rule of law. Economically, it connotes the avoidance of audited revenue payments that would otherwise be available for local authority and government distribution. Politically, it is portrayed as a threat to transparency and accountability, and thus a threat to sustainable democracy. As a social concept, 'crime' indicates moral debasement. Discussions of 'crime' tend to lack a nuanced understanding of its moral variations, its relationship to legitimate activities and the inadvertent role of external policies in its perpetuation. The negative perceptions and representations serve to distance the supposedly virtuous, law-abiding cores of capitalist democracy from phenomena that are categorized as threats to their social well-being. These same cores, and the IFIs, are thereby exonerated from complicity in sustaining the demand for shadow activity.

Economic 'crime' can be deconstructed into at least three varieties of 'shadow economy': organized mafia rackets and trafficking; corruption, fraud and nepotism in business and public life; and the coping or survival shadow economies (including black markets in employment and trade) of the population at large. Moral imperatives demand the elimination of crimes against the person, gang violence and trafficking in women and children. But the reliance of sectors of the population on mafia welfare and petty economic crime is, at least in part, a function of impoverishment and the withdrawal of public safety nets, as well as drawing on traditions of economic organization that resisted the pressures of modern, centralized and audited economic exchange well before the disintegration of Yugoslavia.[51]

The Wider Context

As Simon Chesterman argues, the means used by international civil administrations in war-torn societies are generally inconsistent, irrelevant or inadequate for the ends of human security.[52] They are not, however, inconsistent with the thrust of neo-liberal doctrines which do not place priority on local needs, employment and social protection, since the liberal agenda involves suppression of state-generated growth at the macro-level. On the contrary, in BiH, Kosovo, Afghanistan and Iraq there has been a near paralysis of many public institutions and services.

Also, these war-torn societies have had limited say in the pace and direction of transformation. Contrasts and similarities with the peculiar situation of Kosovo are notable. The Kosovo economy was mapped by the Rambouillet ultimatum of 1999, which dictated its conversion to 'a free market', which was subsequently inscribed in the framework constitution.[53] However, for reasons that probably reflect the history of forcible protection by externals of Albanian interests, of legal and constitutional difficulties in sequestering public ownership, and perhaps also criticism over the impact of neoliberalism in BiH, the EU pillar of the UN Mission in Kosovo prioritized the delivery of public services, institution building, public administration and socially-oriented projects.[54] In Kosovo, therefore, public space was squeezed less vigorously, and social justice was given greater rhetorical weight than in BiH. Experts also consider that processes of privatization in Kosovo, where international administrators have exclusive control over socially- and publically-owned property, were prone to abuse and without safeguards could become a 'de facto money laundering operation'.[55] Indeed, there were concerns that privatization would follow a similar course to BiH.[56]

The social orientation in Kosovo was essentially cosmetic. In spite of faltering growth, declining diaspora remittances and foreign donations, high unemployment and falling purchasing power in 2002–03, the IMF presented its (long-discredited) structural adjustment model of fiscal stringency and deflationary restraints on government expenditure and consumption. IMF advisers welcomed curbs on consumption power and proposed further controls on wages, social welfare, public sector employment and on compensation for workers thrown out of work by privatization.[57] In the last quarter of 2001, an estimated 50 per cent of the Kosovo population lived in poverty and 12 per cent in extreme poverty.[58] In the first quarter of 2003 the unemployment rate was estimated at between 49 and 57 per cent (70 per cent among 16–24 year olds), and about 25 per cent of the population were registered as job seekers.[59] Opinion surveys ranked unemployment and poverty among the greatest problems facing Kosovo.[60] These were not, however, the top priorities of the external agencies.

Like Kosovo, Iraq also had the free market written into its constitution. The post-Saddam political economy may be an extreme example, but it mirrors the neoliberal aggressiveness that has been visited on war-torn societies elsewhere. In October 2003 half a dozen US graduates who could not speak Arabic and had never been to the Middle East took part charge of the Iraqi budget and the awarding of contracts. Of the aid budgeted by Congress – US$18.4 billion – for the period before handing over to the interim government, only 2 per cent had been spent. Yet Halliburton had secured $17 billion worth of contracts (many of them without competitive tender). Of the Iraq Development Fund, based on oil revenues, some $20 billion went missing, and half of it has funded contracts to external agents. The fund was also raided to subsidize furbishment of the US Embassy in Baghdad.[61]

Capitalism is about risk and speculation in the quest for market share. By definition, mistakes and false assumptions about profitability are common. Foreign investors often meet disappointment in their effort to penetrate war-torn markets. But this is not persuasive evidence that a neoliberal agenda has been tempered. Investment failure may be underwritten by government guarantees. Other entrepreneurs make profits: security firms, insurance companies, foreign planners, consultants, experts and administrators.

Conclusion

The political economy of transformation is replete with contradictions, as Bauman notes.[62] The external actors would themselves fail neoliberal tests. The United States and EU subsidize agriculture, steel workers, arms manufacturers and dealers, technological development and the airline industry. The US has a public deficit running into trillions of dollars. No US farmer would tolerate BiH interest rates. The EU and other donors cannot tolerate large public sector wage bills in south-east Europe, but has itself a higher public sector component (at 10.3 per cent of GDP).

In BiH the external agenda of privatization of public space has done little to stimulate growth or suppress and divert shadow economies, and may well increase their grip. The OHR's agenda claims to promote economic growth, but it entails monetarist policies that have a deflationary impact.[63] Privatization has brought benefits to some sectors. In BiH the Zenica metallurgical complex was sold to a foreign company with a contract that guarantees employment protection. But for the most part the process has been a 'slough of despond', and the removal of the state from the economy has reinforced reliance of the poor on the shadow economies. According to Rajko Tomaš, shadow economic activity added about 50 per cent to the economy of the RS in the first three years after Dayton.[64] The external actors claim to be building up state institutions, but deny the state a formative economic role except to facilitate private enterprise. They claim to be protecting individual rights, but deprive the poorest individuals of social protection and public space (or make them pay for it). Dealing with criminality involves greater controls and more policing, but the failure to create jobs forces people to rely on shadow economic exchange.

Investment in public goods, infrastructure, social welfare systems and public employment may be necessary to help redress a situation in which a few individuals flaunt affluence but public facilities are often squalid. No alternatives to the model are entertained. Yet there are plenty of examples of dirigisme, which guided vulnerable societies through difficult times: France, Sweden, Cuba, Asian states (including Vietnam which recovered from war quicker than Cambodia). Such dirigisme entails controls and a degree of authoritarianism every bit as irksome as that employed by the OHR. But a strong and active state role in planning and implementation may be less dysfunctional than the neoliberal model. Expansionist policies to increase employment, income generation and consumption power would wean vulnerable people off illegal activity through investment in public services and social protection. The World Commission on the Social Dimension of Globalization, proposes 'fair market economy' that, at the national level, requires an effective state and a vibrant civil society, with a high priority being the provision of 'decent work'.[65]

In conclusion, the case of BiH since Dayton highlights the reduction of the social and economic spheres. But it has also argued that for BiH this has not been an organic process based in local cultures of political economy, but an aggressive social engineering in which regional war elites have been willing participants in diminishing the public space. As Bauman remarks, it is the job of critical thought 'to bring into light the many obstacles piled on the road to emancipation'.[66] His dimensions of modernity are by no means all evident in BiH. But both the external and local carpetbaggers have created impediments to emancipation in their quest to engineer transformation.

ACKNOWLEDGEMENTS

Research for this paper has benefited from an ESRC research grant (Res: 223-25-0071) and a British Academy travel grant.

NOTES

1. John Kenneth Galbraith, The Affluent Society, Boston, MA: Houghton Mifflin, 1958.
2. Zygmunt Bauman, Liquid Modernity, Cambridge: Polity, 2000.
3. Separation of private and public space is increasingly dissolved. Public goods and public space are often a stage for projecting private relations and emotions, as a kind of salute to individual free expression. Bauman, pp.29, 37.
4. Bauman, p.13.

5. For summaries of the approach and its implementation see: Jens Siegelberg, *Capitalism and War – a Theory of War in World Society*, 1994; Dietrich Jung, Klaus Schlichte and Jens Siegelberg, *Krieg in Weltgesellschaft: strukturgeschichteliche Erklärung kriegerischer Gewalt (1945–2002)*, Wiesbaden: Westdeutscher Verlag, 2003. See also, Jens Siegelberg, *Kapitalismus und Krieg*, Münster & Hamburg, 1994; Dietrich Jung and Klaus Schlichte, 'Why Only Intrastate Wars? Patterns of War and Conflicts after 1945', in Haakan Wiberg and Christoph Scherrer (eds.): *Ethnicity and Intra-State Conflict: Types, Peace Strategies*, Aldershot, 1999, pp.35–51; Klaus Schlichte, *Why states decay. A preliminary assessment*, Working Paper 3/1998, Forschungsstelle Kriege, Universität Hamburg. 'Micropolitics of Armed Groups' led by Klaus Schlichte at the Humboldt University Berlin, at www2.hu-berlin.de/mikropolitik; Münkler, *Die neuen Kriege*, Reinbeck: Rowholt, 2002; Klaus Jürgen Gantzel and Torsten Schwinghammer, *Warfare Since the Second World War*, New Brunswick, NJ: Transaction, 2000.
6. See, Burkhard Conrad and Klaus Schlichte, 'The Hamburg Experience, or Quantitative Research: four limits and one alternative', paper at conference on conflict data, Uppsala, 8–9 June 2001.
7. Berit Bliesmann de Guevara, 'External State Building in Bosnia and Herzegovina – A Boost for the (Re)Institutionalisation of the State or a Catalyst for the Establishment of Parallel Structures?', paper at 7th International Seminar, 'Democracy and Human Rights in Multiethnic Societies', Konjic, BiH, 12–17 July, 2004.
8. Catherine Götze, 'Civil Society Organizations in Failing States: The Red Cross in Bosnia and Albania', *International Peacekeeping*, Vol.11, No.4, winter 2004, pp.664–82.
9. See Béatrice Hibou, *Privatising the State*, London: Hurst, 2004 (forthcoming); Sami Makki, *Militarisation de l'humanitaire, privatisation du militaire, et stratégie globale des États-Unis*, Groupe de sociologie de la défense, École des Hautes études en Science, Paris, 2004. In Iraq during the foreign occupation and interim government, there were about 20,000 private security guards, armed but poorly trained for dealing with civilians.
10. Massimo Florio, *The Great Divestiture*, Cambridge, MA: MIT Press, 2004; Joseph Stiglitz, *Globalization and its Discontents*, London: Penguin, 2002; Amy Chua, *World on Fire: How Exporting Free-Market Democracy Breeds Ethnic Hatred and Global Instability*, New York: Doubleday, 2002; George Soros, *The Crisis of Global Capitalism: Open Society Endangered*, Oxford: Public Affairs, 1998.
11. Robert W. Cox, A useful synopsis of Cox's views on the post-cold war order is in his John Holmes memorial lecture to the Academic Council on the United Nations System (ACUNS), 'Globalization, Multilateralism, and Democracy', 1992.
12. This is explicit in the 'mission statement' of the US State Department's Office of the Coordinator for Reconstruction and Stabilization (at www.state.gov/s/crs) and in the strategy: 'Bosnia and Herzegovina: Towards Economic Recovery' laid out by the World Bank, European Commission and European Bank for Reconstruction and Development in 1996. See also, Roland Paris, *At War's End*, Cambridge: Cambridge University Press, 2004; Michael Pugh (ed.), *Regeneration of War-Torn Societies*, London: Macmillan, 2000.
13. The term 'carpetbaggers' refers to Northerners who went South after the American Civil War to speculate in economic reconstruction and to exert control in the new Republican state governments. Their possessions were often carried in cloth (or carpet) bags. Their political-economic corruption has made the term applicable to outsiders who interfere in the politics of a war-torn society for their own benefit.
14. See examples of 'othering' in Gerald Knaus and Marcus Cox, 'Bosnia and Herzegovina: Europeanization by decree?', in Judy Batt (ed.), *The Western Balkans: moving on*, Chaillot Paper 70, Paris: Institute for Security Studies, Oct. 2004, p.63 (Bosnians as passive); and the foreword by Henrik Kolstrup, UNDP Resident Coordinator, *Human Development Report: Bosnia and Herzegovina, 2002* Sarajevo: UNDP, p.3 (Bosnians as pathologically diseased).
15. Peter Andreas, 'Criminalized Conflict: the Clandestine Political Economy of War in Bosnia', *International Studies Quarterly*, Vol.48, No.1, 2004, pp.29–51.
16. For example, the SDA controls utilities such as the PTT, Elektroprivreda, and Energoinvest, *Dani* (Sarajevo), 6 Aug. 1999, 16–19; European Stability Initiative (ESI), 'Taking on the Commanding Heights', Berlin/Brussels, 3 May 2000.
17. 'Privatizacija Aluminija je potpuno kriminalna', [Privatization of Aluminij is completely criminal] *Dani*, 24 Aug. 2001; 'Scimnjiva Privatizacija Aluminijuma', [The Suspicious Privatization of Aluminij], *Nacional* (Zagreb), 6 Sept. 2001; Jurislav Petrović, 'Position of Croats in Federation endangered', *Dnevni List* (Mostar), 4 Jan. 2005, p.4 (OHR trans.).
18. Žarko Papić, 'Ethička privatizacija: neograničene mogućosti prevare' [Ethnic Privatization: unlimited possibilities for cheating], *Dani*, 6 Aug. 1999, pp.20–21.

19. See International Crisis Group, 'Bosnia's Precarious Economy: Still Not Open for Business', report no.115, Sarajevo/Brussels, 7 Aug. 2001.

20. BiH Media Round-up (OHR trans.), 18 Oct. 2001; Neven Katunarić and Marijan Puntarić, 'Prlic i partnari sada Peru Robu u Pistom Moru Makarske Rivijere' [Prlić and his partners now launder money in the clean waters of the Makarska], *Slobodna Salmacija* (Split), 24 Sept. 2001 (OHR trans.). Conservations with the author Prlić was considered to have the right sort of entrepreneurial skills by top international officials who knew him as BiH Foreign Minister. He went to The Hague to answer war crimes charges but was released on bail in 2004, along with four other Croats, after an intercession by former US Secretary of State, Madeleine Albright.

21. Zdenko Jurilj, 'Real owner of PBS unknown', *Večernji List* (Zagreb), 16 Sept. 2004, p.3.

22. Ivanić claimed that the buyer had to invest KM60 million of additional capital and KM190 million of deposit, 'EURO of millions worth', *Glas Srpske* (Banja Luka), 30 Mar. 2004, p.2 (OHR trans.); *Crna Bosna*, Banja Luka: *Nezavisne Novine*, 2004.

23. Tijana Veselinović, 'Without milk as of Tuesday', *EuroBlic* (Banja Luka), 14–15 Aug. 2004, p.2 (OHR trans.).

24. Enes Plecić, 'Revision being slowed down due to fear: FBiH Govt accelerates bankruptcies and is to dismiss thousands of workers', *Dnevni Avaz* (Sarajevo), 16 Feb. 2004, pp.1, 5. Prewar Prime Minister of Federal Yugoslavia, Ante Marković introduced a limited privatization strategy.

25. A. Dzonlić, 'A comprehensive review will relieve ourselves from burden of illegal privatisation', *Dnevni Avaz*, 4 Jan. 2005, p.2 (OHR trans).

26. Interview by Danka Polovina-Mandić, 'State is not mature enough for privatization of Elektro-privredas and Telecommunications', *Dnevni List*, 7 Jan. 2005, p.3.

27. BHTV1, 3 March 2004; Muhamed Cabrić, 'They will seek the help of anti-corruption unit', *Dnevni Avaz*, 5 Jan. 2005, p.17 (OHR trans.).

28. BH Radio, 1 Dec. 2004 (OHR trans).

29. BHTV1, 5 Jan. 2004; Miso Relota, 'Discussion on changes to Law on bankruptcy postponed', *Dnevni List*, 11 Mar. 2004, p.4; Radio Herceg-Bosna, 31 Mar. 2004; 'Biber announces lawsuit against FBiH Govt', *Dnevni Avaz*, 31 Mar. 2004, p.2; 'New 10 000 workers to end up on street?', *Slobodna Dalmacija* (Split), 31 Mar. 2004, p.18 (OHR trans.).

30. 'Privatisation in RS and FBiH is a theft', *Nezavisne Novine* (Banja Luka), 17 Mar. 2004, pp.1,4 (OHR trans.).

31. 'Privatisation has become a privilege of brokers', *Nezavisne Novine*, 18 Mar. 2004, p.2.

32. Ibid.

33. 'Privatisation as dogma', *Oslobodjenje* (Sarajevo), 1 Mar. 2004, p.3; Federation TV, 1 Mar. 2004 (OHR trans.).

34. 'FBiH Privatisation Agency in deficit of 2,3 million KM', *Dnevni Avaz*, 26 April 2004, p.9; A. Hadziarapović, 'State earned only 345 million KM', *Dnevni Avaz*, 16 Feb. 2004, p.5 (OHR trans). FDI was US$300m in 2002, and from 2003 to mid- 2004 $850m. Fikret Causevic, 'Transition in the Economic Sphere', paper at 7th International Seminar, 'Democracy and Human Rights in Multiethnic Societies', Konjic, 12–17 July 2004.

35. *Bosnia and Herzegovina – the long road back to business as usual*, Economics Department, Bank Austria Creditanstalt, Sept. 2003, pp.8–9.

36. *Strategy for Economic Development of BiH*, Government of BiH, Sarajevo, May 2004.

37. Florio (n.10 above); Hibou (n.9 above).

38. OHR, *Economic Newsletter*, Vol.7, No.4, Oct. 2004, pp.4–5.

39. *Living Standard Measurement Survey in Bosnia and Herzegovina*, Sarajevo: Federal Office of Statistics, 2002.

40. UNDP, *Early Warning System: Bosnia and Herzegovina*, Quarterly Report, April–May 2002, p.16.

41. UN Wire, 'Bosnia-Herzegovina: World Bank Announces Assistance Strategy', 25 May 2000 (at: www.unfoundation.org).

42. Interview with World Bank official, Sarajevo, 12 Dec. 2002.

43. 'Introduction', *Strategy for Economic Development* (n.36 above).

44. UNDP, *Early Warning* (n.40 above), p.16.

45. OHR Economic Task Force Secretariat, *Economic Newsletter*, vol.5, no.3, Oct. 2002.

46. This also excludes workers on firms' waiting lists. World Bank Country Brief for BiH, 2004 (at www.worldbank.org). A broader concept of unemployment places the national rate in 1998 at over 56 per cent: Dragoljub Stojanov, 'Hungary and Bosnia and Herzegovina: a short view of a success and of a failure of transition', unpub. paper (available from the author, Faulty of Economics, University of Sarajevo).

47. 'Poverty Profile in Bosnia and Herzegovina', *Strategy for Economic Development* (n.36 above), p.8.
48. Michael Pugh and Neil Cooper with Jonathan Goodhand, *War Economies in a Regional Context: Challenges of Transformation*, Boulder CO: Lynne Rienner, 2004, pp.170–71.
49. See, e.g., Michel Chossudovsky, 'The Criminalization of Albania', in Tariq Ali (ed.), *Masters of the Universe? NATO's Balkan Crusade*, London: Verso, 2000, pp.285–316.
50. 'BiH is a centre of organised crime', *Nezavisne Novine*, 2 Dec. 2003, p.2 (OHR trans.); Kolstrup (n.14 above) foreword. See, also, the special issue of *Problems of Post-Communism*, 'Transnational Crime and Conflict in the Balkans', vol.51, no.3, May–June 2004.
51. Christopher A. Corpora, 'The Gas Station Blues in Three Parts: The Effects of Organized Crime on Stablity and Development in Southeast Europe', paper at the ISA Conference, New Orleans, 23–27 Mar. 2002.
52. Simon Chesterman, *You, The People: the United Nations, transnational administration, and state-building*, Oxford: Oxford University Press, 2004, pp.238–49.
53. The UN Interim Administration Mission in Kosovo exercises exclusive control and regulation over economic policy and personnel, and over public and socially-owned property and enterprises. Robert Muharremi et al., *Administration and Governance in Kosovo: Lessons Learned and Lessons to be Learned*, Priština/Geneva: Centre for Applied Studies in International Negotiations, Jan. 2003, p.39. For details of foreign control in Kosovo, see Pugh, 'Crime and Capitalism in Kosovo's Transformation', in Tonny Brems Knudsen and Carsten (eds), *Kosovo Between War and Peace*, London: Taylor & Francis (forthcoming, 2005.)
54. European Agency for Reconstruction, '2002 Annual Action Plan', press release EAR/REG/03/01, 14 Feb. 2003 (at www.ear.eu.int/publications/news-a1a23gc4.htm).
55. SELDI Corruption Index Report April 2002 in USAID, p.19.
56. See, Pugh, 'Postwar Political Economy in Bosnia and Herzegovina: the Spoils of Peace' *Global Governance*, Vol.8, No.4, autumn 2002, pp.467–82.
57. Robert Corker, Dawn Rehm and Kristina Kostial, 'Kosovo: Macroeconomic and Fiscal Sustainability', Washington DC: IMF, 2001, p.16. An agreement with the trade unions allows 20 per cent of proceeds of sales of socially-owned enterprises to go to workers employed for past three years. Bertram I. Spector, Svetlana Winbourne and Laurence D. Beck (for Management Systems International), 'Corruption in Kosovo: Observations and Implications for USAID', 10 July 2003, p.19.
58. USAID strategy paper Sept–Dec 2001 survey (at www.usaid.gov/missions/kosovo/pdf/kosovo_strategy_2001_2003.pdf).
59. UNDP, 'Factsheet 1: Unemployment', Communications, Advocacy Team and Policy Team, May 2003 (at www.ks.undp.org); 'Early Warning Report' No.4, May-Aug. 2003, table 2.1, p.11.
60. UNDP, 'Early Warning Report No.4', May–Aug. 2003, table A10, p.31.
61. Details of US carpetbagging in Iraq are in the series of articles by Naomi Klein in *The Nation* (New York), reprinted in *The Guardian* (London): 7 Nov. 2003, p.27; 26 June 2004, p.22; 27 Dec. 2004, p.18.
62. Bauman (n.12 above), pp.132–40.
63. For a critique of the view that integration leads to growth rather than growth leading to integration, see UNDP/Kamal Malhotra, *Making Global Trade Work for People*, Earthscan, 2003.
64. Rajko Tomaš, *Analysis of the Grey Economy in Republika Srpska*, Banja Luka: UNDP, March 1998, p.x.
65. International Labour Organisation, *A Fair Globalisation: Creating Opportunities for All*, World Commission on the Social Dimension of Globalisation, 2004 (at www.ilo.org).
66. Bauman (see n.12 above).

Who Guards the Guardians? International Accountability in Bosnia

RICHARD CAPLAN

If men were angels, no government would be necessary. If angels were to govern men, neither external nor internal controls on government would be necessary. In framing a government which is to be administered by men over men, the great difficulty lies in this: you must first enable the government to control the governed; and in the next place oblige it to control itself.

James Madison, *Federalist Paper* No.51[1]

Long before and ever since James Madison penned these immortal words, political thinkers have been concerned with the question of how to control the power of governments. This concern has led to the development of various institutions and practices of accountability that restrain democratic governments and subject them to public oversight. Indeed, public accountability can be said to be one of the hallmarks of the democratic state.

In Bosnia-Herzegovina (BiH), the High Representative (HR) and other international bodies wield governmental power – power that is exercised ostensibly for the purpose of democratic state-building. Yet, while the power that they possess can be quite considerable, international authorities are not directly accountable to the population whose territory they administer. They are, instead, accountable to the bodies that appoint them, such as the Peace Implementation Council (PIC) and the Council of the European Union in the case of the double-hatted HR (see David Chandler, this volume),[2] the North Atlantic Treaty Organization (NATO) in the case of the Stabilization Force (SFOR),[3] and the European Court of Human Rights in the case of the international judges on the Bosnian Constitutional Court. International authorities serve at the pleasure of these and other bodies and it is to these bodies that they are largely answerable.

There is, then, a fundamental contradiction that lies at the heart of the international administration of BiH – and all international territorial administrations for that matter. While international authorities seek, among other objectives, to enshrine democratic accountability in the local public institutions within their purview, these same authorities are in many ways unaccountable themselves. International administrators are not elected by the citizens of BiH and cannot be removed by them. Nor can the local population contest the decisions of these administrators whose actions, moreover, are not always transparent. Of course, the international administration of BiH operates within a complex international environment in which democratic norms, regional and global institutions, the media, non-governmental organizations (NGOs), and other factors arguably exert a constraining influence on its behaviour. Are these factors adequate, however, to ensure that there is no misuse of international authority? Do they compensate for the lack of international accountability at the local level?

The following sections consider the concepts of vertical and horizontal accountability; how these concepts relate to the operation of the international administration; the limited accountability provided to the citizens of BiH, even in comparison to both historical and contemporary examples of international administrations; and in conclusion, ways of enhancing accountability.

The Concept of Accountability

Accountability refers to the various norms, practices and institutions whose purpose is to hold public officials (and other bodies) responsible for their actions and for the outcomes of those actions. It is concerned, in particular, to prevent and redress abuses of power.[4] Scholars sometimes distinguish between 'vertical' accountability and 'horizontal' accountability. Vertical accountability pertains to the relationship between entities of unequal 'rank', such as a government to its citizens or employers to their employees. Horizontal accountability concerns the relationship among entities of equal 'rank', such as the independent pillars of a government or society (for example, the courts or the media vis-à-vis the executive).[5] Both types of accountability exist in relation to international administrations but only at the international level, where transitional administrations and their constituent elements may be subject to internal audits (horizontal accountability) or to the scrutiny of the secretariat or member states of international organizations (vertical accountability). The 'stakeholders' – those most affected by the actions of an international administration – are largely excluded from these processes.[6]

Accountability entails answerability – the obligation on the part of public officials to inform the public about what they are doing and to provide explanations for their behaviour. Accountability thus requires transparency with respect to decision-making, although this needs to be balanced against legitimate requirements for confidentiality (for instance, with respect to intelligence sources relating to national security). Accountability often also requires effective mechanisms of enforcement. If sanctions for malfeasance are not enforced – if, for instance, corrupt political leaders can disregard election results or court decisions – accountability may be devoid of any real meaning. The sanctions need not necessarily be severe and sometimes disclosure alone can be its own punishment, as when public officials feel compelled to resign over conflicts of interest or individuals testifying before a truth commission suffer shame as a consequence of their actions. Under some circumstances accountability does not entail sanctions at all, as when a central banker is called to appear before a parliamentary committee periodically to explain the reasoning behind interest rate adjustments and other policy actions.[7] As this example suggests, accountability not only guards against abuses of power, it also provides citizens and other stakeholders with information with which they can then make informed judgements, whether or not they are empowered to act on those judgements. (Citizens do not ordinarily elect their central banker, for example.)

One reason to limit the scope of public accountability is to ensure the independence of officials (judges, for instance) who might otherwise be susceptible to electoral or other pressures that would compromise the integrity of their work. Accountability to citizens is also sometimes more broadly restricted in situations of extreme emergency where the suspension of the exercise of certain rights may be thought to be necessary for a limited period of time to restore normality.[8] In effect, this is the basis upon which accountability to stakeholders would appear to be limited in international territorial administrations, the 'normality' to be restored implicitly understood to be that of a stable peace and effective mechanisms of domestic democratic governance. Such reasoning is nowhere made explicit, yet the extraordinary power vested in the administering authority and the absence of significant mechanisms of international accountability would seem to reflect such a view. As Paddy Ashdown explained in a speech to the Venice Commission: 'The High Representative, as final interpreter of the Civilian Aspects of the GFAP [Dayton accord], has been entrusted with the power to take extraordinary measures to surmount the extraordinary obstacles facing peace implementation.'[9] Similarly, the UN Interim Administration Mission in Kosovo (UNMIK) defended its practice of extra-judicial detention in 2001 with reference to the 'internationally-recognized emergency'.[10]

Alternatively, one could liken the administered territories to non-self-governing territories and the administering authorities to trustees who, while obliged to promote the well-being of the inhabitants and the progressive development of their political institutions, are not necessarily obliged to answer to them.[11] However, this justification would be problematic in the case of BiH, because BiH – unlike other internationally administered territories – has its own sovereign authorities. Trusteeship and sovereignty are mutually exclusive concepts.[12]

Although the purpose of the Office of the High Representative (OHR) originally was to 'facilitate the Parties' *own* efforts' to implement the Dayton peace agreement,[13] the hand of the HR has been strengthened considerably as a consequence of a re-interpretation of these powers by the PIC. At its meeting in Bonn in December 1997, the PIC gave the HR greater authority, including the power to dismiss local officials deemed to be obstructing implementation of the Dayton accord and to issue interim laws if the local parties were 'unable' (that is, unwill-ing) to do so.[14] Other international authorities, meanwhile – among them the Governor of the Central Bank (until 1 January 2005), the three international judges of the Constitutional Court, and individuals serving with SFOR and its EUFOR follow on – have from the start enjoyed significant autonomy in relation to the local parties by virtue of the provisions of the Dayton accord. These provisions, it bears noting, were agreed to by the local parties; however, ten years on, as the urgency of the situation in BiH has abated, there has been considerable debate, both within BiH and internationally, about the appropriate exercise of international authority – a debate that has highlighted the limits of international accountability.[15] Nowadays, it is difficult to justify the HR's extra-ordinary powers with reference to 'emergency conditions', although it is clear that certain state-building measures would still not be undertaken by the local parties were it not for the intervention of the HR.[16]

Mechanisms of Accountability

To say that the international administration of BiH is, in many respects, unac-countable is not to suggest that there are no mechanisms of accountability at work at all. To begin with, international authorities must comply with a variety of reporting obligations at the international level. The HR is required to report periodically to the United Nations, the European Union, the United States, Russia, and 'other interested governments, parties, and organizations' on progress in implementation of the Dayton peace agreement,[17] and to brief the PIC and its Steering Board regularly. The reports are available for all to read (in English only, however) on the web page of the OHR. Other international or regional organiz-ations participating in the administration of BiH, such as the World Bank and the Organization for Security and Co-operation in Europe (OSCE), have similar reporting requirements. Of course, reporting on one's own activities has obvious limitations as far as critical examination is concerned, even if these reports often contain candid assessments and, moreover, are subject to scrutiny by higher internal officials and outside authorities. In addition to these reports, interested organizations will often also request the HR to brief them directly, while representatives and delegates from the organizations may visit the territory to observe the work of the administration first hand.

There are other mechanisms of international accountability. The World Bank maintains an Inspection Panel, whose services are in principle available wherever the Bank has projects, including in BiH. The panel is a three-member body estab-lished in 1993 to investigate complaints from local citizens who claim that they have been adversely affected, in a direct and material way, by a Bank-financed project.[18] Yet, although the Bank has had a very extensive presence in BiH, to date the panel has received no requests for inspection from Bosnian citizens (or from citizens under any other international administrations for that matter).[19] This may be because, despite the extent of the Bank's activities in BiH, there is little awareness of the existence of the panel, as the Bank is not very active in promoting knowledge about its work among affected populations.

Other important mechanisms of accountability are the various unofficial bodies, in particular the international and local media and NGOs. The international media have at times been influential in shaping perceptions within donor and other interested states that, in turn, have had a bearing on international policy in the administered territories. The spotlight on alleged corruption, for instance, has at times been especially bright.[20] International coverage, however, has tended to be episodic and, with the passage of time, less and less frequent, although the local language radio services of the major international news broadcasters, such as the *BBC, Deutsche Welle*, and *Radio France Internationale*, have provided regular and sometimes probing coverage of the international administration of BiH. Their coverage has been valuable both for informing the local citizenry and for helping to promote higher journalistic standards among the local media.

The local media themselves have also on occasion been noteworthy for their coverage of the international administration, and there is some evidence to suggest that international policy-makers are sensitive to local media coverage and feel constrained to respond to criticism.[21] But the quality and accuracy of this reporting has been very variable. Although international authorities have expended considerable amounts of funding in support of the local media, these same authorities have been slow to appreciate the importance of establishing an adequate regulatory framework to help develop more effective media. In particular, they have been slow either to promote or impose through executive decision the regulations necessary to facilitate the development of independent and responsible journalism – with, for instance, the promulgation of defamation legislation, the establishment of a transparent licensing regime, and the establishment of codes of practice, among other measures.[22]

International and local NGOs are also important mechanisms of horizontal accountability. Several international NGOs operate in BiH that are orientated specifically towards oversight of the administration – most notably, the International Crisis Group (ICG) and the European Stability Initiative (ESI), whose reports are often available in Bosnian-Croatian-Serbian.[23] Many of the analysts working with these NGOs are well acquainted with the region, know the local languages, and, in some cases, have even served in the international administration. Their analysis has helped to shape the perceptions of key diplomatic 'shareholders' in theatre, such as the United States, Britain and other major donors. Other international NGOs have concentrated on specific areas of the international administration, such as human rights (Amnesty International, Human Rights Watch), refugees (US Committee for Refugees, Refugees International), and democratization (International Institute for Democracy and Electoral Assistance). There are no significant indigenous NGOs, however, that monitor and analyse the work of the territorial administration and associated agencies in BiH. The absence of effective local NGOs working in this area testifies the more general problem in BiH of a lack of citizen engagement in the practice of government.[24]

Lacking, too, in BiH is an international ombudsperson's office. An institution that has its modern roots in nineteenth-century Sweden, an ombudsperson is an independent public official who receives complaints from aggrieved individuals against public bodies and government departments or their employees and who has the power to investigate, recommend corrective action and issue reports.[25] The scope of an ombudsperson's remit can vary significantly, from 'general purpose' (dealing with complaints across a wide spectrum of governmental activities at all levels of government) to 'single purpose' (dealing with only one area or aspect of governmental activity). In other international territorial administrations, the ombudsperson has played a role in holding international officials accountable, although this role has generally been limited to the protection of the human rights and freedoms of individuals and legal entities within the territory.[26] In East Timor, complaints could be filed against the UN Transitional Administration (UNTAET) as well as the agencies, programmes and institutions of the emerging state with respect to policies, procedures and decisions that were thought to be unfair, discriminatory or unjust, or in violation of human rights.[27] In Kosovo, the ombudsperson can receive and investigate complaints from any person in Kosovo concerning human rights violations and actions constituting an abuse of authority by UNMIK as well as by any central or local institution,[28] although the ombudsperson's jurisdiction does not extend to the NATO-led Kosovo Force (KFOR). Even this limited redress is not available in BiH. There are three ombudsperson institutions in BiH – one at the state level (including the District of Brčko) and one for each of the two entities – but their jurisdictions do not extend to international actions except insofar as international bodies may be called upon to facilitate redress of domestic violations.[29]

The Accountability Deficit

The accountability mechanisms that exist in BiH, then, are fairly limited, especially at the local level. As a result, they can only mitigate the international accountability deficit. This deficit manifests itself in several ways, notably a lack of transparency, the absence of local checks on the use of international power, immunities that international personnel enjoy, and the absence of elections or other popular 'referenda' on international performance. The deficit is tolerated to a greater degree both domestically and internationally than would normally be the case within most established democracies because of the extraordinary circumstances that led to the establishment of the Dayton structures. And, yet, in June 2004, the Council of Europe's Parliamentary Assembly observed that:

> The scope of the OHR is such that, to all intents and purposes, it constitutes the supreme institution vested with power in Bosnia and Herzegovina. In this connection, the Assembly considers it irreconcilable with democratic principles that the OHR should be able to take enforceable decisions without being accountable for them or obliged to justify their validity and without there being a legal remedy.[30]

From the standpoint of the affected population, the process of international decision-making in BiH can sometimes seem opaque, notwithstanding laudable efforts by the international authorities to communicate via the publication of various newsletters, reports and press releases, television programmes and the convening of public meetings. Sometimes the simple fact that relevant documents are not always available in local languages creates a barrier to comprehension. There have also been considerable delays in publishing regulations and the tacit assumption that publication on the internet is sufficient even though a large proportion of the population lacks access to computer services. As late as December 2004, the Bosnian Constitution – Annex 4 of the Dayton accord – had still not been published in the Official Gazette of BiH.[31] Transparency is often also lacking with respect to international decision-making. Key decisions are frequently taken without sufficient explanation offered into the reasoning behind them. This practice, too, contributes to the impression of arbitrary rule. As the International Crisis Group has observed:

> Respect for Bosnian authorities and basic notions of reciprocity argue for at least the degree of transparency necessary for the Bosnian authorities and people to understand the basis for decisions, and the decision-making processes, that so affect them. If the point of the international encampment in Bosnia is to 'teach' democracy, tolerance and good governance to the Bosnians then there is no better way to start than by example.[32]

This admonition was made in 1996 but in important respects it is as apt today as it was then.

The immunities that international personnel enjoy, however necessary, further exacerbate the accountability deficit. The NATO-led international security forces (IFOR and then SFOR) have benefited from the same protections as those extended to 'experts on missions' by the Convention on the Privileges and Immunities of the United Nations. The Convention accords the relevant personnel 'immunity from legal process of every kind' in relation to 'acts done by them in the course of the performance of their mission'.[33] International personnel serving with IFOR/SFOR have been subject, therefore, to the exclusive jurisdiction of the respective sending state with regard to any criminal or disciplinary offence that they might commit in BiH.[34] Some of the personnel serving with the security forces in BiH have been implicated in human rights violations: Amnesty International has documented illegal and arbitrary arrests by peacekeeping troops, their ill-treatment of detainees, and the failure of the forces to respect local court decisions regarding detainees.[35] In no case known to Amnesty International, however, has a peacekeeper been brought before a national judiciary in an instance where alleged human rights violations have occurred.

International civil personnel also enjoy broad protection from prosecution. The HR and his staff, for instance, benefit from the same privileges and immunities as are accorded diplomatic agents under the Vienna Convention on Diplomatic Relations.[36] This is not to say that international personnel operate in a legal vacuum: they are bound by the provisions of international human rights and humanitarian law. International personnel, however, are subject only to the jurisdiction of the international organizations with which they serve or, if on secondment, of their respective sending states. In neighbouring Kosovo, by comparison, the situation is marginally better: there the ombudsperson has jurisdiction to investigate a range of complaints against UNMIK although these are very limited and the ombudsperson can only forward complaints against KFOR to KFOR for its consideration. Partly in recognition of the need to be more accountable, UNMIK established 'claims offices' to consider claims for compensation as a result of injuries or damages caused by the organization. However, UNMIK provides no opportunity for individuals to be represented by legal counsel before these offices, and all decisions are taken by a panel of UNMIK staff members, against which the only possible appeal is a memorandum to the UNMIK Director of Administration.[37] (KFOR has established similar offices but its appeals process, according to the ombudsperson, 'incorporates many elements of proper judicial proceedings'.) The deficiencies of these practices notwithstanding, they represent an improvement over the situation in BiH.

The lack of transparency and the absence of appeal mechanisms combine in respect of the dismissal of local authorities. HR's have it in their power to dismiss local authorities in almost every position (mayors, judges, legislators, bank officials, and even presidents) who are deemed by them to be obstructing implementation of the Dayton peace agreement. They are able to carry out these dismissals without offering any evidence in support of their actions and there is no scope for appeal on the part of the individuals affected. Alija Izetbegović, then a member of the Bosnian presidency, observed in late 1999: 'In Sarajevo, they remove a man, label him dishonest, do not present any proof of this, and then talk to us about human rights... They want us to take their word for it.'[38] Such practices can hardly be said to be an object lesson in democratic governance.

Enhancing Accountability

International territorial administrations are not representative democracies; they are institutions created and sustained by international processes – processes, which, though themselves democratically deficient in certain respects, establish a legitimate basis and parameters for the exercise of international authority. International transitional authorities should not be expected, therefore, to function as governments answerable *primarily* to the people whose territories they administer. Nevertheless, greater effort can and should be made to ensure a greater degree of accountability to the local population.

There are several measures that can be taken to strengthen international accountability. One is to enlarge the institution of the ombudsperson. The Ombudsman of Bosnia and Herzegovina, now concerned exclusively with human rights violations, could conceivably be empowered to receive and investigate complaints from citizens about the process of international administration – for instance, procedural improprieties, bias or the lack of due process – and make recommendations to the transitional authority on the basis of their findings. The ombudsman would not be able to strike down the HR's and other internationals' decisions but the recommendations might carry some weight. There is a precedent for such an enlargement of responsibilities: elsewhere ombudspersons deal with complaints across the whole spectrum of governmental activities.[39] The more fundamental problem is that too often transitional administrators view the ombudsperson as an irritant rather than as a vital institution. A high-profile appointment might help to enhance the stature of the office, but the problem is not an easy one to resolve.

A second mechanism for strengthening accountability is expanded jurisdiction of the Bosnian high courts. As these courts demonstrate that they are capable of deciding issues in a fair and impartial manner, they might be given authority to review international authorities' exercise of powers if and when these seem to be incompatible with locally enacted legislation. The Bosnian Constitutional Court, for instance, has jurisdiction over issues concerning whether a law is compatible with the constitution, international human-rights law, and general rules of public international law.[40] In November 2000, for the first time, the court reviewed a decision of the HR (regarding the creation of a unified border service for BiH), which, though the legislation was found to be in conformity with the constitution, established a precedent for a local institution (or, more accurately, a mixed institution) to challenge the legality of an international act.[41] Before local courts can assume more authority, however, it may be necessary to amend the international legislation defining the powers of the HR and other international administrators to allow for some form of judicial review.

International officials might also find it instructive to revisit some of the parallel experiences of the past. Under the League of Nations administration of the Saar Basin, for instance, the League Council followed the work of the Governing Commission closely and intervened on at least one occasion – in reaction to a decree restricting civil liberties – to check the authority of the Commission.[42] In addition, the League had a dedicated supervisory body, the Permanent Mandates Commission (PMC), whose principal role was oversight of mandatory administrations. Under the United Nations Trusteeship system, there was also a dedicated supervisory body – the Trusteeship Council – that had responsibility for the review of reports submitted by the administering authority of trust territories.[43] The Trusteeship Council could also accept petitions from inhabitants of the trust territories and from third parties as well, marking an innovation over the functioning of the PMC.[44]

In theory, a similar function could be performed by an *ad hoc* body that would be established by the Security Council. (The Security Council already oversees the work of other international administrations, but the burdens on the Council mean that its oversight is cursory.) Indeed, the UN Secretary-General's High-level Panel on Threats, Challenges and Change, in its December 2004 report, recommended the establishment of a Peacebuilding Commission, one of whose functions could be to oversee the work of UN territorial administrations.[45] The Panel envisaged that national representatives of any country receiving peace-building support would be invited to attend the meetings of the commission; it might also consider accepting petitions from local residents, in the manner of the UN Trusteeship Council.

The accountability deficit could also be reduced if there were a clear (though not rigid) sense of the limits of international executive authority. To a certain extent HR Paddy Ashdown began to delineate such limits with the articulation of his Mission Implementation Plan (MIP) in January 2003, which identified the core tasks which the OHR proposed to focus upon in order to accomplish its mission. The MIP acknowledged that it was neither possible nor desirable for the OHR to do everything. 'Our job is to bring BiH to the point at which it can continue its journey, like other transition countries, with substantial support from the international community, but without the unique and highly intrusive, and potentially dependency-inducing post-war support structure that OHR represents'.[46] More significantly, the MIP identified the transition point for each of its core tasks by which they could be judged to be either completed or in a position to be handed over to the Bosnian authorities. Here, then, was a potential gauge for assessing whether the OHR was working within or exceeding specified limits.

The problem with this approach, however, was two-fold. First, it left it to the OHR to identify both the tasks and transition points and, more importantly, to make the determination as to whether these points have been reached. There is thus the danger that the goal posts can be moved indefinitely. Indeed, as the OHR itself has acknowledged, rather ambiguously, it may be necessary to add tasks or programmes 'in the light of developments'.[47] Second, there was no mechanism by which Bosnian citizens could challenge the HR's assessments of progress towards transition, just as there are no mechanisms for the review of other decisions that he may make.

The flipside of restraint in the exercise of international authority is local ownership of the processes of governance. HR Wolfgang Petritsch made ownership the cornerstone of his new strategic approach to the international administration of BiH in 1999: 'The overriding objective of the International Community must now be to substantially accelerate the rate at which responsibility for governance and particularly the creation and effective operation of state institutions is assumed by local political leaders', he told ministers of the PIC's Steering Board on 22 September 1999.[48] However, what Petritsch and other international officials clearly have had in mind when they have spoken about ownership is a greater sense of local responsibility for *domestic* governance. Missing from the equation is any sense of ownership of international processes. And yet, local ownership is arguably difficult to achieve without meaningful participation in international as well as domestic decision-making.[49] As Joseph Stiglitz, the former chief economist of the World Bank, has observed in relation to development assistance programmes:

> Broad participation in the vital activities of a developing society, like shop-floor participation in a company, is at least helpful, and perhaps even necessary to foster a lasting transformation. Active involvement brings commitment to the lessons being learned and ownership of the results. Participation and involvement is not just a matter for government officials or managers; it needs to reach deeper to include those who are often excluded and who are key to the strengthening of social and organizational capital. *Outside experts can encourage 'ownership' of 'best policies' through persuasion, but the degree of ownership is likely to be much greater if those who*

must carry out the policies are actively involved in the process of shaping and adapting, if not reinventing these policies in the country itself.[50]

Active local involvement in the process of shaping international legislation with respect to BiH has certainly been limited. Formal consultative mechanisms – a feature of other international administrations – have been lacking from the start, if only because BiH, uniquely among international 'protectorates', has had a sovereign government and it would not have been appropriate for an international administration to establish formal consultative links with anyone other than government or government-sanctioned representatives. Indeed, in Kosovo and East Timor, the formal local consultative mechanisms were disbanded once the provisional institutions of self-government were established.

For similar reasons, arguments in favour of the 'Bosnianization' of the OHR are somewhat misguided. While it might seem desirable to increase the degree of local responsibility for the execution of OHR tasks, a truly Bosnianized OHR would represent something of an unelected parallel Bosnian government, which would clearly be unacceptable. The fact that the OHR is not accountable to the Bosnian public is problematic enough; how much more fraught would be the relationship between a Bosnian head of the OHR's Economic Department and the Federation's *elected* Finance Minister?

There are also legal impediments to local ownership of international processes. The HR and other international officials are accountable to an international constituency and have an international mandate to ensure the integrity of particular governmental operations. There is, in short, an inescapable contradiction between the requirements of international administration, on the one hand, and the imperative of local ownership, on the other, which can only be overcome with the eventual transfer of responsibility to Bosnian authorities and the concomitant relinquishment of international authority over those same areas.

The Bosnianization of internationally controlled governmental functions has in fact occurred in a number of areas – some of them very sensitive – as local authorities have satisfied the international authorities that they have the capacity to execute their responsibilities in a competent and impartial manner. After six years of direct management of all electoral activity in BiH, for instance, the OSCE in 2001 transferred its responsibility for the administration of elections to a mixed Bosnian Election Commission (comprising four Bosnians and three internationals) that derives its authority from and reports to the Parliamentary Assembly of Bosnia and Herzegovina. Similarly, in December 2003, the OHR terminated the Reconstruction and Return Task Force and transferred its responsibilities to the relevant domestic authorities.[51] And on 1 January 2004, three Bosnian citizens succeeded Frank Orton, a Swedish national, as the Human Rights Ombudsmen of Bosnia and Herzegovina.[52] The Central Bank of Bosnia and Herzegovina, too, has undergone a steady Bosnianization: its staff of more than 250 is made up now almost entirely of Bosnian nationals. While the head of the bank has been a foreign national, as stipulated by the Dayton accord, a Bosnian will serve as governor from 1 January 2005.[53] In all cases the domestic bodies are subject to continued international supervision but, in effect, international control has withered away.

Conclusion

The fact that there is a fundamental contradiction at the heart of the international administration of BiH is not to say that the administration is fundamentally flawed. 'All international administration, however benign, is to some extent illegitimate', David Harland has observed. 'In a world in which sovereignty is understood to flow from the will of the people, the very idea of an administration brought from the outside runs against that of sovereignty.'[54] A lack of international accountability at the local level can be justified on the grounds that emergency situations require extraordinary measures that may extend to the temporary suspension of the norms of democratic governance. To accept that radical measures may be necessary under such circumstances, however, does not mean that there is no scope for the enhancement of accountability. Indeed, as the situation in BiH improves and BiH's problems begin to approximate those of other transition states, greater international accountability becomes not simply desirable but imperative. To the extent that greater international accountability can be achieved, it will help to ensure the legitimacy of international actions.

ACKNOWLEDGEMENTS

This paper draws from the author's *International Governance of War-Torn Territories: Rule and Reconstruction* (Oxford: Oxford University Press, 2005). The author gratefully acknowledges the Leverhulme Trust and the United States Institute of Peace for their support of this research. The opinions, findings, conclusions, and recommendations expressed here are those of the author and do not necessarily reflect the views of the Trust or the Institute.

NOTES

1. James Madison [attributed], 'The Federalist No.51', in A. Hamilton, J. Jay and J. Madison, *The Federalist: A Commentary on the Constitution of the United States*, New York: Modern Library, 1941, p.337.
2. With the appointment of Paddy Ashdown as HR, the HR also became the European Union Special Representative in Bosnia and Herzegovina.
3. On 2 December 2004, the EU-led EUFOR succeeded SFOR.
4. A. Schedler, 'Conceptualizing Accountability', in A. Schedler, L. Diamond and M.F. Plattner (eds), *The Self-Restraining State: Power and Accountability in the New Democracies*, Boulder, CO: Lynne Rienner, 1999, p.14.
5. Ibid., pp.22–5. See also G. O'Donnell, 'Delegative Democracy', *Journal of Democracy*, Vol.5, No.1, (1994), pp.55–69.
6. On the notion of 'stakeholder accountability,' see R.E. Freeman, *Strategic Management: A Stakeholder Approach*, Boston: Pitman, 1984.
7. Schedler (n.4 above), pp.17–18.
8. *International Covenant on Civil and Political Rights*, Art. 4.1 reads: 'In time of public emergency which threatens the life of the nation and the existence of which is officially proclaimed, the States Parties to the present Covenant may take measures derogating from their obligations under the present Covenant to the extent strictly required by the exigencies of the situation, provided that such measures are not inconsistent with their other obligations under international law

and do not involve discrimination solely on the ground of race, colour, sex, language, religion or social origin,' at www.unhchr.ch/html/menu3/b/a_ccpr.htm.

9. Speech by the High Representative, Paddy Ashdown, to the Venice Commission, 8 Oct. 2004, at www.ohr.int/print/?content_id=33344.

10. 'Regarding the Administration's retention of the right to extend pre-trial detention through Executive Orders, i.e. outside the jurisdiction of the courts system, UNMIK reminds critics that Kosovo still ranks as an internationally-recognized emergency. For such circumstances, international human rights standards accept the need for special measures that, in the wider interests of security, and under prescribed legal conditions, allow authorities to respond to the findings of intelligence that are not able to be presented to the court system.' *UNMIK News*, No.98, 25 June 2001, at www.unmikonline.org/pub/news/nl98.html.

11. Compare with *Charter of the United Nations*, Chapter XI ('Declaration Regarding Non-Self-Governing Territories') and Chapter XII ('International Trusteeship System'), at www.un.org/aboutun/charter/.

12. See further, W. Bain, *Between Anarchy and Society: Trusteeship and the Obligations of Power*, Oxford: Oxford University Press, 2003.

13. *General Framework Agreement for Peace in Bosnia and Herzegovina*, Annex 10, Art. I(2), emphasis added, at www.ohr.int/dpa/default.asp?content_id=380.

14. Peace Implementation Council, 'Bosnia and Herzegovina 1998: Self-sustaining Structures', Bonn, 10 December 1997, Art. XI(2), at www.ohr.int/pic/default.asp?content_id=5182.

15. See, for instance, G. Knaus and F. Martin, 'Travails of the European Raj', *Journal of Democracy*, Vol.14, No.3, (2003), pp.60–74; International Crisis Group, *Bosnia's Nationalist Governments: Paddy Ashdown and the Paradoxes of State Building*, ICG Balkans Report No.146, 22 July 2003, at www.crisisweb.org/home/index.cfm?id=1474&l=1.

16. For a discussion of the HR's exercise of authority, see R. Caplan 'International Authority and State Building: The Case of Bosnia and Herzegovina', *Global Governance*, Vol.10, No.1, (2004), pp.53–65.

17. *General Framework Agreement* (2004) (n.13 above), Annex 10, Art. II.1(f). The UN Security Council requires the Secretary-General to submit the HR's reports to the Council. See UNSCR 1031 (15 Dec. 1995), §32.

18. Details about the operations of the Inspection Panel, accessed at http://wbln0018.worldbank.org/IPN/IPNWeb.nsf?OpenDatabase. See also, I.F.I. Shihata, *The World Bank Inspection Panel*, Oxford: Oxford University Press, 1994.

19. Author email exchange with Mr Serge Selwan, World Bank Inspection Panel, 4 Feb. 2004.

20. See, for instance, C. Hedges, 'Leaders in Bosnia are said to steal up to $1 Billion', *New York Times*, 17 August 1999. In this particular case the *New York Times* was reporting on findings by the OHR's own anti-fraud unit, which the OHR did not wish to publicize.

21. A. Buric, 'The Media War and Peace in Bosnia', in *Regional Media in Conflict: Case Studies in Local War Reporting*, London: Institute for War and Peace Reporting, 2000, p.71.

22. Ibid.

23. The reports of the two organizations can be accessed at www.crisisweb.org and www.esiweb.org respectively.

24. This problem is discussed in European Stability Initiative, *Governance and Democracy in Bosnia and Herzegovina: Post-Industrial Society and the Authoritarian Temptation*, 11 Oct. 2004, at www.esiweb.org/docs/showdocument.php?document_ID=63.

25. R. Gregory and P. Giddings, 'The Ombudsman Institution: Growth and Development', in R. Gregory and P. Giddings (eds), *Righting Wrongs: The Ombudsman in Six Continents*, Amsterdam: IOS Press, 2000, p.3.

26. In the case of Kosovo, consideration had also been given to the inclusion of 'maladministration' within the remit of the ombudsperson but these provisions were omitted from the final regulation. See P. Koskinen, 'Workshop Background Paper on Human Rights Institutions', paper prepared for Kosovo International Human Rights Conference, 10–11 Dec. 1999, in *Conference Documents and Report* (Kosovo: OSCE Mission in Kosovo, 2000), Annex F, p.120. The so-called Crossman Catalogue defines 'maladministration' as including 'bias, neglect, inattention, delay, incompetence, ineptitude, perversity, turpitude, arbitrariness, and so on'. The 'catalogue', which was not intended to be a comprehensive definition, cites examples offered by Richard Crossman, then leader of the House of Commons, when the Parliamentary Commissioner Act of 1967 was being taken through Parliament. *House of Commons Debates* [Hansard] 734, 1966–67, 18 Oct. 1966, cols.51–52.

27. 'Twenty Cases Examined by Ombudsperson', *UNTAET Daily Press Briefing*, 1 June 2001, at www.un.org/peace/etimor/DB/UntaetDB2001.htm.

28. UNMIK Regulation No.2000/38, 'On the Establishment of the Ombudsperson Institution in Kosovo', 30 June 2000.
29. *General Framework Agreement* (n.13 above), Annex 6, Art. IV, mandated the appointment of a Human Rights Ombudsman for a non-renewable five-year term, which the three signatory parties agreed to prolong until 31 December 2003, when responsibility was transferred to an all-Bosnian institution. The Ombudsmen of the Federation of Bosnia and Herzegovina was established under the Federation Constitution of 1994, while the Ombudsmen of Republika Srpska was established through legislation adopted in February 2000.
30. Parliamentary Assembly of the Council of Europe, Res. 1384, 26 June 2004, Art. 13.
31. Author email exchange with Dr Zoran Pajić, Office of the High Representative, 23 Dec. 2004.
32. International Crisis Group, *Aid and Accountability: Dayton Implementation*, ICG Bosnia Report, No.17, 24 Nov. 1996, p.16, at www.crisisweb.org/home/index.cfm?id=1566&l=1.
33. *Convention on the Privileges and Immunities of the United Nations*, Art. VI, Section 22(b). The UN Secretary-General can, however, waive the immunity of any official.
34. *General Framework Agreement* (n.13 above), Annex 1A, Appendix B, Art. 7.
35. Amnesty International, 'The Apparent Lack of Accountability of International Peace-keeping Forces in Kosovo and Bosnia-Herzegovina', AI Index: EUR 05/002/2004, 1 April 2004, at http://web.amnesty.org/library/pdf/EUR050022004ENGLISH/$File/EUR0500204.pdf.
36. *General Framework Agreement* (n.13 above), Annex 10, Art. III.4(b).
37. Ombudsperson Institution in Kosovo, *Third Annual Report 2002–2003*, p.4, at www.ombudspersonkosovo.org.
38. Izetbegović, cited in Knaus and Martin (n.15 above), p.66.
39. Gregory and Giddings (n.25 above), p.8.
40. *Constitution of Bosnia and Herzegovina*, Art. VI, at www.ccbh.ba/?lang=en&page=texts/constitution/article06.
41. Constitutional Court of Bosnia and Herzegovina, Decision U 9/00, 3 Nov. 2000, at www.ccbh.ba/?lang=en&page=decisions/byyear/2000.
42. S.R. Ratner, *The New UN Peacekeeping: Building Peace in Lands of Conflict after the Cold War*, Basingstoke: Macmillan, 1995, pp.92–3.
43. For a discussion of the supervisory roles of the Permanent Mandates Commission and the Trusteeship Council, see N.C. Crawford, *Argument and Change in World Politics: Ethics, Decolonization, and Humanitarian Intervention*, Cambridge: Cambridge University Press, 2002, Chs. 6 and 7.
44. *Charter of the United Nations* (n.11 above), Chapter XIII, Art. 87.
45. *A More Secure World: Our Shared Responsibility*, Report of the High-level Panel on Threats, Challenges and Change, UN Doc. A/59/565, 2 December 2004, §261-65, at www.un.org/secureworld/.
46. Office of the High Representative, 'OHR Mission Implementation Plan', 30 Jan. 2003, at www.ohr.int/ohr-info/ohr-mip/default.asp?content_id=29145.
47. Ibid.
48. Wolfgang Petritsch, 'Speech by the High Representative for Bosnia and Herzegovina. at the Steering Board Ministerial Meeting', New York, 22 Sept. 1999, at www.ohr.int/ohr-dept/presso/presssp/default.asp?content_id=3339.
49. See M. Baskin, 'Between Exit and Engagement: On the Division of Authority in Transitional Administrations', *Global Governance*, Vol.10, No.1, 2004, pp.119–37.
50. J.E. Stiglitz, 'Participation and Development: Perspectives from the Comprehensive Development Paradigm', *Review of Development Economics*, Vol.6, No.2, 2002, p.169 (emphasis added).
51. '25th Report by the High Representative for Implementation of the Peace Agreement to the Secretary-General of the United Nations', 3 March 2004, §52, at www.ohr.int/other-doc/hr-reports/default.asp?content_id=32024.
52. Human Rights Ombudsman of Bosnia and Herzegovina, 'Preliminary Monthly Report', 31 Dec. 2003, at www.ohro.ba/articles/cs.php?id=183.
53. The first 'Bosnian' Governor of the Central Bank, Peter Nicholl, was appointed in May 2003. Nicholl was already serving as the Governor of the Central Bank – and had been since the bank was established. In order to extend his position, beyond the six-year restriction on foreign nationals, the New Zealander was made a Bosnian citizen and his appointment extended a further 18 months. 'Nicholl Extends His Stay', Newsmakers, *Central Banking*, 26 May 2003, at www.centralbanking.co.uk/newsmakers/archive/2003/may26.htm#2.
54. D. Harland, 'Legitimacy and Effectiveness in International Administration', *Global Governance*, Vol.10, No.1, 2004, p.15.

INDEX

Printed in the United States
121279LV00002B/28-30/A

9 780415 463829